GREENWICH FORUM VI

GREENWICH FORUM VI

World Shipping in the 1990s

Records of a Conference
at the Royal Naval College, Greenwich

23–25 April 1980

Edited by **Commander M.B.F. Ranken**
Chairman and Managing Director
Aquamarine International

Published by Westbury House, IPC Science and Technology Press Limited, PO Box 63, Bury Street, Guildford, Surrey GU2 5BH, England.

Greenwich forum V
1. Merchant marine — congresses
I. Ranken M.B.F.
387.5   HE735

ISBN 0 86103 049 4

Printed in Great Britain by Thomson Litho Ltd, East Kilbride, Scotland.

CONTENTS

II   Background Papers

III   Study Groups

THE GREENWICH FORUM

In September 1973, the Royal Naval College Greenwich held a Conference to celebrate the 100th anniversary of the establishment of the College. Its theme was 'Britain and the Sea', and it was from that Conference that the Greenwich Forum originated.

The Conference was unique in that it provided an opportunity for representatives of virtually all Britain's maritime concerns to exchange views and information and to establish where their interests met — and indeed sometimes clashed. At the end of the Conference there was a strong feeling that its work should be continued, which led to a meeting in February 1974 on board HMS Belfast.

Those who attended this meeting were drawn from an equally wide range of official, academic, industrial and technological institutions and associations; all were interested in the furtherance of Britain's interests in the sea and on and beneath the seabed. It was agreed at the meeting to set up a small working party to report on how the purpose of the meeting might best be pursued. This working party became the Greenwich Forum, formed with the objects of:

a. Transcending the boundaries between business, scholarship and public affairs, as well as those between academic discipline and sub-disciplines.

b. Establishing and strengthening informal links between all those most active in the various organizations already interested in fields peripheral to, impinging on or likely to be affected by the increasing and widening importance of maritime and offshore affairs.

c. Bringing the increasing importance of Britain's maritime interests to the attention of a wider public by organizing conferences, seminars and lectures at which information could be exchanged and common viewpoints developed.

The Greenwich Forum is particularly interested at the moment with the proper planning and management of the marine and submarine resources of the North Sea and of the 200 mile exclusive economic zone around our shores. These resources include fisheries, hydrocarbons exploitation, dredging, maritime transport and recreation; and their management involves, for example, traffic control, control of pollution, care for the marine environment, communications, joint surveillance of ship movements, policing these activities and safety at sea. The aim of the Greenwich Forum has been to persuade the British Government to view those problems of the sea as a whole, not as a number of unrelated extensions into the marine element of separate land-based problems, and to urge on it the need for interdepartmental coordination of policies. There is the further consideration that, as far as the North Sea is concerned, the real framework for policy making is becoming that provided by the European Community rather than the purely national; and the Greenwich Forum is developing contacts with groups in the European Community whose interests are analogous.

Activities

The activities of the Greenwich Forum since 1974 have included:

a. A seminar on the Third UN Conference on the Law of the Sea (UNCLOS), held at the Centre for International Studies, London School of Economics and Political Science (LSE) in the summer of 1974.

b. A Conference on 'The Exploitation of the North Sea', held at the Royal Naval College Greenwich in April 1975.

c. Two series of public lectures given at University College London in the Lent Terms of 1975 and 1976.

d. A series of evening meetings for invited audiences, aimed particularly at Members of both Houses of Pariliament, held at the Council of Engineering Institutions in the winter of 1975/1976.

e. A Seminar on 'Britain and the North Sea', held at the Centre for International Studies, LSE, in the academic year 1975/1976.

f. A meeting on 'The 200 miles Exclusive Fisheries Limit: how is the Government to meet its external obligations afloat?', held at the House of Lords in November 1976.

g. A further seminar on 'Britain and the North Sea', held at the Centre for International Studies, LSE, in the Lent Term 1977.

h. A Conference on 'Britain and the Sea: the 200 mile zone and its implications', held at the Royal Naval College Greenwich in October 1977.*

j. A Seminar on 'Britain and the Sea', held at the Centre for International Studies, LSE, in the Lent Term 1978 and including discussion on 'The Politics of the Seabed' and 'Britain and the UNCLOS'.

k. A meeting on 'Offshore Kit: the Export Potential' held at the House of Lords in May 1978.

l. A Conference on 'Britain and the Sea: Deepwater Exploration and Development Ten Years On' held at the Royal Naval College Greenwich on 4 and 5 October 1978.*

m. An International Conference on 'Europe and the Sea: the case for and against a new international regime for the North Sea and its approaches' held at The Royal Naval College Greenwich on 2, 3 and 4 May 1979.◆

n. A Conference on 'Britain and the Sea: The Challenges for Shiping in the 1990s' held at the Royal Naval College, Greenwich on 23-25 April 1980.

* Copies of the Proceedings for these Conferences may be obtained from the Institute of Marine Engineering, London.

◆ Copies of the Records of Greenwich Forum V are available from Westbury House, PO Box 63, Bury Street, Guildford, Surrey GU2 5BH, UK. Westbury House titles are distributed in North America by Ann Arbor Science Publishers Inc, 10 Tower Office Park, Woburn, Mass 01801, and in Australia by Butterworths Pty Ltd, 586 Pacific Highway, Chatswood, NSW 2067.

Membership

The members of the Greenwich Forum (at April 1980) are:

Professor D.C. Watt (Chairman)	Professor of International History London School of Economics and Political Science
Dr Pat Birnie	Lecturer in Public International Law University of Edinburgh
Professor R.E.D. Bishop CBE	Kennedy Research Professor of Mechanical Engineering, University College London
Professor A.D. Couper	Professor of Maritime Studies UWIST
Mr. C.C. Fielding	Chief Scientist (Royal Navy)
Mr C.P.B. Hardcastle	Managing Director Scrimgeour Hardcastle & Co
Captain L.A. Holder	Head of Maritime Studies Liverpool Polytechnic
Lady Kennet (Elizabeth Young)	Writer
Mr. F.G. Larminie	General Manager, Environmental Control Centre British Petroleum Co Ltd
Mr. D.E. Lennard (Honorary Treasurer)	Director D.E. Lennard and Associates Ltd
Dr C.M. Mason	Lecturer in Politics Glasgow University
Vice Admiral Sir Ian McGeoch KCB DSO DSC	Editor, *The Naval Review* Managing Editor, *Naval Forces*
Professor P. Nailor	Professor of History and International Affairs Royal Naval College
Mr. J.A.H. Paffett	General Manager National Maritime Institute
Professor B. McL Ranft	Senior Research Fellow King's College London
Commander M.B.F. Ranken	Chairman and Managing Director Aquamarine International
Mr J. MacN Sidey DSO	Director P & O Energy
Professor A.J. Smith	Professor of Geology Bedford College London
Lieutenant Commander C.R.K. Cameron, Royal Navy (Honorary Secretary)	Senior Lecturer Department of History and International Affairs Royal Naval College

Further information may be obtained from the Honorary Secretary of the Greenwich Forum at the Royal Naval College, Greenwich, London SE10 9NN, UK.

MESSAGE OF WELCOME

From the Rt Hon John Nott MP, Secretary of State for Trade

"The theme for this year's Greenwich Forum is challenges for shipping. This is a topic of world-wide scope. As an island, we are especially dependent on shipping for our trade.
As possessors of the world's fourth largest fleet we are committed to working towards the most effective use of the world's shipping resources. I believe that the interests of all countries — developed and developing, North and South — are best served by an international competitive market which is as free as possible. Where regulation is necessary — as in safety and pollution matters — it should be by international agreement in the interests of all.
These objectives need the greatest possible mutual understanding, so that we all appreciate each others problems and objectives and can work towards reasonable solutions.
The expression "full and frank exchange of views" has become a diplomatic cliche, but I hope that in this Forum it will mean exactly what it says. I cannot do better than wish you every success in a constructive debate".

SHIPPING IN THE 1990S:
THE PRESENT POSITION

The Greenwich Forum

International trade by sea increased almost six and a half times between 1950 and 1977 when the total had reached 3 380 million tonnes, although this was only 5% above 1973, the year of the first OPEC price 'shock' doubling oil prices and restricting production, so that, on top of greater commercial and political pressures, bunkers prices and availability are additional long-term problems with which shipowners increasingly have to contend; presently crude prices and supply are at the whim of the producing countries, but the availability of usable bunkers is further aggravated by much greater refining by the oil companies, leaving increasingly heavy fractions to be burnt in ships' engines and boilers. Possibilities for new or modified propulsion systems need to be studied now, so that they are available when needed towards and beyond the end of the century.

World shipping has carried through revolutionary changes, particularly over the past 15 years. The ocean passenger liner is extinct as a result of the vast expansion of air travel, and only cruise ships remain in this sector. Bulk cargo ships have become much more specialized and many are much larger than in the past. Several ultra-large crude oil carriers (ULCCs) now exceed 500 000 dwt and tankers totalling over 175 million grt (around 325 million dwt) carried at least 1 440 million tonnes in 1968. Variations on these are oil/bulk/ore (OBO) and oil/ore carriers, mostly in the range 50 000-100 000 dwt, which seek to maximize loaded time at sea. Liquefied natural gas (LNG) tankers up to 125 000 metres^3 capacity, and liquefied petroleum gas carriers (LPG) are other new types of vessel. Bulk chemical carriers have also become a major class in their own right. Timber and animal carriers have likewise become much more specialized.

By far the most revolutionary has been the change from port-to-port operations to fully integrated transport systems carrying goods in closed containers from door-to-door, and in which the ship is but one link in the chain, albeit the largest single investment; variations on this theme are barge carrying ships like LASH, BACAT, and SeaBee. The modern shipowner has become a transport manager controlling road vehicles, river and canal barges and towage, inland and port terminals, warehousing, ship repair and a host of related services. Many refrigerated reefer trades have converted to containers, though some like bananas and fish may still be carried in bulk; today's major reefer fleets follow the seasonal patterns of trade much more than in the past, in a highly specialized operation.

Other vessels include ferries, now very specialized and self-contained, coastal trading vessels, fishing vessels and fish factory ships, offshore supply boats, heavy-lift crane ships, lay barges, cable layers, dredgers, research vessels, tenders etc.

The emphasis has been on keeping vessels at sea for most of the time, on the principle that any piece of load-carrying equipment is only profitably employed when moving and loaded, preferably completely full. This compares with 50-60% of a ship's time, which used to be spent loading, unloading, or simply waiting, and earning nothing. Port work was also very labour intensive, slow, and therefore costly, with many problems of labour relations. Labour in UK ports has dropped from 90 000 to about 30 000, and will go lower; the traditional ports are almost empty of ships. Most cargo is now stacked in unit loads four or five high, or placed directly on wheeled trailers, by large mechanical handling systems or cranes in the ships themselves or on the dockside, and there is little or no waiting time by trucks. 50 or more containers can be handled every hour, and a large cellular container ship can be discharged and reloaded in a tide or two. Cargo is loaded at the suppliers' works and unloaded in the customers' premises, with no intermediate individual handling except of non-standard, usually very large loads.

Fewer, larger and more specialized ships, also requiring smaller crews, are needed to move a given volume of cargo. The world fleet of ships over 100 grt is something over 65 000 in number, and the UK still has the fourth largest tonnage of ships, though in common with most other OECD fleets it is shrinking, as those of various emerging countries, the USSR, and one or two flag-of-convenience countries continue to increase. London remains the world centre for shipping, its markets, finance, insurance, trade associations, consultancy and admiralty law, as well as the Inter-governmental Maritime Consultative Organisation (IMCO).

Despite the very commercial and highly competitive nature of the world shipping industry, it is very vulnerable to recessions in world trade, such as has occurred following the 1973 oil crisis, leaving many shipowners with too many ships in service or on order to meet greatly reduced cargo requirements, most especially in the tanker trades, where individual ships are extremely costly units in capital, interest and operating terms. The impact of recession on the world shipbuilding industry has been disastrous, and the UK's own industry is no exception, though perhaps worse affected than some by its generally poor condition and overmanning.

The advent of the very large tanker introduced major hazards to the environment and community at large, as exemplified by the *Torrey Canyon* and the *Amoco Cadiz*, but also by the need to eliminate operational oilspills while loading and discharging, and most especially while tank washing on passage. Other hazards were increased by reduced crew sizes and particularly by deteriorating standards of seamanship in a period when there is increasing reluctance to go to sea. The increased volume of traffic in many congested shipping lanes has led to new regulations, routeing and traffic separation, as well as greater intervention by governments in enforcing higher standards, in surveillance and policing, and in providing better navigational information.

Restraints on shipping

Private restraints on shipping take many forms, principally to improve the service given and avoid cut-throat competition. These are exemplified by the long-standing liner conferences of which some 360 are in operation covering all major liner trades worldwide. But many trades rely on the charter system and the spot market, where charter rates are geared to supply and demand. In general the two systems operate to the benefit both of the cargo customer and of the shipowner, at highly competitive and reasonably stable rates. Nationally controlled fleets like that of the USSR, however, may threaten commercially sensitive rates, and competition from overland routes, like the Trans-Siberian railway, may be undesirable, as it certainly is strategically if it eliminates the alternatives by sea, which would be needed urgently in times of tension.

International restraints on the free operation of the world shipping market have become a major concern in recent years, first through the actions of individual governments providing heavy subsidies and privileges to their own flag ships, or trying to apply domestic legislation to shipping which is international, and secondly through unrealistic collective action at UNCTAD and elsewhere, mainly instigated by the Group of 77 to limit cross-trading in as many types of trade as it can achieve. Most of these restrictive practices only serve to increase shipping costs, which tend to be more detrimental to the developing than to the industrial countries, and are hardly at all offset by increasing the cargo carried in the developing countries' own ships. The EEC and other major trading groups could apply collective pressure to offset or resist unacceptable moves within UNCTAD, but in general the traditional free trade in shipping has stood the test of time and should not be lightly discarded.

Despite the rapid reaction to changing methods, and great ingenuity in adapting to commercial, financial and restrictive pressures, most shipping has for a long time been only barely profitable. Thus UK shipping companies were averaging no more than 3.5% profit before tax between 1958 and 1969, and several in 1978 made 1% or less. Also the earnings of foreign exchange from their worldwide operations are no longer thought to mitigate this low profitability in times of rapid inflation; some doubt whether they really did in earlier times.

The UK shipping industry is vital to the country's role as a major trading nation, and how to increase its profitability to acceptable levels is the primary problem to be solved in the future, at the same time as tackling and beating nationalistic and international restrictive practices, increasing commercial and operating costs, the difficulties of maintaining high standards of contented manning, and deteriorating energy supplies at ever-rising prices.

All these and other problems of today's shipping industry need to be taken into account in considering likely trends and patterns in the 1990s and what needs to be done from now on to ensure the health of the industry in the closing years of the 20th century and beyond.

OPENING ADDRESS

Sir Frederick Bolton (President, International Shipping Federation)

I usually find myself struggling against the popular notion that tomorrow will be quite different from today and yesterday, and arguing instead that life is usually more evolutionary than revolutionary. But in considering Britain and shipping in the 1990s, whether the changes are violently revolutionary or more peacefully evolutionary, I do not think there can be much doubt that things will indeed be different.

We have a remarkable set of papers before us, by a remarkable set of experts, discussing the sort of changes and causes of change which are likely to happen – some in the 1980s rather than in the 1990s, I feel – and it seems that their messages are woven round perhaps only a couple of simple strands, the changing role in the world of the UK and of the West in general, and the energy crisis. These are large enough, positive enough, real enough, factors to mean that something different really is bound to happen – even if it happens over the next 20 years slowly enough for us all to be able to adapt to it in an evolutionary way, rather than recoil from it shattered by a revolutionary confrontation.

Britain's changing role

It is of course a truism that Britain has retained for a little longer in shipping than in other industries and branches of commerce, something of the world dominance that it had at the beginning of the century – not, of course, the 45% of the world's industry that it had in 1900 but still a high enough leading ranking, third or fourth, to enable us still to think of ourselves as world leaders. But although our original development may have been based on the carriage of our own UK trade in the days when we were world leaders in that too, we quickly established ourselves in the cross-trades so that our fleet became and still is very much larger than would be needed for any bilateral or UNCTAD code 40–40–20 arrangement to deal with our own cargo alone in and out of the UK.

We must remember this when we complain about the excessive size of the Russian fleet, and limit our complaints not to the size but to the way it is used.

But our past and present success in carrying other peoples' cargoes simply means that we and other similarly placed traditional maritime nations must be the losers in any redistribution of opportunity for carrying cargo – anyone's gain is likely to be at our expense.

So long as the trend is away from a determination that cargo shall be carried as cheaply and efficiently as possible – from trading, market-oriented, conditions for the real benefit of all – and in favour of a manipulated share with a variety of motivations, none of which is cheapness and efficiency, ours is a rearguard action; never a retreat, but a deliberate withdrawal from one position to another in the hope, if not the expectation, that the hostile pressure will slacken and that the 'variety of motivations' will switch its attention somewhere else, and cheapness and efficiency will again be needed, so that we can advance again from the position we managed to hold.

Of course, this argument means that even if the forces against us, the non-commercial forces, strategic in the case of COMECON and largely emotional in the case of less developed countries, are insurmountable by us without the support of our own national authorities, we must still maintain our technological and organizational hold on our own industry, so that we can still offer cheapness and efficiency when it is once more required. And it is a nice point how far and what sort of government help encourages or stifles capabilities of operating with cheapness and efficiency. I have always thought that we should try to avoid that sort of government support which aims to maintain a nucleus of the industry in being no matter how uncompetitive it is (as some other countries have done for decades), until our fleet is down to or below the size which would be needed to carry our own trade in and out of the UK shared bilaterally with our trading partners. This might mean a reduction to not much more than half its present size. Of course, defence considerations might require government intervention before the industry shrinks to this size, if the size and nature of the fleet required for defence purposes is in fact determinable.

This means that I do not go along with the suggestion that we can no longer hope to be competitive with much of the rest of the world. On the contrary, I believe we can be confident about our ability to compete with anyone else, if we try hard enough, provided the dice are not loaded against us by governments: in the long run, the world will require us to do so. So we should be determined to sit it out until then, somehow.

Energy – the real issue

With the adoption of the theme of this conference as 'Shipping in the 1990s', we may have been enabled, just, to avoid the real issue here, of what is going to be the effect of no oil for energy. We clearly do not have to discuss a 'no oil for shipping' position for the 1980s – probably not, equally, for the 1990s – but, surely, by the end of that decade, the issue will be stark. There is a paper before us which calls for fuel economy, technologically and organizationally, and envisages a growing use of coal.

It is possible to argue that oil will be reserved for those uses for which other sources of energy cannot be (or so easily be) used – coal and nuclear power for land use and electricity generation, and, perhaps, with the radically improved battery, for road transport – but oil for the larger part of worldwide shipping, and the air. But even if this were to happen, and it would mean for us throughout the 21st century – and I am not sure that I accept that myself – there are bound to be very far-reaching consequences of a major change in the relative price of oil.

So far the world has adjusted once after 1973-74, and may well do so again after 1979-80, to the 'real' price of oil, but even if there is no such adjustment after these most recent increases, they have not yet really altered the balance fundamentally; we have not yet seen the car abandoned for rail because the higher energy cost of the car outweighs the other costs and convenience; we have not seen the reversal of the trend from lo-lo to ro-ro in the short-sea trades, nor a major movement to process raw materials at the place of extraction rather than carting them across the world, and then carrying the finished product back again, because the change in the relationship of the costs of energy and the rest of costs makes it more economical to do so.

The end of oil for transportation, whenever it comes, will mean a whole range of changes. Even if it is not actually with us by the year 2000, we shall surely be planning for it by then.

If these two broad strands of thought on the future of our industry are a gross oversimplification, a corrective to them lies in the papers now before us, which expose some complexities which underlie the simple truth whether it is as I see it or not. I hope that this session of the Forum will provide indications of what individual companies and the various institutions connected with the industry could do to improve the industry's position in the world for the next couple of decades.

I. Main papers

1. TRADE AND SHIPPING PATTERNS IN THE 1990s

Peter Goodwin (Economist Intelligence Unit)

> 'International trade permits a more efficient employment of the production forces of the world'. (John Stuart Mill)

The logic behind this statement needs no explanation. However, Mill should probably have gone on to point out that the interdependence created between nations to achieve these benefits is self-propagating unless artificially constrained. In general, economic prosperity has improved through history, not least because of this growth in interdependence. However political as well as economic relationships between countries do not remain static and threaten the pattern and degree of interdependence which has become established. Imbalances built up within and between national economies now pose increasing problems for the future. The shipping industry is very much a football in the scheme of things. As such it has had to adapt rapidly and sometimes painfully to an ever-changing environment. Some changes that will determine the activity of the shipping industry in the 1990s are being effected now, many more may materialize which cannot be foreseen today.

This paper sets out to provide pointers to the shape of the industry in the 1990s by describing the general world economic outlook and prospects for international trade based on how development has progressed in recent times.

THE PAST 25 YEARS

The world population increased from 2 500 million in 1950 to 4 000 million in 1975. During that time world production grew at an average annual rate of 5% resulting in per capita income growth of 3% per year. Growth in the developed countries was more rapid than in the developing countries partly because of the high rate of growth in industry, more than 6% per year. In the developed market economies, agricultural production doubled, while in the developing countries an increase of 130% was achieved. This sustained rapid growth, achieved partly by specialization in production, generated an even greater rise in the volume of world trade, which by 1973 was six times greater than the growth in world production.

The dominance of the USA in western politics played a major role in these achievements. Backed by the support of the European nations, a new order was established which facilitated an effective reallocation of production factors at the international level. Among the components of the international economic order were: freedom of trade, internationalization of capital movements, transfer of technology, an international division of labour favouring economic growth, a monetary system encouraging stability of exchange rates, and the establishment of intergovernmental institutions to maintain and promote the new order.

Furthermore, the upheavals of war had created increased adaptability within many nations, in particular those which had suffered most. Countries such as Germany, France and especially Japan, found themselves in the mood to grasp new opportunities for development in the sympathetic environment being created by the new order.

In the developed countries the new order has tended to narrow per capita income differentials, and remove the wide disparities that previously existed. Through more free exchange of technologies and shifts in industrial structures and trade flows, faster rises in productivity have occurred in Japan and Europe compared with North America. Not only have the disparities in wealth been reduced but also the developed nations have tended to become more alike in character. In particular national governments have become more directly involved in both the distribution of wealth through 'the welfare state' and in the organization and control of the productive sectors.

It can be argued that policies orientated towards more equitable distribution of wealth have restrained growth in national wealth and the rate of investment in productive sectors. Unlike the developed world, the developing world is becoming increasingly disparate in character and yet increasingly dependent for its development on the developed world. At the one extreme some, particularly south-east Asian nations like Korea and Taiwan, have nearly accomplished their own techno-industrial revolutions, while others are persistently failing to stem the rise in their populations suffering from malnutrition. Although growth in per capita income for Korea and Taiwan has been maintained at over 5% per year, in Bangladesh negative growth still persists.

Although the developing world is disconcerted by possible undermining of their cultural and ethnic characteristics, it recognizes that interdependence with the developed world is an essential prerequisite for survival, let alone development. The developed world provides a market for developing countries' exploitable natural resources and the source of the technology and capital goods necessary for their growth. For the foreseeable future the developing countries would be unable to achieve real progress independently, although trade between them has been increasing rapidly, and their rate of progress is inextricably linked to growth in the developed world. About two-thirds of all exports from developing countries were purchased by industrialized nations: 70% of fuel, 65% of primary products and 60% of manufactures.

In recent years economic growth in the developed world has declined; their combined gross domestic product (GDP) is now increasing annually by between 3% and 4%. Strong inflationary pressures and unstable foreign payments' positions having their origins in the recession of 1974-75 have obstructed the reattainment of concurrent rapid growth, full employment and price stability in developed countries. There is little evidence to suggest that the prospects in the immediate future are more encouraging.

The sensitivity of world trade to the economic health of the industrialized world has been demonstrated by the reduction in growth between 1975 and 1977 to a little over 4% from 9% annually. Furthermore, the growth in the exports of the developing world fell to 3.6% per year compared with 6.4% before 1973. Part of this reduction, however, can be accounted for by the stagnation of primary commodity exports in volume terms caused by adverse weather conditions in several countries producing agricultural exports. It could also be argued that the primary sector has been under-served in the allocation of priorities for investment by governments seeking to break into other sectors too early, and possibly being misled by good early returns on investment from manufactures.

Developing countries' exports of manufactures were expanding by 15% per year before 1973. Subsequently the rate of growth slowed to 11% as a result of the economic downturn and also because of protectionist measures taken in the developed countries whose industrial base was coming under threat of new competition. Among the products most affected by increased protection have been textiles, footwear and steel.

ECONOMIC GROWTH PROSPECTS

The most reasonable estimate of future growth in the developed world is for GDP to grow at between 4.0% and 4.5% annually (see Table 1). The North American

Table 1. Growth of gross domestic product 1970-90 (average annual % growth rates, 1975 prices).

	1970-78	1978-80	1980-90
Industrialized countries	3.4	3.4	4.2
North America	3.4	3.0	4.0
Japan and Oceania	5.1	5.1	5.9
West and North Europe	2.8	3.3	3.8
Developing countries	5.5	5.2	5.5
Low income countries	2.5	4.7	4.8
Africa	2.9	3.7	3.7
Asia	4.1	4.9	5.0
Middle income countries	5.9	5.3	5.7

Source: Based on World Bank estimates.

economies will probably grow at or slightly below this rate, while the European economies are considered more likely to fail to achieve this average, and Japan remains the most likely candidate to exceed the average. The USA, being richly endowed with natural resources and with a lead in technology, is able to enjoy relative indpendence from the economy of the rest of the world. The EEC is less independent and will continue to wrestle with its own problems of industrial reconstruction having lost most of the adaptability which its currently strongest members enjoyed 25 years ago. Japan has lost less of its adaptability and is also on the doorstep of some of the fastest growing markets for its goods and of present and potential sources of raw materials. The future of the centrally planned economies is more difficult to predict; their present share of world GDP is about 19%, and opinions about their share by the turn of the century vary from 25% to 30%. China, which is included in these forecasts, is expected to increase its share of global GDP from 4% at present to 9% during this period, assuming that its present open-door policy is not reversed during the present or subsequent regimes.

The developing world as a whole is likely to maintain a higher rate of growth between 5% and 6%, and may attain 20% of global GDP by 1990 and nearly 25% by 2000. These forecasts mask the variations in the likely fortunes of particular countries within this group and wide contrasts in growth are expected. In low income countries of Asia, a growth rate of about 5% is expected. This is higher than previously attained and is based in part on the recent acceleration of agricultural investments and production in India, and on the prospects for Indonesian oil revenues. However, this region faces a massive increase in population despite declining fertility, and by 1990 over 120 million will be added to the workforce.

A less promising outlook confronts the low-income countries of central Africa. Population increases will be rapid and agricultural productivity cannot be raised rapidly as a result of deficiencies in agricultural research, physical infrastructure and climatic conditions. Rapid industrial development also cannot be envisaged. The middle-income developing countries could well improve on this recent growth rate of about 5%. Population growth has been high, enhancing their domestic markets, and, given favourable conditions to market their manufactures abroad and appropriate investment decisions, productivity increases should be more readily attainable.

PROSPECTS FOR INTERNATIONAL TRADE

As mentioned above, the slow and unstable growth of the industrialized countries, combined with increased protectionism, international inflation and exchange rate instability, reduced the growth of world trade, in volume terms from 9% per year before 1973 to little more than 4% subsequently. Trade in primary commodities has grown little in volume terms since 1973, although over the period since 1960 average growth rates of 6.7% and 4.4% were recorded for energy fuels and other primary products respectively. The growth in trade volumes for manufactures increased by over 9% per year between 1960 and 1976.

Before making judgments about the future rates of growth in trade on the basis of the growth in global economic activity described above, a number of factors distinguish the post-war past from the future. First, the reduced adaptability of industry in the developed world may persist and lead to sluggishness in developing new industries, restraint in economic growth, and further protectionist measures. Second, the growth of multinational corporations will cause international divisions of single company activities and more closed-loop systems of international trade. Developing countries will face increasing problems of urbanization and intensify their requirements for manufacturing industries and policies aimed at protecting the domestic markets for manufactures. The effect on the world economy of quantum rises in the price of energy fuel was clearly demonstrated in 1973; future similar actions of the OPEC countries and other countries producing vital primary goods cannot be foreseen but should not be ruled out.

Although the Eastern bloc countries are largely self-sufficient, they do need to participate in international trade for certain imports and for foreign exchange earnings. As a means of exerting greater influence, particularly in the developing world, their participation in world trade could be expanded; certainly the recent build-up of their national fleets indicates a desire for greater involvement.

Finally, the emergence into world affairs of China under the present regime represents a new factor in any prognosis of future world trade. The cautious would point out that a second U-turn in their policy towards the rest of the world could occur as rapidly as the last. However given the recent past, and in the foreseeable future as China builds up its interdependence with other countries, its ability to revert back to isolationism will become more difficult.

Assuming that the developed world regains some of its lost momentum through improved economic management and a determined effort not to give in to protectionist measures, growth in GDP (see Table 2) should recover to between 4%

and 4.5% per year which would indicate a growth in exports of goods to about 6% per year. Developing countries are increasingly looking to each other for mutual trading

Table 2. Growth of exports, by product category 1960-76 and 1976-90 (average annual growth rates in volume terms).

	1960-76 World	Industrial-ized countries	Developing countries	1976-90 World	Industrial-ized countries	Developing countries
Fuels	6.7	4.5	6.3	3.1	3.3	3.2
Other primary products	4.4	5.1	3.7	3.3	3.3	3.3
Food and beverages	4.4	5.1	3.5	3.3	3.9	3.1
Non-food agricultural products	5.1	6.3	3.4	1.8	1.1	2.8
Minerals and non-ferrous metals	3.9	3.4	4.7	3.5	3.0	4.5
Manufactures	9.1	9.1	12.7	7.0	6.5	10.9
Machinery	9.9	10.0	17.5	7.6	7.1	15.3
Other manufactures	8.5	8.3	11.8	6.5	6.0	9.0
Total	7.4	7.8	6.3	5.7	5.9	6.1

Source: World Bank data.

exchanges, and international trade within this group will continue to expand rapidly. The volume of this trade will depend on foreign exchange positions, economic growth and policies towards trade rather than on special trading agreements, although a number of international trading groupings have been arranged. Their trade will still remain highly sensitive to changes in their trading volume with the developed world, on whom they will depend for their overall export performance.

The Tokyo Round of multilateral trade negotiations was a mixed blessing for the developing countries. The agreements provide a series of detailed codes designed to constrain the development of non-tariff barriers to trade which could enable improved access to markets in the developed world. On the other hand, certain exemptions relate directly to the infant industries of the developing world, and there are proposals for further safeguards for exporters in the developed world, again in sectors of special significance for the developing world.

Protectionist measures which inhibit world trade will adversely affect the economies of both the developed and the developing world. The structural changes that should constantly be under way in the developed world will tend to take place too slowly, and the adverse effect of lower trading volume between the two groups of countries will adversely affect the growth of trade between the developing countries by reducing their international liquidity. The worst result of increased protectionism would be to both slow down the rate of growth between developing countries and also to reduce their ability to import the goods and services they require to pursue development programmes.

On the assumption that the developing world continues to make further progress in its efforts to feed itself, and develops further its agro-processing industries, its trade in non-mineral primary products and agricultural products will grow slowly. Even slower growth is likely to be recorded in fuels, as oil resources closer to consuming areas are developed and the output from traditional sources is restrained.

International trade in manufactured goods will continue to increase at a faster rate than primary products (see Table 3). Exports from industrialized countries

Table 3. Distribution of population, production and export trade 1976 and 1990.

	World total	Industrialized countries	Developing countries	Capital surplus oil exporters	Eastern Europe and China
Population (million)					
1976	4 078	661	2 129	12	1 276
1990	5 192	714	2 955	18	1 505
GNP per capita (US $)					
1976	1 673	6 414	538	6 691	1 061
1990	2 798	10 261	831	8 933	1 774
Value of exports ($ billion)					
Fuels					
1976	187	29	77	64	16
1990	285	46	119	97	23
Other primary products					
1976	206	119	69	neg	18
1990	326	187	110	neg	29
Manufactures					
1976	578	468	55	1	55
1990	1 499	1 133	234	4	127
Share of global exports trade (% by value)					
1976	100	63	21	7	9
1990	100	65	22	5	8

Source: World Bank data.   *Note:* Values at 1975 prices.

would be expected to increase by between 6% and 7% per year given the annual growth in GDP of between 4% and 4.5%. Since 1960 the developing countries have increased their exports by over 17% per year. In the future this high rate of growth is unlikely to be sustained for the reasons given above.

SHIPPING PATTERNS

Having considered the bare bones of world economic development by the 1990s, it now remains to add some flesh to produce an animal which corresponds to the form and characteristics of the shipping required to service this global trade. This is best accomplished by looking at groups of commodities separately: these are liquid bulks (mainly oil), dry bulks, and lastly other cargoes.

Forecasts of global energy consumption are plentiful and varied, depending as they do on a large number of assumptions regarding supply and demand. The conclusion generally arrived at is that the energy balance will remain tight and will be a matter of concern for both the developed and the developing world for the rest of this century. It is widely believed that the world supply of oil will reach a peak well before the year 2000. During this period the distribution of reserves will probably change such that the USSR and China may well control over one-third.

The main movement of crude oil will remain that from the Middle East to Europe, followed by that from the Middle East to Japan. Other OPEC producers are likely to find their exports of crude oil being reduced as domestic demands soak up production.

Outside OPEC the main hope for export production is Mexico. If Mexico can achieve 5-6 million bbl/day production, exports could reach 3 million bbl/day, of which some 70% would probably be consumed in the USA and the remainder in Europe. Still an unknown quantity, but very much the hope for the future, is the potential of the Chinese coast. Given that substantial reserves exist, exploitation for the world market seems likely as China's role in the world economy increases and for earning foreign exchange to pay for the massive import requirements that development would require. Elsewhere there are hopes of discoveries in the North American and Russian Arctic.

In terms of a requirement for shipping, the most optimistic forecasts envisage an increase in tonnage from around 230 million dwt at present to about 280 million dwt by the year 2000, still below the presently available capacity. More pessimistic assumptions indicate a fall in demand to around 200 million dwt. It is unlikely therefore that dramatic changes will take place in the size of crude oil tankers that will be built, and new tonnage for crude oil carriage may be concentrated in the 80 000-120 000 dwt range.

The prospects for seaborne trade in oil products, LNG and LPG are quite different. The continuing development of Middle East refineries in particular will generate a demand for additional and larger products carriers. Shipping requirements for LPG could increase fivefold by the year 2000 calling for a fleet of over 300 vessels. The future pattern of movements of LNG is impossible to predict; the resources are large and widely distributed, little is known about the timing of developments, and the pattern of distribution between pipeline and ship is uncertain. By the 1990s the size of shipping fleet could vary between 12 million m^3 and 20 million m^3 with vessels averaging over 100 000 m^3.

Growth in the seaborne trade in the five major bulk commodities historically remained just above the rate of growth in global GDP but has remained fairly static since 1974 at about 650 million tons/year. By the mid 1990s the volume of these trades could reach 1 500 million tons/year assuming a growth rate between 4% and 5%. Coal and iron ore are likely to grow more rapidly, and grain more slowly than the other major bulks. Coal will increasingly be called on to contribute to future energy supply, and the trade between suppliers in the Pacific area, principally Australia and consumers in Europe, will become a major trade route with a large demand for shipping tonnage.

The tendency in the major bulk trades has been for newer larger vessels to displace older smaller vessels as trade has grown and intensified on particular routes. More recently this trend has been moderated both because the position of oversupply has reduced the rate of new building, and because of physical limitations at the terminals. A further factor which in the future may restrain the growth in the average vessel size will be the development of new supply sources and a more even distribution of supply from different sources to consumers.

Growth in the grain trade is expected to be less rapid with the year-to-year variation experienced in the past repeated in the future as harvests fluctuate. North America's share of the world market is likely to remain at about 70%. On the consumption side, east Asia, particularly Japan and China, is likely to increase its importation faster than the other main net importing regions of Eastern and Western Europe and South America. Although there are widespread restrictions on vessel size within the grain trades, particularly at the discharge terminals, the trend towards larger vessels will continue. The North American export trades will become more dependent on vessels over 50 000 dwt particularly if steady and regular trading between the USA and China develops.

UNCTAD debate

Before considering the general cargo prospects, the current debate being carried on within UNCTAD on the role of open registry shipping and the related question of cargo-sharing requires examination. The concern of the developing countries about the present 'inequitable' distribution of world shipping (see Table 4) has been taken up

Table 4. Distribution of world tonnage, tonnage on order and world trade.

	Share of world fleet (% of dwt)		Share of tonnage on order (% of dwt)	Share of world trade (%)	
	1970	*1978*	*1978*	*1970*	*1978*
Developed countries	65.0	53.4	53.6		
			}	54.8	55.4
Open registry countries	21.6	31.2	14.8		
Developing countries	6.3	8.6	22.0	40.4	39.4
−Asia	3.3	4.9	6.2		
−Africa	0.4	1.0	2.4		
−other	2.6	2.7	13.4		
Centrally planned economies	6.6	6.4	6.7	4.8	5.1
−E Europe	6.2	5.3	6.4		
−other	0.4	1.1	0.3		

Source: UNCTAD.

by the UNCTAD Secretariat, whose Director stated at the 'Shipping 2000' conference in London that the next 20 years ought to see an end to the domination of a small group of ship-owning countries and the phasing-out of flags of convenience. It is less clear how this would be achieved, although the Group of 77 nations remained united in their support in January 1980, despite the financial and managerial problems that they would face in building-up their own fleets. Whether, and how rapidly, newly emergent fleets under the flags of the developing nations will become established remains to be seen, whether in their own long-term national interests or not, a new generation of ship-owning nations is likely to be in existence during the 1990s. Many would necessarily have to operate under the umbrella of protectionist measures such as cargo reservation, cargo-sharing and state subsidization. Examples of such protection would be new, and several South American countries provide precedents.

Phasing-out open registry operations seems unlikely and, it has been argued, the scope of such operations may in fact increase to embrace lower-cost OECD countries in which shipping is subsidized, either directly or indirectly. Assuming that the range of countries and commodities for which cargo reservation measures are taken increases, the operational flexibility of the bulk shipping fleet as a whole must be reduced and the associated increases in shipping costs passed on to the producers or the consumers. The best interests of many countries lie in buying in relatively low-priced bulk shipping in a free market. It must be assumed that this will have been well demonstrated during the present decade by the example of at least some of the pioneers, such that during the 1990s enthusiasm for establishing national shipping fleets is dampened and more rational policies for the allocation of national resources are favoured.

Type and structure of shipping

Trade between nations in the developed world has been estimated to grow by between 5% and 6% per year. This growth, compounded with the higher rates of growth of trade in manufactures by the developing world, is likely to produce a total traded volume of high-valued cargo of about 300 million tons by the year 2000. That forecast compares with a present volume of 100 million tons. The type of shipping and the organizational structure of the industry which will be developed to cater for this trade is indicated by trends in the recent past.

During the past 15 years the most dramatic development in general cargo shipping has been the growth of highly productive shipping systems, particularly container and roll-on/roll-off systems. The world container fleet, including roll-on, roll-off/container and barge/container vessels has grown from almost zero in 1965 to about 15 million dwt.

Further inroads into liner services will be made by container services. Once thought to be limited mainly to trades within the developed world, the benefits of their application to the trades of the developing world are increasingly being realized often through the development of a feeder service system operating out of entrepôt ports. By the end of the century container vessels will dominate liner trading, possibly carrying over 80% of the trade in manufactures.

There are many problems to be overcome in introducing these capital-intensive systems into the trades of developing countries. The physical infrastructure requirements at the ports and inland are obvious, but the cumbersome bureaucracy associated with trading to and from many of these countries may be a more lasting deterrent to the development of containerization. Other objections are also cited, in particular the employment aspects, but opposition is likely to be more easily overcome than it was in the developed countries. Also, these countries that have already committed themselves to the purchase of conventional tonnage for their national fleets may wish to protect their share of trade without replacing their new vessels too soon. Such protection could be offered, and the emerging environment for liner shipping operations would appear to be a sympathetic one.

Implementation of the UNCTAD Code of Conduct for Liner Conferences has become almost inevitable. Within the Code each nation will have access to seaborne transportation in its own flag fleet of 40% of its trade carried within the Conference system. Given this market allocation and the growth in the container and vessel-leasing industry, emergent national fleets have every opportunity of establishing themselves in liner trades with conventional or more sophisticated vessels. The learning process will not be without difficulties, and success may depend on the ability of Conferences themselves to survive the necessary change-over from being clubs for the traditional operators to political institutions representing and coordinating the views of a more disparate membership. It is not clear that this change will be effected with success, and in recent times several Conferences, often those in the major liner trades, have come under threat of collapse. To succeed will require a determined effort from within their secretariats and their memberships, and the encouragement of UNCTAD.

There will also be an increased demand for more versatile ships, that will combine the movement of containers at one extreme and bulk cargoes at the other. I am not competent to assess if and how rapidly this demand can be met, but perhaps other papers presented at this meeting will be revealing. However, until such vessels become commonplace there could develop underutilization of shipping capacity which can only lead to rising freight rates and an inhibition of trading growth, and hence economic growth.

To summarize the general cargo prospects, by the end of the 1990s the volume of trading will have grown by a factor of three over the present level. The role of conventional general cargo liners will be diminished and restricted to peripheral services and as support services to container services. Container services will dominate the movement of general cargo trading and will operate between fewer ports of call than the conventional services they replace but will be supplemented by feeder services. Liner Conferences should have become more comprehensive in their role and have a stronger part to play in the interface between governments, operators and customers.

In the midst of a downturn in the world economy, much of the above may be regarded as too optimistic and the case for a less sanguine view can readily be made. However as wars are never won by planning for defeat, plans for economic prosperity and the role of shipping in these plans should not be based on assumptions of permanent recession. I am confident that old mistakes will be repeated less frequently and that new problems will be faced in the light of greater experience, with the end-result of growth in the developed world resuming and providing a steady basis for continual development of the poorer countries. The shipping industry worldwide will help to sustain that growth and will share in that growth, but with some redistribution of shipping activity.

Table 5. Future development of world international seaborne trade (million tonnes).

	Total	Oil	Major bulks	Other bulks	Other
1960	1 080	540	228	87	305
1970	2 530	1 420	504	80	526
1980	3 700	1 900	750	450	600
1990	5 225	2 300	1 200	700	1 025
2000	7 020	2 300	1 870	1 100	1 750

Source: Fearnley and Egers data and author's estimates.

DISCUSSION

Growth estimates

The paper states that the most reasonable estimate of future growth of gross domestic product (GDP) in the developed world is 4-4.5%, and in Table 1 the author used 4.2%, as opposed to about 3.5% in the 1970s. But many of his comments, particularly about protection and other tendencies, make one sceptical that it can be as high as that. Recovery is not occurring anywhere near as fast as in the 1950s, and there is great uncertainty in the immediate future. Higher and lower growth rates might be more helpful, together with a longer-term perspective.

Author's response. In my estimates of GDP growth, I put forward a single scenario for the simple reason that to explain three, or perhaps five scenarios, takes up more time and may be more confusing than trying to develop just one. Of course, one could postulate high and low scenarios with a wide range of assumptions about, for example, the price of energy, or the price of oil within the energy production sector, but in general the growth in global GDP or global wealth will very much depend on progress in the developed world which makes up so large a proportion of global wealth.

There is a tendency, in my view, for the developed world to become more inflexible in realizing new investment opportunities, partly because there is a greater development of the non-productive sectors of the economies – through development of the welfare state, for example. Obviously, the development of the non-productive sectors can increase the welfare of people within an economy, but this does not necessarily increase their productive capacity nor their level of production.

There are many reasons why growth may not be so high. Equally, there are many reasons why perhaps a higher rate of growth would be postulated. I have merely put forward one scenario as a base case – perhaps my own best estimate. Let us each adopt an attitude or a view and express our thoughts in relation to what other people think.

Pay differentials

The British shipping industry's unanimous report on the employment of non-domiciled seafarers resolved that pay differentials should be phased out, and that if the Indian, Pakistani and Bangladeshi governments objected, the remedy lay in their own hands to claw back the income as far as their own comparatively well paid seafarers are concerned. The present UK government has not changed the policy of its predecessor.

Author's response. It is believed that the aims of the Agreement of the General Council of British Shipping are: to phase out wage differentials over a five-year period; to employ expatriates as and where necessary in agreement with the trades unions; and to man new vessels with British seamen to the extent possible. The effect of this will be to further raise the cost of operating UK flag vessels, enabling low-cost operators to make further inroads in the trades in which the UK operates, and possibly speeding the decline of the British fleet. It will probably also advance the progress of more automated shipping, reducing manning scales and so forth, with the overall result being a lowering of employment prospects for both British and expatriate seamen.

2. PROSPECTS FOR THE LINER INDUSTRY

L. G. Hudson OBE
(Past Chairman, India, Pakistan and Bangladesh Conferences)

One regular theme in discussions about UK industries concerns the difficulties in competing successfully in the international field. That fear, or fact, has been an ever-present – almost commonplace – problem for the UK merchant shipping industry, so that the constraints and challenges of today, while perhaps more severe and requiring somewhat different answers, are not unexpected problems to the shipowners, nor are they totally incapable of reasonable solution. Proper consideration of where the UK shipping industry stands today, and estimation of where it might be, or could be, in the future, require some historical background, because the lessons of yesterday can sometimes be applied usefully to the likely problems of tomorrow.

To that end the practical development and problems of the liner industry are considered. That part of the shipping fleet has been chosen for discussion because it is the part which has so far suffered the greatest extent of attack by major influences outside the UK and these influences may also soon be echoed in other parts of the shipping fleet. Much of this paper comprises quotations from published works or speeches by others from which are drawn conclusions related to the probable future of the UK shipping industry.

Development of Liner Conferences

A 'liner' may be defined as a vessel which plies on a fixed route or routes, sailing according to a predetermined schedule and offering cargo or passenger space at fixed rates to those who wish to have goods transported or to make journeys. This definition is made to differentiate clearly between liner shipping and tramp/bulk/tanker shipping, a distinction which is referred to below in more detail.

The regularity of service and the fixed rate for each commodity arose as a necessity for traders despatching parcels of cargo on a routine basis. An automatic outcome was competition – competition in service, and competition in rate by the various contending shipowners. That competition produced devices to eliminate financial disaster – either by cooperation or by compulsion. Although such outcomes may appear self-evident, the fundamentals therein were evident in the beginnings of the liner trades, and are reechoed today and will be tomorrow, but by different devices which nevertheless produce similar regulatory results. In effect, the requirements are the same: the methods are different.

The first device to regulate liner shipping was invented in the trades between India and Britain in the 1870s, *viz* the Conference system. This arose from coincidence of factors unique to the Indian trades: first, the development of the steamship coincident with the opening of the Suez Canal caused pressures of competition with the sailing ships going via the Cape to Europe, and also between those new steamships going via the Cape to Europe, and also between those new steamships transitting the canal for the same destinations; second, some major shippers of tea owned their own vessels and shipped their own cargoes, using the freight rate to manipulate their tea selling prices. As an alternative to elimination by competition resulting in a residual monopoly, the contending parties agreed to cooperate and formed a Conference.

It is interesting to read the preamble to the Conference Agreement dated 1875:

> *This agreement is for the purpose of working the steam shipping trade with India, in the way most advantageous to the trade and those engaged in it...[1] with this object it is intended to maintain a regular and sufficient supply of steamship tonnage to meet the requirements for Calcutta, Madras, Colombo, Bombay and Karachi; to distribute this tonnage in such a way as to avoid waste; to regulate by tariff the rates of Freight and Passage Money and the dates of departures; and generally to consider with a desire to meet, the reasonable wishes of Government, Merchants and shippers, in the hope that they, equally with the parties to this Agreement, may find it to their interest to keep the business in its present channels.*

Many other industries are now similarly suffering from extreme competitive pressures brought about by technical changes. The response of the shipping industry in forming a combination of owners to regulate both prices and output is not unique. Much of the debate on Conferences both now and in the past has concentrated however, on the theoretical properties of Conferences, without due regard to the economic and technological characteristics of the liner industry.

One result of the Indian Conference Agreement quoted above was the same challenge that has been made ever since – that this represented the creation of a monopolistic cartel. There may appear to be cartel similarities, but no liner Conference has been able to act as a monopolistic cartel to date; yet strangely, the UN Code of Conduct for Liner Conferences makes this more of a possibility in the future. It has not been possible for a Conference to enforce prohibitive or extortionate freight rates or to provide restricted services, because such limitations have immediately invited commercial outsider activity or governmental interventions.

The members of the Indian Conference Agreement were all British (eight different companies), and they continued in that fashion for the next 40 years – gradually increasing the membership and, as a result, diminishing their own individual shares of the trade to make room for the newcomers – all of whom were European nationals.

There were many researches into the Conference system during this period and many will be familiar with, for example, the British Government Enquiry into 'Shipping Rings' in the early 1900s, or the almost coincidental US government Alexander Committee report, or the more recent UK government Rochdale Enquiry. These all concluded that the Conference system fulfilled a policy of self-interest not necessarily contrary to the public interest. To quote Churchill in another context, 'They are the worst alternative, save all the rest', ie if they are an evil, they are an acceptable and necessary evil. The Conference system continued to exist and expanded. It continues today because it answers a necessary requirement enabling cooperation between nations engaged in seaborne trade.

However, many developing countries have since claimed that such cooperation existed then to the exclusion of some, and, in particular, often to the exclusion of the national in his own trade. The fight has been for a rightful share and a voice in the carriage of national liner cargoes. Many of these objectives have been achieved partially because those aims seemed right and justified, but also because world opinion was changing.

The changing context of liner shipping

Over the past 50 years, world opinions affecting political, social and international relationships have changed more rapidly than during any other period in, perhaps, the previous 1 000 years. To some extent, this has also been hastened by technological changes – Harold Macmillan, a former UK Prime Minister, remarked that if one listed the great technologists of the world since, say, Leonardo da Vinci, 80% are alive today, thus indicating a rate of technological change such that ten years of current development probably covers as much change as perhaps 100 years of development did 400 years ago.

This may mean that we face change faster than we are capable of absorbing it – because human nature changes but slowly – and it may also mean that if, as a nation, a people, an industry or a company, we do not keep pace with changes, then we shall fall behind.

The developing countries' objectives and achievements have been to ensure their own full participation in the carriage of their national liner cargoes. The methods they adopted to induce those changes were, in the first instance, the national pressures of traders supported by government – as they saw it, necessary instruments with which to face the opposition pressures of capital and possession.

Although it needed that pressure to start the reaction, my experience of those times testifies that, fortunately, there were at that time, on both sides of this problem, men of vision and sense who realized that change in this direction was inevitable and that it was just. The result – slow, and probably wisely so in the sense of needing to learn as well as being able financially to support the task of walking before running – was a cooperative development between all parties involved.

However, the parties directly concerned were shipowners, not governments or traders. This left unsolved the problem of belief in a cartel influence and, perhaps more relevant in many quarters, a belief in a foreign-dominated cartel influence. Because the seaborne carriage of cargo is the most economic long-haul transport system, the liner industry is here to stay. Despite cargo reductions through airlines creaming-off the top-rated cargoes and the bulkers taking the bottom-rated cargoes, the major commodities tend to increase in quantity, and it thereby becomes increasingly necessary for governments to ensure a satisfactory system preventing any abuse in the transport of a nation's seaborne cargo.

World changes affecting political outlook, social structures and technology, and the speed of these changes, have produced a greater desire in many countries for a regulated liner shipping industry, going beyond the original Conference system and beyond the objectives set by the earlier British pioneers.

If the political economy of most countries is concerned with two basic issues, *viz* security (ie the prevention of disruptions by conflict), and the monetary value of trade and services, then the transport chain falls especially and importantly into the latter category. It is evident, however, that changes in the world's economic structure and relationships necessitate a greater centralization of interests if developments are to occur in an orderly fashion.

The evidence of the past is that efficient and reliable liner services can only be maintained in a regulated market, and the alternative to the method of regulation by the Conference system is a complex and costly system of multinational governmental regulation. Unregulated liner trades, or those only partially regulated by weak Conferences, generate excess tonnage, poor load factors, low returns on capital and an inability to effect replacement of fleets, especially in an inflationary climate. The economic characteristics of the liner industry are such that an efficient resource allocation in the industry can only be achieved through some form of market regulation. Efficient performance and the assurance of adequate service on a continuing basis and at acceptable rate levels flow from a rational organization of each of the principal trades.

Current constraints on the liner shipowner

The cost of transport, like all communication costs, demands heavy investment and is becoming more capital-intensive. The resultant freight cost creates antagonisms which require machinery to prevent breakdowns and unfairness. There are other factors which tend to discipline or limit the extent of freedom of the liner shipowner to control his own activities.

Soviet penetration of liner trade

One important influence is the pressure of the USSR liner fleet breaking into established world trades. The USSR has the largest conventional liner fleet in the world, far larger than its national cargo requirements, and is thus seeking employment in the trades of other nations, ie as a cross-trader, but with a costing basis usually well below that of other nations. An example of the implications of this can be gauged from the fact that the major liner trades of the world are containerized; they comprise at present about six trades, the longest of which is between Australasia and Europe. A monthly sailing, ie a regular identity, can be provided in the Australasia-Europe trade, and thereby likewise in any other trade with two container vessels. Thus, with 12 container vessels it would be possible to encroach into the major liner trades of the world and disrupt these by intensive rate action. The power to do this is certainly there, and it could be used either for earning foreign exchange or for political reasons, or for both.

A major criticism of the Soviet fleet is that it charges much lower rates of freight and thus competes – some say unfairly – in others' trades. At the same time its own national trade is largely protected itself by the cargo booking system or by the method of bilateral trading and shipping agreements – the latter agreements carefully, or artfully, excluded from the UN Code of Conference Practice by such nations. In all probability however, the Soviet fleet does operate at lower internal costs than many other nationals, just as, for example, the UK fleet operates more cheaply than US flag vessels or German flag vessels. The economic and social structures of such countries are different and it is not possible for equity or fairness in 'cost' to be made effective by commercial methods alone.

Developing countries' objectives

The second major influence is the growing demand of the developing countries to participate in the carriage of the world's trade. Insofar as any country may dominate freight levels in its national trade, a national share below 50% at uneconomic rate levels ensures a majority subsidy of that trade by the non-national carrier, which then benefits the trade, but not necessarily the shipping industry of the nation at the other end. Participation in the carriage of the world's trade implies a fleet size and usage greater than necessary for national trade alone; it can also produce foreign exchange earnings, as opposed to participation solely in the national trade producing only foreign exchange savings – both cases assuming the operations are economic.

The UK liner fleet, being long-established, has built up a chain of trade memberships, which enables the liner fleets of the major UK companies to operate a linked system of voyages covering contiguous areas and thus operating their vessels with the least unused or unoccupied space. Many of these voyages are therefore in cross-trades – an opportunity not readily available to newcomers, but an area where they will increasingly seek membership.

The UN Code of Conduct for Liner Conferences gives encouragement to universal cross-trade membership, and if any application is refused, even for the practical reason that the slices of cake otherwise become uneconomic to all, there arises then the challenge of discrimination among what are apparently equals in right.

The consideration in the UN Code for claimants to join a third flag trade is without concern for the volume of that trade to support more vessels out of limited freight: a conflict of interests must thereby arise.

An interesting sidelight concerning many minor cross-trades is that service patterns and rate levels are largely dictated by occurrences and results in the major trades with which they may be related. It is uneconomic to deviate or delay for a lesser return than can be made in the major trades, and some minor trades may suffer in consequence.

US policy

Mention must be made of the special attitude of the USA concerning liner trades, because it concerns both participation in their trades and the freight rates applied in them. That influence dominates a large section of world trade in a particular way, protective according to some, restrictive according to others.

An increasingly restrictive interpretation of the US Shipping Act of 1916, largely in response to the highly interventionist role of the US Department of Justice, has hampered liner operations. This has been to the disadvantage of US lines more than it has to their European competitors. It has prevented coordination and rationalization as well as mergers, among US lines, and is largely responsible for the excess capacity, and hence the high level of rates in the US trades.

Resource ownership, cargo generation and trade shares

The OPEC principle of applying enforced prices for limited material resources has so far applied especially to oil, but it is possible to see this being applied in respect of other basic but limited resources, possessed by a few nations but required nowadays by all (eg iron, manganese, cobalt, chromium, tin, grain, coffee, meat etc). In this regard in the early part of the 19th century, England supplied about 40% of the world's requirements of copper from its nationally mined resources. That type of resource contributed extensively to its consequent trade development and shipping development; but it is non-existent today.

This aspect introduces another influence increasingly affecting the shares of trade held by liner companies in Conferences. Demands are increasing for the shares of a trade to be related to the amount of cargo generated by the nation concerned. This puts a premium on nationality and reduces the need for efficiency. Even though the EEC has excluded its intra-national trades and seeks to exclude its intra-OECD trades from control and division under the UN Code, there is no doubt that with the

EEC trades, whether intra-EEC or inernational trades with other nations, some EEC nations which have a large trade-generating capacity will seek to proportion their fleet size in keeping with the proportion their trade bears of EEC trade. The growth of a German or French fleet and the consequent decline of a UK fleet in the EEC trades would be a result of such pressure. Conversely, the right of establishment under EEC rules does open the possibility of joint ventures or operating procedures beneficial to the low cost countries in the EEC.

The 'Valente' principle

Mr Valente, the Brazilian government representative at earlier UN Conference for Trade and Development (UNCTAD) shipping committee meetings, often acted as spokesman for many developing countries at those meetings and was the author of an article in the journal of the Carnegie Institute Foundation, and because of the serious implications in his theory – perhaps practice – it is worth quoting verbatim.

> *The common Measure of Understandings was adopted [by UNCTAD] unanimously, though with certain reservations. This agreement considered: 'that the development of merchant marines in developing countries, as well as their participation in Liner Conferences as full members on equitable terms, is to be welcomed' [and that] 'the question of development of merchant marines by developing countries should be decided by such countries on the basis of sound economic criteria'... Obviously there was no doubt that economic considerations should be taken into account by any country planning the establishment or expansion of its merchant marine – no rational planner could consciously base decisions on unsound economic criteria. But the insistence on the obvious seemed to confirm the fact that the expression might be used to denote mere commercial profitability at the level of the enterprise.[2]*

Mr Valente's last phrase is the fundamental point of his subsequent commentary that 'the expression might be used to denote mere commercial profitability at the level of the enterprise'. He then states that, 'interpreted in this restricted sense, it would encompass the establishment of a merchant marine in a developing country only as an industry among others, losing sight of the all important implications of shipping for national security and the development of the economy as a whole'.[3]

Mr Valente's understanding of the province of a national merchant marine can thereby be translated as a public utility. Because all international trades have at least two independent nationals involved it follows that under this method if a national is content to subsidize its trade through its shipping industry (incidentally also for the benefit of the cargo recipient of the other national) it must anticipate that countermeasures will be induced by the nation at the other end of the trade to protect its shipping industry.

Social and technological changes

Regarding changes in social structures, it is possible to see the influences on the shipowners' previous freedoms now exerted by trade unions, in addition to the complete revolution in manpower requirements both at sea and on shore resulting from the technological changes in ship-handling, cargo-working and port facilities. The reduction in manpower requirements creates problems particularly in countries with an excess of manpower but with limited capital resources. There is no doubt, however, that most capital-intensive substitutes for manpower are proving themselves to be a cheaper cost item in the long term than manpower; thus the problems of redundancy or unemployment for many must be faced and solved. One must probably accept also that there will be levelling upwards of wage scales induced by international union pressures so that the previous benefits of some countries using or supplying low-cost labour will diminish.

The liner industry is characterized by a very high proportion of fixed and inescapable costs. This entails steeply falling (and rising) average and marginal cost curves. In these circumstances great importance attaches to optimum capacity utilization, and the unit cost of the service falls rapidly with improved utilization of vessel space. The path to reduced unit costs and cargo rates is the attainment of higher load factors. Far greater benefits accrue from high vessel utilization than from increased competition generated by adding to the number of line services operating in a trade. The latter increases the vessel tonnage operated without increasing the aggregate of cargo tonnage available to be handled, hence increasing the unit cost of doing business. That method is apparent in US policies causing wasteful competition, excess resources in their trades and unacceptably low load factors.

Technological advances have developed and changed radically the customary manner of handling cargo; a simple illustration is the development of the container system. This method necessitates a different type of ship, of cargo working gear, of cargo-booking and freighting, of port facilities and of inland collection and delivery facilities. Apart from the wholesale change of method the question arises – as it did with the change from sail to steam – whether we have the courage, the faith and the resources to make such a change. Further, can the trade support the cost of such necessary capital expenditure, and will the trade sustain the employment and investment?

It requires a considerable act of courage and faith, in addition to willing financial backers, to make such enormous investment, particularly if there is evidence of past losses or inadequate return on investment, or inadequate understanding by shippers and traders of the need for their support in what must prove to be a joint adventure. Happily, the growth of the UK Shipper Council provides a forum where the leaders of the shipowners and the shippers industries can meet, discuss, consider and plan on a large scale for mutual benefit.

The aim then becomes, not, as in the past, the shipowner following a policy of self-interest, but the shipowner and the shipper following a policy mutual self-interest. There is another important facet to the march of unitization. A liner service of the breakbulk type, if replaced by a container service, will if planned for full economy of operation, probably replace perhaps six to eight breakbulk ports by direct service and, by reason of aggregation of cargo to reach the economic cargo load, probably produce a less frequent service, although it may be a faster service. If this is applied to eg the Indian Conference service with Europe, this means a reduction, if the trade were wholly containerized, from about 80 breakbulk vessels presently employed in the Conference service, to, say, ten container vessels. The impact on seagoing manpower requirements alone is immediately apparent. But at present that trade covers some 18 different countries in India and Europe, each of which has and would be accepted as entitled to employ a national shipping line in that trade. If there are to be only ten vessels covering the whole trade and there are 18 entitled participants, then the answer is that individual ownership is not practicable but has to be replaced by a consortium, international and cooperative.

For many developing countries there are difficulties in embarking on a wholesale change to unitized cargo movement: the high cost of large-scale financing requirements; the lack of adequate infrastructure (an absolute necessity if the full benefit of unitized cargo movement is to be obtained); the displacement of labour already in excess in such countries. For these reasons the trade of such nations can develop but slowly towards the full unitized movement of cargoes. Unitized cargo movement afloat tends to broaden the range of cargo movement when ashore with the resultant widening of the coastal sphere of operations, so that many Conferences now overlap or combine, and rate levels become uniform over a wide area irrespective of port performance, cost or quality. This is likely to provoke claims by better ports for rate priority, ie a type of despatch money as opposed to the shipowners' demurrage-type surcharges on inefficient ports.

Such developments would seem on today's experiences likely to affect adversely most UK ports against their continental rivals. However, the merging of ocean services with inland services has also stimulated competition and diminished the effectiveness of Conferences to protect their chosen sphere.

As part of the technological changes to come it seems likely that alternatives to the now very expensive fuel oil and diesel oil will be developed, entailing different ship design – even a change as limited as a return to pulverized fuel will have considerable repercussions on design, supply, manning and facilities.

Regulation of pollution

Increasing applications of technology, more sophisticated and hazardous cargoes, larger vessels and reliance on automation, enlarge the danger of likely pollution of the world's sealanes and require greater control against the liabilities of inadequate vessel-operating procedures. The history of merchant shipping spawning the legal concept of limited liability and the insurance industry, may be repeated by its causing the development of greater international regulation of vessel design and operation.

DEVELOPMENT OF THE UN CODE OF CONDUCT

The over-riding influence which will have the major impact on the liner shipping industry is the UN Code of Conduct for Liner Conferences. An understanding of the background leading to its introduction is necessary to appreciate whether it can or will attain the intended objectives, and to examine what those objectives are.

The UK government's Royal Commission on Shipping Rings was an example of concern as to whether the Liner system as operated through Conferences satisfied the public interest. That enquiry, like all subsequent enquiries and investigations, concentrated on two basic matters which recur constantly: first, how much of a trade is held by each participant – which takes into account the extent of privilege, of right, of claim, of competence etc; second, what is that trade worth to a participant which takes into account the extent of profitability or loss, the levels of freight charged and the ability of trade to sustain any freight level.

There are two main reasons why this industry in particular should be subject to so much enquiry and research. First, it is suspected of having cartel influence capable of being exercised perhaps to the detriment of public interest. Second, it is suspected that the freight levels are applied arbitrarily by the shipowners without regard to the public interest, which is usually interpreted as also meaning the shippers' interest. To say that these are wrong suspicions does not eradicate them, but it is not easy for non-shipowners to appreciate why the shipowners in Conferences act as they do and how these fears can arise.

Rate levels in liner shipping

Rate levels in the liner trades – externally the main contentious issue – are represented by a freight tariff which is usually the sum of the trading results of all the lines in a Conference. It is generally a balance between the income and expenditure of all members, assessed partly on past results and to some extent on probables. It includes a cross-subsidy of commodity freight earnings and probably a cross-subsidy of voyage legs. Because it is generally more economic to sail a vessel full than part empty – assuming that marginal costs are covered – it means that some goods will pay more freight than it costs and likewise others will pay less. The freight tariff is published for a fixed period ahead and the rates therefore contain an element of forward price risk. Not all merchants, especially large merchants, necessarily wish to pay for the absorption of the risk; they might prefer a discounted rate and run the forward risk themselves. That, however, is a method of benefit perhaps to large shippers but not to small shippers.

The carriage of bulk cargoes, liquid or solid, is usually the result of a negotiation either cargo-by-cargo or on a contract basis for a full ship carrying one commodity. The rate of freight is then fixed by market forces, ie by the relationship between the demand for ships and the supply of ships at that moment. This is constantly changing. Each fixture is a separate bargain. Rates may double or treble or diminish in a few weeks. Nobody screams if this happens. No extortionate shipowner is blamed. None claims his business is ruined. None blames the market. It is above criticism, like an Act of God.

Unfortunately, liners cannot rely on this simple method, partly because they are carrying a miscellany of commodities, the mix of which they cannot predict, partly because one part of their service to trade is to quote rates fixed for some period ahead so that forward business may be transacted, and partly because they are fixed in the trade concerned and cannot follow whatever is the best business available worldwide at the time, as do the tramps and the bulk carriers.

Because of the miscellany of cargo which liners may be asked to carry during the course of a round voyage and because they never know just what its mix will be, two points emerge. First, one can seldom say what the exact cost will be on which to assess the rate on any item of cargo. The earnings of the ship will depend on all the cargo and what the mix is. Second, if we are to judge whether rates are too low or too high we cannot judge it by one voyage or one shipper: it is necessary to look at the results of the overall service. This means that the rates on individual items of cargo interact so that, if total revenue/expenditure is to remain in a constant relationship, then if one rate is reduced another must be increased, but not necessarily by the same amount because the volume of one may differ from the other. If such a method of adjustment were followed logically, then rates would vary continually at short intervals – a situation unacceptable to most shippers of liner cargoes. Apart from this there are the problems of politics, or outsider competition, or international comparison, or the difficulty of altering differentials which have been long established, however well justified an alteration may be.

Liner rates have to be fixed consciously, and they do not fix themselves almost entirely by the level of the freight market or the commodity market as happens in the bulk trades. Perhaps it is part of the burden which the liner industry must bear, but it always seems to be the reasoning of the shipper (and frequently governments) that freight adds to the cost of an article but not to the value of an article. Thus the activities of liner Conferences will always be a source of friction and suspicion. Because the shipowner has to be the arbiter of the rate level and the service which he is willing to provide at the price, taking into account the ability of the trade to pay his price and the alternatives of competition from other shipowners or other commodity markets, the suspicion naturally grows that the shipowner – or more probably the Conference – has ultimate power over freight levels and, of course, over the amounts of cargo which its various members or aspiring members should lift.

The charge of cartel influence

The shipowner cannot attain a despotic position from financial power or from monopoly power. As for financial power, it is interesting to see that the P&O SN Company, one of the world's largest liner companies, is financially smaller than IBM's French subsidiary company. Monopoly power, if ever attained by commercial means, has always been attacked immediately by non-Conference outsider operators who, surprisingly, seek not to defeat the Conference but to join it.

The international membership of Conferences also creates a moderating influence on rate levels because the member line of each nation concerned is also interested in ensuring that the goods of that country are not priced out of the market by unreasonable freight levels; thus a mutual discipline results.

An examination of the membership of any Conference over a period will illustrate the considerable changes in membership. The growth of the Indian Conference from eight UK members to 26 international lines from 16 different nationalities was cited above. The membership of the Atlantic Conferences today bears almost no resemblance to the pre-war membership; change is continuous, despite the Conference system.

However, it is this aspect of belief of cartel influence contrary to the public interest which induced the research into the Liner Conference system resulting in the several Codes of Conduct subsequently introduced.

Rochdale Report

The first attempt at such a regulatory system arose in the UK government's Rochdale Report of 1970, leaving aside for the moment the regulatory methods applied by the US government (because they were particular to the US trades), and other recent examinations, such as the Grigor report of the Australian government (which is particularly concerned with the production of cost data to support the application of rate levels).

The Rochdale Report did not suggest that an alternative to the Conference system was necessary either in the public interest or in the traders' interest. It did, however, propose that Conference members should collectively accept a published Code of Practice to be evolved from negotiations between government, shipowners and merchants. In general it proposed that the Code should cover:

(1)   the admission or otherwise of new members to the Conference;
(2)   the availability of Conference tariffs;
(3)   a revenue/cost system to establish the fairness of rate levels;
(4)   a system of consultation between merchants, governments and shipowners;
(5)   and specifically, that freight levels should be adjusted commercially between ship-owners and merchants, without government intervention.

The proposal was accepted generally by European and the Japanese governments, and at a meeting in Tokyo in 1971 they asked their shipowners to develop a code alorg somewhat similar lines to those in the Rochdale Report. The shipowners acting as a body negotiated with their combined national shippers associations and produced an agreed Code, acceptable to their governments. The theme of that Code was self-regulation made effective by consultation. A study of its clauses shows that the subsequent UN Code copies many of the European Shipowners and Shippers Code clauses but includes also a prescribed cargo-sharing system.

PROVISIONS OF THE UN CODE

The UN Code is a remarkable document, both in what it achieves and in being such a badly drawn document, because it is intended to have international legal standing. It is criticized for being too rigid and at the same time for being too ambiguous. Both criticisms are valid and their consequences are of great moment for the future of the liner trade.

The reason for this is perhaps best explained if an extract is cited from the speech of the US representative at the final plenary session of the UN meeting at Geneva when the great majority present signed the Code. He stated that:

> This Conference was unavoidably caught up in these obstacles, which were a major factor preventing adoption of a universally acceptable Code, despite the great talent, best intentions and the herculean efforts of the principals involved. It remains almost incredible thus, that the major issues were worked out in a compromise attended by a handful of delegations four days before the end of the Conference. Their product was not discussed in Committee or Plenary for lack of time. There is a totally inadequate record. There was insufficient time for essential drafting chores even after the limited compromise was reached. A proper legal drafting group, common to all diplomatic Conferences, to finalise textual language referred to the Plenary, could not be established for lack of time and the quality of the final text reflects this... A different source of basic problems in our attempt to negotiate this convention was the ever present potential clash between Code rules to govern liner conference conduct and the scope of Government freedom to regulate in the same area. We did not, until the end of the Conference, squarely address the issue of the extent to which the code might be construed not only as regulating Conferences but also as limiting the actions of Government. However, we have still not clearly resolved this critical issue one way or the other.

I believe that his speech derived not from antagonism to the Code but from the poor quality of the product which resulted. The Code's implications, merits, faults, and its ultimate effect on the industry, can be assessed in relation to the main problems faced by the parties involved in liner shipping – how much of the trade one has, and what it is worth. Table 1 therefore specifies the proposed solutions for these issues in what may be termed the 'regulating Codes' mentioned above. This illustrates a development towards the ends which the liner industry will face and how these two issues are suggested or ordered for reconciliation.

The descriptions used are of course abbreviations of the methods, and it is necessary to realize that a Panel or an Arbitrary decision can be enforced, but the result of a consultation or a conciliation cannot be so enforced. This having been said, it is difficult not to accept the result of conciliation without flying in the face of public opinion and thereby accepting the consequences of that pressure.

The results of acts taken as a signatory to the UN Code are equally and legally applicable to all sides, ie on national shippers and shipowners and on ratifying governments. The different devices for settlement of these two major problems all move around the issue of regulatory control, inducement, self-regulatory acceptance,

Table 1. Provisions of regulatory Codes.

Method	Membership (share)	Rate levels
Rochdale	Panel decides	Negotiation
Tokyo	Conciliation	Panel decides
European Shipowners/ Shippers Code	Conciliation	Consultation
UN Code	Arbitrary	Conciliation

or of hoped-for reasonableness. None, so far, goes to the length of legislative domination of the financial freedom of the shipowner to determine his own future. That could well be the next step if the present objectives fail, but such a step then involves the problem of national legislation being above or subservient to international legislation, a question which greatly concerned the developing countries in their preliminary discussions on the Code at the Santiago UNCTAD III meetings; this is an issue on which not all developing countries, like many other nations, have yet come to any common conclusion, or are likely to for some years to come.

The US government delegate at the signing of the Code in Geneva also referred to the inadequacies of drafting. This is particularly important to shipowners, because the consequences of those inadequacies will fall on them when different countries adopting the Code as part of their legal framework (which must happen because the Code is an international convention) either interpret the wording of the Code differently, or the contending parties in a dispute arising under the Code choose to read the wording in a manner which suits their particular objective. These can be real fears causing delay and heavy cost in settlement.

In respect of each clause of the Code, it is possible to find several examples of the need to seek and thereby demand legal interpretation by case law of particular words or phrases; further, it is not especially useful to quote the 'Objectives and Principles' set out at the beginning of the Code to obtain an adequate guideline, which were, in fact, written after the Code clauses had been drafted. Eg, Article 2, clause 8, gives a right to join a pool: does it also give a right not to join a pool, and, if so, how does this conform with the national lines being considered as a group under clause 9 of that Article? Article 2, clause 17, states that the goods concerned are regardless of origin or destination. This opens the question of the ability of land-locked countries to obtain a national share trade. Article 7, clause 3 (a), allows the introduction of royalty systems provided the shipper does not violate those by evasion or subterfuge, a wording which is clearly nonsensical.

Thus, the document, although well intended and the result of great compromise, is a legal hotch-potch which will cause the liner shipowners far more costly troubles than it is intended to secure – although it will become a goldmine for lawyers. Those costs will have to be paid for – out of freight.

The method of sharing cargo adopted in the UN Code undoubtedly opens the door to many new applicants to the detriment of the present shareholders. Whether the Code is operative by agreement or not, it is more than probable that most trades will tend to be regulated in that pattern, ie right and precedence in national trade and a widening of membership in non-national trades. Such developments must react to the detriment of the UK fleet overall.

The method of regulating rate levels under the UN Code offers, however, the prospect of a return consistent almost with a cost plus basis; the difficult area is the lengthy period of fixed forward rate cover during an inflationary era. As yet there is no definition of a fair level of profit; nor is there any definition of the extent of capital involved, or whether depreciation of existing assets or replacement of existing assets must be covered out of freight earnings.

Developments in bulk trades and prospects for liner shipping

The change from the small tanker and from the small berth bulk tramp to the VLCCs, the OBOs and the specialist bulkers has been as dramatic as the advent of the unitized system has been in the liner trades. The pressures against the existing bulk/tanker fleets are similar to those already experienced, and to some extent met, by established liner fleets. It is possible to see from the progress and pressures in the UK Shipping Committee a similar attack being mounted for national cargo rights, and on a claim that flags of convenience are especially contrary to the interests of many developing countries. The arguments on which these attacks are based ignore the prime interests of the cargo to secure the best and most economic terms for world interests. This aspect is covered in detail in the paper by Mr Robin Pender.

CONCLUSIONS

(1) The liner industry will enlarge by way of quantity of cargo movement.
(2) The trend will be towards unitized cargo movement, afloat and ashore.
(3) Automation will take over largely in vessel-manning and cargo-handling.
(4) Fleet numbers will diminish and individual companies will tend to be absorbed into consortia.
(5) Labour redundancies will arise with consequent union and social problems.
(6) Trades will tend to be allocated nationally and there will be little room for newcomers.
(7) The size of a national fleet will tend to be limited by the size of the national trade.
(8) The allocation of trade under the UN Code will not promote efficiency of operation or minimize cost.
(9) Low-cost operating countries will tend to provide or operate vessels for high-cost countries possessing ample trade, on a joint venture system.
(10) Large capital expenditure will be necessary and an adequate return on that investment must be assured or it will not be made by the private sector, and trade could decline.
(11) Freight levels will be determined from a costing basis, providing the shipowner with a steady but not very encouraging return on capital.
(12) A certain amount of protection will be afforded by national governments covering their fleets against excessive intrusion by others into their national trade.
(13) That protection will produce, conversely, a greater measure of government intervention in the operation of its merchant fleet both in respect of financial matters and employment.
(14) Finally, the UN Code will cause numerous legal battles, costly to the contending parties, and an early Review Conference of the Code will be necessary.

These conclusions perhaps suggest an unhappy future for the industry. That, however, is far from my expectation, for one main reason. Those who are connected with the sea, like those who are connected with the land, are close to and have to recognize the forces of nature. They therefore become, and are, tolerant, ingenious and resourceful people. They are also in the business of shipping not essentially for the mundane reason of profit, but because it is also a chosen way of life.

These attributes produce a type of person who, as shown by the survival and increase of the Conference System over the past 150 years, will find an answer to these problems. That answer will be a happy one, of that I am certain.

References and footnotes

1   Note that the trade is placed first and the shipowners second – an important realization of precedence which becomes even clearer in more recent times.
2   M. G. Valente, *Shipping and Developing Countries' Participation,* Carnegie Endowment No 582, March 1971.
3   *Ibid.*

DISCUSSION
UK business interests

(1) Capital development can be put in by a country and then used by somebody else to undercut the rate. There is a considerable threat to container services posed by the double OCL line on three counts:

- they get cheaper manning;
- they get cheaper bunker fuel;
- they have had cheaper building facilities than could possibly be obtained by a British shipowner.

This is all good competition, but on the other hand the people who invested in the facilities, invested in the container units, and invested in all the systems for supporting a container transport system were in most cases British. Are there any benefits for British interests?

(2) It has been suggested that British shipping is likely to continue to decline because of the UNCTAD agreements etc. One possibility is perhaps for British shipowners to concentrate on offering ship management services – which they do at present, but which could be developed – for ships under the flags of Third World developing countries.

There is also the requirement for financing ships. This can quite well be done through the London market. If the British shipowners have a contribution to make which includes the financing and the managing of ships, then this is something which would enable us to keep a fair share of the shipping market.

Author's response. With regard to ship management services, I suggested in the latter part of my paper the likely development for British interests of joint ventures as being a means, perhaps, of bringing in expertise, finance and other things useful to those other countries seeking to benefit from trade that they wish to ship. The benefits for the UK are outlined in that part of my paper.

Pay differentials

What is this speaker's view on pay differentials between the British industry and others?

Author's response. On the question of the parity of wages, for example for Indian seamen, it was my recollection at the time that this was introduced that the wage rates – quite correctly, probably, from the Indian government's point of view – were not as high as European rates should be, because otherwise a pattern is set for other demands in India itself for equality of status – policemen, postmen, stevedores, for example, all sorts of people – and this can create wage chaos in that country. The way in which it was overcome was to create a welfare fund with the differential being paid into a fund which was paid into India and then allocated by the government, possibly with the agreement of the trades unions, to the men concerned for retirement and so on. At least that was how it was supposed to work in theory. What I could never understand, however, was that the same system was not applied to an Indian seaman serving on an Indian ship. So if an Indian ship was alongside a British ship, the man could be employed on either, and a higher wage rate was paid by the owner of the British ship than by the owner of the Indian ship to the same man. This always seemed to me to be anomalous.

UK policy in UNCTAD

When one looks back at the attitudes of government in the UK towards the UNCTAD-proposed Liner Code, were we right to have embarked upon almost total opposition to the concept, or should we have tried more realistically to come to terms with the inevitable?

Author's response. I myself have always had some thoughts about that. At the time it was discussed at the plenary negotiations in Geneva there was a group called the packeteers and another called the non-packeteers, and the UK was a member of the non-packeteers, whose proposals were not accepted. To that extent we then lost influence in terms of subsequent negotiations.

Cost of running a Conference

How much does it cost to run a Conference? The secretariat is small, cheap and efficient, but when it comes to the auditing of all the cargoes and commodities which are carried, the freights that are put on them, the accountancy staff, the bills of loading etc, which must all be accommodated, accounted for and then audited, it would be interesting to know how much a Conference actually costs.

Author's response. My own experience of running a major Conference was that the cost would be about 0.5% of the freight income. It is minimal, and is certainly less than the cost of running the Federal Maritime Commission in the USA. A Conference does not deal with making out bills of loading and that kind of thing – that is a matter for the shipowner himself, or his forwarding agents, or his agents. A Conference is simply a centralized body for the organization of Conference operations, not for the material booking and transfer of cargo.

Official representation in Conferences

Is any role seen for official representation within the Conference Secretariat, at Conference meetings, discussions and so on, as advisers to or observers of Conference procedures – maybe to advise on, for example, the effect on trade of freight rate increases, etc? Is a role seen for political observers in Conference negotiations and Conference secretariats?

Author's response. At major Conference meetings where there is a national line involved, which is often the case with developing countries, this is tantamount to official representation from government. Maybe it is not made explicit, but certainly the national line sits as a representative of government. I do not think it would be a good idea to set up such a forum to include political representatives from all the governments concerned, because this would undoubtedly tend to transform a commercial organization seeking reasonable viability into a political forum, and thus change the whole concept; even if representatives sit simply as observers, their influence is undoubtedly felt.

3. UNCTAD PROPOSALS IN RELATION TO THE BULK TRADES

R. R. Pender (Director, Stag Line Limited)

Most of this paper is devoted to examination of the practical effects of UNCTAD Secretariat proposals for the development of the merchant fleets of developing countries, as we in British shipping see them. A brief history, however, serves to put the subject into perspective.

In its efforts to engender and promote the development of the Third World's merchant fleets, UNCTAD first concentrated on the more valuable general-cargo trades. The result of this was the formulation of the UN Convention on a Code of Conduct for Liner Conferences, already described in detail by Mr Hudson.

UNCTAD then turned its attention to the bulk trades in a two-pronged attack which concentrated first on open registries and, second, directly on the bulk trades. To some extent, the debate on open registry shipping has been a curtain raiser for the more important question of the bulk trades. The two issues were brought together at the Fifth Session, UNCTAD V, at Manila in May 1979.

It may at first appear that the debate on open registry shipping is quite separate and self-contained, but this is not in fact the case. The UNCTAD proposals to phase-out open registries represent a circuitous approach to the same objective as that embodied in the proposals on the bulk trades. This objective is to ensure for the developing countries an equitable participation in the carriage of their seaborne trades, particularly in bulk commodities.

Open registry issue

I consider the open registry issue first, before coming to the bulk trade proposals themselves. However, at the outset I wish to emphasize that this whole issue is in fact a purely political matter. The outcome of the debate in UNCTAD is not likely to depend on the relative merits of each argument in commercial or economic terms, for it is entirely dependent on the strength of the political groups within UNCTAD. The Group of 77 (the developing countries) have 116 votes between them and therefore have an overall majority with which to pass any resolution through UNCTAD. The OECD countries (Group B) have only 30 votes with which to stop the developing countries or suport an alternative resolution. Group D (the Eastern bloc) also have minority voting power with ten votes. Viewed in this light, it is not difficult to see how the fate of the bulk shipping industry lies in the hands of the Third World governments.

The intertwining of the open registry and bulk issues is based on the fact that a high proportion of vessels registered under flags of convenience are bulk carriers and tankers. Indeed, according to UNCTAD statistics, 83% of the world's open registry tonnage was engaged in the bulk trades in mid-1977, which is the equivalent of about one-third of the world's bulk fleet. A large proportion of this tonnage is beneficially owned by a few developed countries, which, according to the Secretariat, are unable to operate their vessels competitively because of prohibitively high crew costs. These shipowners therefore register their ships in countries which do not have strict regulations governing the ownership of vessels (these are known as open registries or flags of convenience). The UNCTAD Secretariat maintains that these shipowners are thereby able to employ cheap shipboard labour from the developing countries and can offer a competitive and profitable service. Thus, the Secretariat reasons, if open registries were eliminated, owners of open registry vessels would be obliged to transfer their operations to joint ventures with developing countries to remain competitive. The Third World countries would thereby increase their participation in the bulk trades and acquire finance and expertise for the operation of their own vessels.

It is an interesting tactical point that the UNCTAD Secretariat chose to initiate the open registry debate long before the opening debate on the bulk trades in Manila, where the connection between the two issues became apparent.

The open registry question arose in UNCTAD as early as 1968, but it was not until 1974 that any action was initiated. It was then agreed that the economic consequences of the existence or lack of a genuine link between a vessel and its flag of registry should be examined. An *Ad Hoc* Intergovernmental Working Group was convened in February 1978 and concluded, among other things, that certain economic elements were normally relevant in determining whether or not a genuine link existed between a vessel and its country of registry.

Immediately prior to UNCTAD V in May 1979, the emphasis of the debate on open registries had changed. The UNCTAD Secretariat report on 'Merchant fleet development' for discussion at UNCTAD V linked the open registry question to that of the bulk trades. Among the policy recommendations, it proposed that: first, agreement should be reached 'on the principles relating to the economic elements of the genuine link which *must* exist between a vessel and its country of registry ...', and second, that measures should be taken by governments 'to prevent the establishment of new open registers, and to phase out flag of convenience operations over a period of years ...'.

Resolution 120 (V) called on the UNCTAD Secretariat to undertake studies on the repercussions of phasing-out open registries, and on the feasibility of establishing a legal mechanism to effect the phasing-out.

The *Ad Hoc* Intergovernmental Working Group on Open Registries examined these studies in January 1980. Essentially the session was inconclusive. The Group of 77 took a great deal of time trying to agree on a joint view. This eventually emerged as a draft resolution concluding that open registries should be phased-out within a reasonable period of time. Liberia and Panama dissented from this 77 Resolution.

Group B, with France alone dissenting, concluded that the material provided by the UNCTAD Secretariat did not establish the case for phasing-out open registries and that considerable doubt remained as to whether such action would be to the overall economic benefit of the developing countries.

Instead, Group B recommended that individual developing countries wishing to build-up their bulk fleets should report in detail to the Committee on Shipping any specific 'barriers' that they had encountered in seeking to enter the bulk trades. Group B also recognized the need for greater transparency about the ownership of vessels under open registry or other flags to enable flag states to fulfil their responsibilities under international law, particularly in respect of marine safety, protection of the marine environment and the training of seafarers.

The meeting decided that both the Group of 77 and Group B resolutions should be sent forward to the UNCTAD Committee on Shipping at its next meeting in September 1980, when there will be further substantive discussion on this subject.

UK bulk shipowners and operators have no particular urge to fight for open registry owners – far from it, for they are competitors in many cases. It could be argued that the British fleet might well be one of those to benefit if open registries were to be phased-out. Nevertheless, we are firmly opposed to the UNCTAD proposal for two main reasons.

Critique

First, we object to any interference in flag-of-convenience operations which is purely politically motivated. Second, we agree with the UNCTAD Secretariat's conclusion that the phasing-out of flags of convenience would have a profound effect on the structure and operation of the international bulk shipping industry, but we are not convinced that it will have the effect that the Secretariat believes or, indeed, desires.

The UNCTAD Secretariat's studies nowhere give any evidence to support the presumption that shipowners of developed countries, if denied the opportunity to register their vessels under flags of convenience, would opt to transfer their operations, even in part, to developing countries. If these shipowners would not participate in joint ventures with developing countries, the principal purpose of phasing-out open registries is negated.

Studies undertaken by other research organizations, which have examined the question in far more depth and detail than the UNCTAD Secretariat, suggest that the Secretariat's presumption is substantially incorrect. A study by the Economic Intelligence Unit, for instance, indicates that owners of open registry tonnage are unlikely to redeploy it in joint ventures with a developing country unless that country is politically stable and can offer adequate financial guarantees of security for the investment.

In the light of the conflicting conclusions of the few studies undertaken on the effects of phasing out, we are very reluctant indeed to see governments embark on a course which may well fail to achieve its objective, and additionally may prove detrimental to the world's bulk shipping industry. Before taking such a drastic measure, it is essential for further studies, and indeed for some conclusive evidence, to be produced to indicate that phasing-out open registries will be beneficial to the bulk shipping industry in general, and to the incipient bulk fleets of developing countries in particular.

The second line of argument used by the UNCTAD Secretariat to justify its proposals for eliminating open registries concerns substandard shipping. This is a matter of great concern to many, not least to British shipowners. It is also a matter which has regrettably lost much of its potency through being linked, and indeed confused, with the open registry issue.

The Secretariat claims that because the owners of flag-of-convenience tonnage reside outside the territory in which their ships are registered, these governments have no effective jurisdiction over the owners and are unable to enforce adequate shipping standards. This is not in fact strictly the case.

Statistically, it is true that the flags of convenience have the worst safety record. However, there are many ships of high standard operated under open registries, and substandard ships operated under other flags. Our criticisms and actions against substandard shipping must be directed against all such operations, irrespective of flag. There is already a widely accepted package of international instruments covering these aspects. What is important now is that they should be comprehensively adopted and effectively implemented.

Our second main objection to the proposal is that it is linked with that to introduce cargo-sharing into the bulk trades. Because we oppose the latter proposal, for reasons set out below, we also object to any interference in flag-of-convenience operations which is motivated by the same political considerations.

UNCTAD approach to increasing Third World participation in bulk trades

The first studies and recommendations were reported to UNCTAD V. At this conference, Group B (the OECD countries), maintained that the international bulk trades provided one of the most perfect examples of a situation in which free-market conditions prevailed. There were no 'barriers' to the entry of any fleet into these trades, provided that the shipowner was able to satisfy the demands of producers, consumers and charterers for economical, safe and efficient transportation. If, however, the developing countries had encountered any obstacles to entry into these trades, the governments of Group B were prepared to discuss them, and examine how they might be eliminated.

The Group of 77 (the less developed countries) rejected Group B's approach and formulated a Resolution on the basis of the guidelines given in the UNCTAD Secretariat's studies. This Resolution was passed by majority vote. With the exception of Turkey, all Group B countries voted against the Resolution, while Group D (the Eastern bloc) abstained.

Among the features of the Resolution (Conference Resolution 120(V)) were requests for the UNCTAD Secretariat to undertake in-depth studies on the bulk and refrigerated cargo trades, and the controls exercised by transnational corporations. Some of these studies have now been produced and will be discussed at the Ninth Session of the UNCTAD Committee on Shipping, due to meet in September 1980.

Our particular fears about the detrimental effects of the implementation of UNCTAD's proposals are perhaps best illustrated by examining the central recommendation of Resolution 120(V). But first it may be helpful to clarify the distinction between the bulk and the general cargo or liner trades.

Bulk/liner trades distinction

The most important difference in this context is that, in the liner trades, vessels operate along regular trading routes, like bus services. The bulk trades, on the other hand, are largely irregular, and vessels are often chartered on a single voyage basis, and infrequently repeat a voyage pattern. Further, the liner trades are tightly organized Conferences, whereas pure market forces control the provision of bulk shipping. In addition, there is a fundamental difference in the types of cargo shipped – liners carrying relatively small parcels of a wide variety of cargoes, and bulk shipments consisting of homogeneous cargoes such as oil, ore and grain.

UNCTAD Resolution 120(V): critique

Any problems encountered by the developing countries in increasing their participation in bulk shipping are not inherent in the current structure and operation of the trade. They are those of any entrant into a free market economy industry. In short, they are the problems of acquiring finance for the acquisition of modern and efficient vessels and gaining the expertise in the management and operation of them. These are not 'unfair' in any way. They are faced by owners of all nations who continually have to strive to become and to remain competitive. The thesis expounded here is that in this struggle there are no short cuts that do not have very grave consequences. In my view UNCTAD is proposing short cuts, and ignoring the consequences.

The central provision of the UNCTAD V Resolution on the bulk trades calls on governments, 'to take steps to ensure for developing countries equitable participation in the transport of all cargoes, and more specifically bulk cargoes generated by their own foreign trade by national vessels of the respective trading countries or by vessels otherwise operated by them'. The phrase 'equitable participation' has been interpreted by the UNCTAD Secretariat and developing countries to mean 'equal share' or a 50:50 cargo split between vessels of the trading partner countries.

We fully recognize, and have never disputed, the freedom of developing countries to participate, if they so wish, in international bulk shipping. However, we do not accept that it is appropriate for countries to be given automatic rights to cargo shares in their bulk trades, as implied in the central provision of Resolution 120(V). We take this view because we believe that the present free-trade mechanism provides the world's economy with an unsurpassably economic and efficient bulk transport mechanism.

We regard the ability to adjust supply to meet demand as a prime objective in attaining economy and efficiency in any industry. In the bulk trades, shipping is able to do this because ships are not generally tied to a particular trade, except if perhaps there is such a regular flow of traffic that a regular service is the most economic method of providing for it. Importers and exporters are able to charter vessels as and when the need arises, and owners can endeavour to obtain freights so that their vessels spend the minimum of time on ballast voyages.

If prescribed cargo shares were introduced into the bulk trades, vessels would be restricted in the number of trade routes in which they would be allowed to operate. This would increase the number of ballast passages which would have to be made. In many cases, it would probably increase the amount of time that vessels are idle, waiting for a cargo which they are permitted to carry. All in all, prescribed cargo shares in bulk trades would restrict the operational flexibility of the shipowner, and also the charterer, the shipper and the receiver, and would thereby decrease the efficiency of shipping in the international transport of commodities.

In addition, prescribed cargo shares would severely limit the action of competition and would protect the operations of inefficient and costly shipping services. This would be particularly detrimental where a country has only one national shipping company. Irrespective of the service that such a company offered, or the cost of the service, 50% of the cargoes traded by the country would automatically be reserved to this one enterprise, and the shippers would inevitably have to bear the cost. Many developing countries have only one, often state-supported, shipping enterprise.

Conclusions

Prescribed cargo shares in the bulk trades would therefore give rise to uneconomical and inefficient use of shipping both by restricting the operational flexibility of the shipowner, charterer, shipper and receiver, and by curtailing competition among shipping companies. The additional cost of these inefficiencies would have to be borne by the producers and consumers of the traded goods. This would fall on developing and developed countries alike.

Several papers have now been produced by the UNCTAD Secretariat for discussion by the Committee on Shipping in September 1980. One of these entitled 'Merchant fleet development: guidelines for developing countries' is significant not only because of its content, but also, and particularly, because of its tone and flavour. Its purpose is to provide the developing countries with a set of guidelines to increase the competitiveness of their merchant marines in all sectors, especially in the bulk sector. In the latter regard, the report reiterates the principal provisions of Resolution

120(V) as policy guidelines. Essentially it recommends that the carriage of bulk trades should be equally shared between the ship operators of each trading partner country and that this should be enforced by developing countries through joint ventures and bilateral agreements between trading partner countries, in the contracts for the sale or purchase of bulk commodities and through the abolition of open registries.

For reasons already stated, we find such a policy not only objectionable, but dangerous. Equally objectionable and, in my view, detrimental, is the tone of the report. The paper seems to have been written in a spirit of confrontation. It suggests that the Third World should milk the developed countries of all it can get before rejecting them. The blatant bias and contentious approach of the Secretariat really makes one wonder what happened to the so-called independent body of international civil servants, and the concept of cooperation. Frankly, if the Third World will not pledge itself to cooperation in the long term, there is no reason why Western shipowners should cooperate in the short term.

My views on UNCTAD's bulk trade proposals are not governed solely by altruism. Their effect on the established bulk shipping industry would be very damaging. The success or otherwise of shipping enterprise would become less dependent on its ability to attract business through offering a good service to shippers at competitive rates, and more dependent on the size and nature of its country's international trade. The interests of countries which in effect export their shipping services, as the UK does, would be damaged a great deal.

The British bulk shipowner has painfully gained expertise – often over many years – in the harshest possible environment: an international free market. As a result, he is able to offer a competitive and economic service and is thus reluctant to see the results of his labours taken away purely on the basis of political considerations.

When UNCTAD and the UN generally are working so energetically towards liberalizing trade and reducing protectionism in every field other than shipping, it seems anomalous that the UNCTAD Secretariat should be endeavouring to *introduce* protectionist measures into an almost perfect free-market industry.

Discussion

Decline in free trade?

The paper ends by arguing that it is incongruous that the UNCTAD Secretariat should be endeavouring to introduce protectionist measures into what is described as 'an almost perfect free market industry'. Given that worldwide the completely free market market is generally in retreat, is there not perhaps something to be said for any rate considering how British shipping can successfully operate in a market which is not completely free? That is, thought should be given to a world where the free market is not in operation. A free market may continue to some extent, but is it wise to expect it undoubtedly to continue?

Author's response. A future decline in free trade may well come about, and, if it does, shipping is always adaptable. Either one can go along with it, or if one does not like the new regime one can sell the ship tomorrow and go and make ice cream. The arguments produced in support of what could be regarded as the decline in free trade so far as bulk shipping is concerned do not seem to many to give an adequate reason – at present anyway – for upsetting what is regarded as essentially a very free and unbridled competitive market.

UK policy in UNCTAD

If UK policy in UNCTAD concerning the liner trade has proved to be wrong as far as the UK and other EEC members are concerned, are we now going down the same dangerous course with the bulk trade, having regard to the political realities that exist?

Author's response. Those who were involved in this matter some two to three years ago came to the conclusion that perhaps all the government officials who had been involved in the Liner Code discussions – and they had been involved in that for about ten years – might perhaps not know too much about how the bulk trades worked, and so we suggested that they might like to attend a day's seminar so that it could be explained how the market worked and how we try to make an honest living. A very successful one-day seminar took place and it was from then that the Consultative Shipping Group (CSG) governments took the line they did in Manila in 1979 and to date have supported that line.

Merchant shipping and defence

In the shipping business who is it who considers the adequacy of the UK merchant fleet for defence purposes? Does anyone do so at all? The clear impression is that the merchant fleet is developing along present lines purely for commercial purposes, but in doing so it is becoming totally unsuitable for defence purposes. No one appears to be thinking about this: someone should be.

CHAIRMAN'S REMARKS

Need for coherent UK policy

If this Conference is to achieve anything, then some of the questions that have been posed as to choices will have to be answered. Indeed, if we find ourselves unable to answer them, we must at least be able to state what the implications of each of them are: how far we believe that the freedom of the market for bulk trade is likely to disappear entirely – which I find a little difficult to believe – under the influence of the UNCTAD proposals; and how far British shipping can, and ought, to go along with it.

What we obviously cannot do is to emulate the courtiers of King Canute who, on the seaside, advised him that if he simply sat there the waves of the sea would not wet his feet because he was so powerful a king that they would retire before him. Speaking as an entirely unbiased outside observer, I have the feeling that there have been some of King Canute's courtiers active, both within and without the British government, in advising them on marine policy in the past, and I have observed that the sea has, as so often before, failed to take any notice of the advice that they have been given.

I hope that in the next sessions we shall hear more to enable us to answer some of the questions.

The First Presentation of Papers (1-3) and Discussion Sessions were chaired by Professor D. C. Watt, Chairman of the Greenwich Forum.

4. Ships of the 1990s and Their Operation

THE IMPACT OF FUEL COST AND TECHNOLOGICAL DEVELOPMENTS

Marshall Meek (Technical Director, British Shipbuilders)

So much has happened over the past ten years that it is difficult to project forward to the 1990s with any confidence. We find ourselves more easily thinking of the shorter-term 1980s. Nevertheless, at the pace historically found in marine progress it could take until 1986-87 to develop a new item of shipboard machinery or equipment such as a fluidized bed boiler, to the stage where it can be considered as reliable for a new vessel. The ship could then be built by 1990 but it will certainly take longer for such an installation to become widely accepted.

The decade 1968-1978/79 saw rapid changes and new ship types such as the containership and the ro-ro, arriving well within a ten year span. However, these changes stemmed from the need to handle the cargo more efficiently, and that was more easily achieved than the developments we expect in the next 10-15 years. The latter will be associated with fuel cost and the search for new propulsion systems. It has always taken a relatively long time for new engineering systems to be adopted in shipping, eg the process of change from steam reciprocating machinery to steam turbine or diesel, or from coal burning to oil. Some would suggest that there is a 20 year cycle in marine developments between a concept and general acceptance into service in the form of a tried and tested product.

There will of course still be conventional ships in large numbers in the 1990s. Air transport, being less efficient and therefore relatively more costly than sea transport, will not now make the inroads into seaborne trade that at one time seemed likely. Figure 1 shows a generalized comparison of transport efficiency for several types of transport vehicle. The superiority of cargo-carrying surface vessels is apparent provided modest speed is accepted. A cargo vessel is 20 times more efficient than an aircraft which might be carrying similar types of cargoes.

For marine craft it would appear that there is unlikely to be, by the 1990s, a move away from relatively slow displacement type craft. Table 1 shows simple specific power values that illustrate how the slower and larger vessel always shows to advantage, and this is more important than ever with higher fuel costs.

It is not clear, however, what impact land transport such as the Trans-Siberian railway will have, especially if it is not run on a normal commercial basis. As to the volume of trade by sea and the actual numbers and tonnage of ships required, I refrain from comment in this particular paper, other than to suggest that ships will probably have a shorter lifespan, because they will be designed down to minimum scantlings and strength for cheapness, because of more rapid changes in trade requirement, and because of the more onerous and frequent changes in legislation.

Acknowledgments
The views expressed are the writer's alone and do not necessarily represent those of British Shipbuilders, with whose permission, however, it is presented.

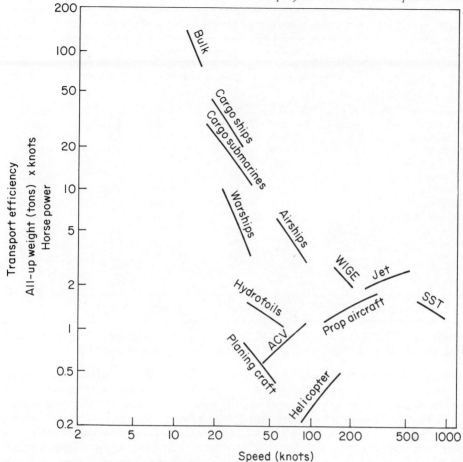

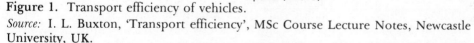

Figure 1. Transport efficiency of vehicles.
Source: I. L. Buxton, 'Transport efficiency', MSc Course Lecture Notes, Newcastle University, UK.

It seems that the dominance of the UK fleet will be less in world terms following the severe and permanent-looking run-down of the late 1970s, unless of course by the 1990s we are such a low-cost country, or have such other financial attractions, that foreign owners will find it beneficial to register and operate from the UK.

The 1990s will clearly be a more difficult era than the years that are past. A high level of international and national legislation is here to stay, with the environmentalists being ever more demanding. At the same time the cargoes carried will be even more hazardous, with nuclear products probably featuring more largely. Shipping must be prepared for tighter controls on many activities. It is remarkable that in 1980 the number of casualties to ships has been increasing year by year in spite of all the talk and recommendations concerning greater safety. By the 1990s it can be expected that there will be closer control over the way ships are navigated and managed. In some areas such as the English Channel this is happening as to navigation already.

But it remains astonishing that in 1980, the position is much the same as in 1972 – that the largest vehicles can sail over vast areas of the world with the scantiest evidence of true identity.[1] A motor car must by day or night be capable of immediate

Table 1. Typical values of specific power for ships and other marine craft.

Ship type	Displacement Δ tons	Speed $V\,kn$	Power $P\,hp$	Speed coefficient $V/\Delta\ 1/6$	Specific power $P/\Sigma V$
Tanker or bulk carrier					
Mammoth	600 000	15	60 000	1.6	0.01
Large	250 000	15	30 000	1.9	0.01
Medium	30 000	15	12 000	2.7	0.03
Coaster	4 100	12	2 100	3.0	0.04
Dry cargo	17 000	17	11 000	3.4	0.04
Container ship	36 000	22	32 000	3.8	0.04
Trawler	1 800	14	2 400	4.0	0.01
Cargo liner	18 000	21½	20 000	4.2	0.05
Vehicle ferry	5 000	20	16 000	4.9	0.16
Passenger liner	44 000	29½	110 000	5.0	0.08
Destroyer	4 000	30	40 000	7.5	0.33
Frigate	1 200	40	48 000	12.3	1.0
Patrol craft	90	50	11 000	25	2.5
Foilcraft	70	50	3 500	25	1.0
Sidewall hovercraft	16	32	360	20	0.7
Amphibious hovercraft	160	65	13 000	28	1.2

Source: A. Silverleaf, 'Ships of tomorrow – some possibilities and prospects', *Transactions NE Coast Inst of Engineers and Shipbuilders,* December 1969.

identification in the event of misdemeanour. A VLCC of 250 000 dwt can sneak through some precarious strait endangering countless miles of coastline with a fair chance of being unidentifiable. Some would say she can even change her name at sea and dispose of her vast cargo illegally with at least some prospect of success in avoiding identification. It is not clear why ship operators should not be seeking, in this era of modern communications, to have the position of their valuable assets reported daily, or even more often. No other item of such value as a large ship and its cargo is allowed to range so widely and in such a relatively hazardous environment without its owners immediate cognizance. *Berge Istra* and *Berge Vanga* lost at sea subsequently involving massive and futile searches are cases in point – not to mention the strange case of the *Salem* where there is some suggestion that she actually off-loaded her cargo in an unscheduled port without the rightful cargo-owner's knowledge.

The 1990s could be a period when new propulsion systems will be entering service; when there will be (following the rather premature and ineffective efforts of the 1960s) increased automation controlling machinery and reducing manpower with electronic systems; tighter control of all shipping activities; and even fewer men on board, with the corollary that when emergencies occur on board they will be real.

On this last point the writer believes that there is some danger in proposing to reduce a ship's crew below some practical minimum limits. It is intellectually exciting, technically challenging, and apparently feasible, to develop a degree of automation which will cope with bridge, engine room and cargo working systems and make it possible to reduce crews almost to single figures. But there can still be illness or physical accident among the crew on a long voyage, and it is not unknown for more than one person to suffer from the same complaint. Data on such occurrences must be available now in shipowners' records and should be analysed in any consideration of minimum numbers. Likewise, the number of times a vessel is involved in an emergency such as a rescue operation, should be analysed to show with what probability it could happen that with a very reduced crew it might be impossible to fulfil the normal obligations of seafarers to each other. There would seem to be need for an international approach involving an honest dialogue with Masters and Officers on such a vital subject to avoid unfair pressures on sea-going folk, or dangerous competition betwen shipping companies.

SHIP DEVELOPMENT SCENARIOS

All pressures affecting shipping activities end in expressions of cost – unless it be the less easily quantifiable sociological aspects of which we are now more aware.

These cost pressures can, in terms of importance, be separated into energy costs and other costs. The other costs will be cost of labour both ashore and afloat and all that relates to employing people – the cost of the ships themselves and the servicing of the associated finance; the cost of repair and maintenance, port and harbour dues; and the cost of insurance.

Before we seek the solutions to these cost pressures we should study them a little more closely. Energy costs must come first because in the overall expenditure of running present-day ships the fuel cost outweighs all others. For a typical Panamax bulk carrier under the British flag, excluding capital costs and depreciation, the fuel cost can represent well over half of all running and voyage costs, say 55% or something over £1 million/year, remembering that every operator will have a different figure depending on average speed, days at sea, weather conditions, actual draught etc. The next largest item is crew costs which can run at 40% of fuel costs.

This is followed in order of importance by maintenance and repairs, and port and harbour expenses, each of which can represent 30-50% of crew cost. It is clear therefore, that the main endeavour is to reduce fuel cost, and then labour/manning costs. All this applies fairly generally to most types of vessel, although faster and more powerful vessels would of course have an even higher percentage of expenditure on fuel.

On the whole, ships' machinery is remarkably reliable and time out of service is low. One UK shipping company averaged 20 hours lost due to breakdown at sea per ship per year in 1978 for a fleet of 59 ships of mixed type, ie container ships, tankers, bulkers etc.[2] Such figures do, however, imply a rigorous approach to initial design and to maintenance procedures.

There is considerable point in trying to quantify more carefully the relative merits of the various savings in operating and first costs of vessels. The calculations are not necessarily simple but using well recognized cost-revenue sensitivity computer program comparisons such as Table 2 can be developed. This refers to a Panamax bulker of 60 000 tons dwt whose particulars are given in Appendix I. Other ship types will require separate investigation, and indeed even this design of bulk carrier will require careful scrutiny if the main assumptions given in Appendix I are significantly altered. Nevertheless, the important features are clear, remembering that the figures shown relate to 10% variation in each of 23 items and the comparison is based in the first instance on differences in net present value. Other criteria such as required freight rate also need to be considered where applicable.

A change in freight rate has the greatest direct effect on profitability and its improvement must always be the aim; but it should be noted that higher freight rate is often associated with higher ship speed, a complication referred to below. The desirability of increasing the load factor is obvious, but it is not easy to alter this without incurring other adverse effects such as increasing distance steamed.

Table 2. Overall net present values and freight rates.

Case	Description	Merit order	NPV	Difference in NPV	Equivalent FR Rate	RFR of shadow price
1	Basis	22	214 682	0	8.0000	7.9254
2	First cost decr by 10.0%	7	735 991	521 308	7.8189	7.7443
3	Decr steel weight	9	699 593	484 911	7.8343	7.7609
4	Decr cost of steel	20	318 944	104 262	7.9638	7.8892
5	Decr hull labour costs	19	323 288	108 606	7.9623	7.8877
6[a]	LW Decr by 1.0% of payload	14	444 975	230 293	7.9208	7.8470
7	Decr horsepower	6	743 809	529 127	7.8200	7.7470
8	Decr specific fuel cons	4	959 476	744 794	7.7417	7.6672
9[b]	Decr speed loss from new	17	351 124	136 442	7.9529	7.8787
10	Decr building time	11	633 644	418 962	7.8577	7.7848
11	Ship life incr by 4 years	10	678 356	463 674	7.8336	7.7566
12	Ship life decr by 4 years	24	−465 271	−679 954	8.2644	8.1809
13[c]	Decr time out of service	21	284 785	70 103	7.9758	7.9016
14	Decr port turnround time	8	728 983	514 301	7.8273	7.7552
15	Decr steaming distance	3	2 040 326	1 825 644	7.4002	7.3397
16	Decr crew costs	13	563 666	348 984	7.8738	7.8042
17	Decr upkeep costs	12	622 063	407 381	7.8535	7.7839
18	Decr fixed costs	18	337 298	122 616	7.9574	7.8828
19	Decr registered tonnage	15	380 031	165 549	7.9426	7.8680
20	Decr port charges	16	355 119	140 437	7.9512	7.8766
21	Decr cargo handling cost	23	214 682	0	8.0000	7.9254
22	Decr bunker costs	5	942 120	727 438	7.7473	7.6727
23	Incr load factor	2	2 517 608	2 302 926	7.2727	7.2049
24	Incr freight rate by 10%	1	2 517 608	2 302 926	8.8000	7.9254

Source: I. L. Buxton, *Engineering Economics and Ship Design,* BSRA Publication, 1976.

Differences in distance steamed have, in fact, the next most important effect. It will not of course be possible to reduce distance by 10% on any voyage, but a 2% reduction might be possible and will still give a significant benefit, equal for example to reducing crew cost by 10%. This is why operators should look more readily at satellite navigation systems probably combined with weather routeing to make sure that every possible mile is shaved off the voyage by more accurate position fixing and more precise navigation.

The benefits from reducing the specific fuel consumption are roughly similar to reducing bunker costs, although it is not easy to design a diesel engine to give a 10% better consumption – and there is little chance of a 10% reduction in bunker cost! Only by making the step change to a cheaper fuel such as coal will any gain be made under this heading.

Next, a 10% reduction in horsepower would be significant – but again unlikely. Yet in all these items the summation of a few per cent here (such as obtained with a smooth hull) and a few per cent there (perhaps coming from a more efficient propeller) represents the way in which overall savings can build up to an appreciable total.

The current pressure for smaller crews is explained by the change produced by a 10% reduction of crew costs; but a 33% reduction from 30 men to 20 is more likely to be attempted by operators. The saving is then very appreciable, and equals, for example, a 20% reduction in total ship horsepower.

In this way a picture can be obtained of the best route to follow to achieve savings for any particular set of circumstances. It is possible to get a feel for the value of fitting, for example, a waste heat recovery system where the additional cost, lost deadweight and increased upkeep can be balanced against the fuel saving. However, such calculations need continual updating with the latest fuel and other costs.

Figure 2 shows the possible scenarios for the 1990s and resolves the solutions to the above cost pressures into (a) the technical solution and (b) the organizational solution.[3] For the rest of this paper we go down the chart first on technical, and then on organizational prospects in more depth and detail.

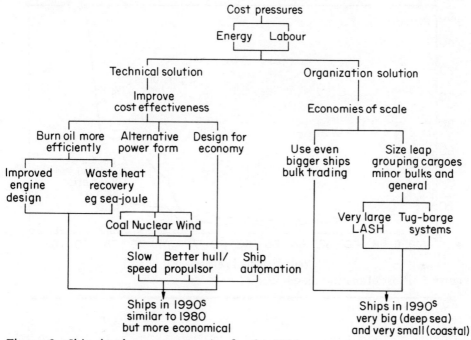

Figure 2. Ship development scenarios for the 1990s.

The technical solutions will embrace a vast range of interesting developments, and much research and design development will be applied before general unanimity is achieved on the most economic form of propulsion. But by the 1990s the ships themselves will still be similar in type to those we see today although propelled relatively more efficiently; and because no improvements or innovations will succeed in cancelling out or even balancing the increases in operating costs, there will be no option but to see these costs passed on to the shipper in the form of increased freight rates.

However, if the organizational solution is followed as the alternative way of achieving cost savings of the magnitude required, we could envisage an attack via fundamental principles, ie a further effort to achieve the undoubted economies of scale which apply to surface ships; a rational appraisal of the optimum speed for a given trade; and a renewed appreciation of the benefits of reducing time in port, involving, perhaps, new methods of consolidating cargoes into very large units. So it could be a choice between (a) leaving aside the cargo consderations as having been developed as far as possible over the past decade, and concentrating on energy saving; or (b) renewing the quest for more far-reaching ways of consolidating the cargo and adopting a transportation system to suit, while still incorporating as far as possible the energy saving concepts.

THE TECHNICAL SOLUTION

Cost of fuel and where it goes

Transportation by water uses 3% of all the energy used in the world,[4] ie it is by no means a major user, and it is nearly all oil. Ships' bunkers consume about 4% of total

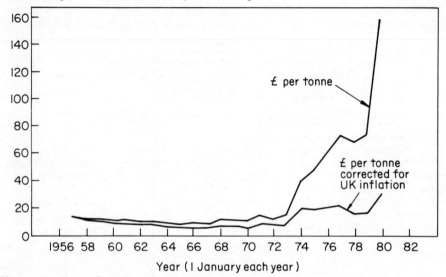

Figure 3.   Cost of marine diesel oil.

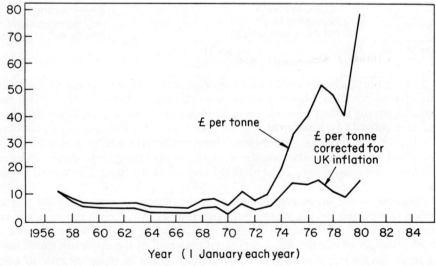

Figure 4.   Cost of marine residual fuel.

oil consumption. The shipping industry therefore has little muscle in effecting any change in the pecking order in the 1990s.

The cost of ships' fuel (diesel and residual) over recent years is shown in Figures 3 and 4, both in straight money terms and also corrected for inflation.

When inflation effect is taken into account the rise over the 'oil shock' year of 1973 is not too drastic. It is the more recent rises of 1979 that give the reason for the current urgency in seeking cost savings. We must ask ourselves what could happen in the 1990s. Clearly the price of oil will go up and not down; and in view of the uncertain political nature of many producing countries it is a fair question whether it will be available freely and reliably in any case. We must therefore use it more efficiently to look elsewhere for cheaper fuels.

The energy consumed in a modern diesel driven ship is illustrated in Figure 5. There are many points of energy loss to examine. These are expressed in another way

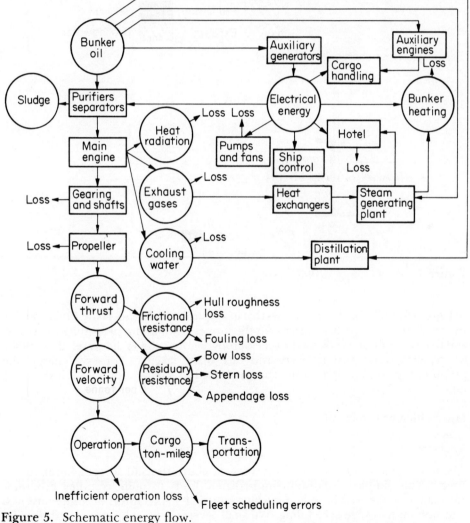

Figure 5. Schematic energy flow.
Source: Energy Saving in Ships, BSRA Technical Memorandum S69, 1979.

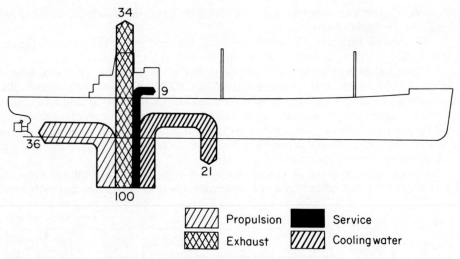

Figure 6. Heat energy – 1960 vessel.

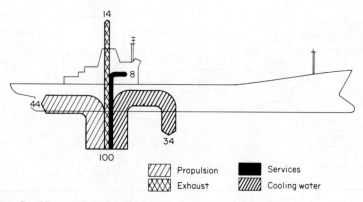

Figure 7. Heat energy – 1980 vessel.

in Figures 6 and 7. The former shows that in a typical diesel vessel of the 1960s roughly the same heat energy disappeared up the funnel as went into propelling the vessel, and that was only one-third of the total output. Figure 7 shows the vessel of the 1980s where, with waste heat recovery and care being taken to conserve energy, the proportion going into propulsion has increased to 44% and only 14% lost up the funnel.

More efficient use of oil

Lower speed

The most obvious way to reduce oil costs is to burn less and accept a lower voyage speed. This simple proposition immediately leads to quite complex economic calculations if the vessel is still to satisfy conflicting market forces of competitiveness and optimum voyage scheduling. We shall revert to the subject under design for economy, and merely note in passing that fuel savings from slow speed running, provided the ship can still satisfy the charterer, are much more readily achieved than by any other combination of fuel saving features. It is suggested, therefore, that in the 1990s we shall not see ships running much faster than they are now.

Lower quality fuel

The quality of available fuel has lowered recently and the likelihood is that this trend will continue, accompanied by redesign of marine machinery to accommodate the heavier residual fuels rather than the distillates, yet still to keep maintenance costs at a reasonable level. There will be stronger pressure for effective ways of purifying the residual fuels and the present conflict between centrifugal separation and homogenizers will no doubt be resolved; as will the vexed subject of oil additives which, although presently suspect as to their effectiveness, may indeed be developed to give enduring benefits by reducing corrosion and inhibiting acid formation.

More efficient operation

There is no doubt that fuel savings can even at present be achieved by improved operating practices. For one five year old steam-driven tanker of 250 000 dwt operating at design heat balance, the fuel consumption was 8% higher than at sea trials

Table 3. Common areas of recoverable fuel losses.

Area	Equivalent fuel loss tonnes/day	Power range
Maintenance		
Main condenser		
air leakage	3	Full
fouling	5	Full
Main boiler		
1.5% efficiency	2.3	Full
55% air heater leakage	1.0	Full
CO_2 fan running	1.0	Full
Worn burner tips	–	
Main turbine		
internal by-passing	–	
large gland leaks	0.7	Full
Evaporator fouling feed pump		
using extra nozzles	0.15	Full
high discharge pressure	1.0-0.5	½-Full
Operation		
Keeping extractions in use with deaerator floating	up to 7.0	½ or less
Reducing boiler pressure	up to 3.0	½ or less
Reducing electrical load by 10%	0.7	Full
FD fans at slow speed	1.0	Full
Pump drains to condensate line	0.1	All powers
Modifications		
Keeping feed heaters in use	2.0	½ or less
Keeping evaporator on exhaust steam	2.0	½ or less
FO recirculation before heaters	0.3	All
Auxiliary condenser by-passing	–	All

at full power.[5] 3% was recoverable by improved operation and 5% was due to deterioration in equipment which could be retrieved by suited maintenance. Table 3 shows common areas of retrievable fuel losses for such a tanker normally designed to burn 158 tonnes fuel/day at full power.

It is clear therefore, that operators will in future learn the importance of good housekeeping in the engine room.

Energy recovery

Efforts must in future be made to recover some of the 60% of calorific value of fuel that is lost in a typical diesel engine. Exhaust gas losses can account for 30-40% of this and jacket, lubricating oil and scavenge air cooling about 25%. But this waste energy must first be converted to mechanical or electrical energy and the problem is that it is largely low-grade heat from which the energy must be extracted. However, various systems are already being developed and there will certainly be still more effective devices. Fresh water distillation, utilization of cooling water generally, and more careful use of power for ventilation are all worth more consideration. One successful system for recovering energy from the higher-grade heat in exhaust gases is the British 'Seajoule' package where energy extracted from both exhaust gas and cooling water is converted into propulsion power by using an electric motor to give additional power to the propeller shaft or for auxiliary power. It is claimed that there can be a net improvement of 3½-4% of work output.

There is little doubt that further progress will be made over the next ten years in finding better materials to take care of the greater corrosion that will occur when exhaust gas temperatures are lowered and when energy is extracted below acid dew point.

Energy reducing systems

There are still several ways in which the conventional machinery design can be revised to yield energy savings. These will all need to be developed fully over the next ten years or less. At the moment cooling pumps and fans operate at fixed speeds independently of the main engine output. There can therefore be excessive cooling or unnecessary pumping. This can be improved by using variable speed pumps and fans with a control loop incorporating temperature or pressure sensors. It is claimed that 10-15 kw can be saved on a sea water circulating pump delivering 200 m³/hour.

Insulation

There is room for a closer look at insulation on board ship, both to conserve the degree of heating in cold weather and the air-conditioning in hot weather. In addition there are invariably steam pipes both internally and on deck that need examining for efective insulation. Uninsulated deck steam lines can lose 3 kw per metre of length.

Navigation and steering

As we have seen above, it is very beneficial to reduce steaming distance by accurate navigation as far as possible. But both the satellite navigator and the practice of the weather routeing are still not accepted completely by the mariners. The writer is firmly of the opinion that cost of such aids to more efficient operation should not figure prominently. They are small compared either with the capital cost of ship and cargo or with the possible energy savings. In the next ten years there will be development of a reliable microprocessor approach to the whole subject of navigation.

There are also benefits in efficient steering. It is known that the use of adaptive autopilots can produce 1% or 2% saving in fuel by optimizing the rudder and main engine performance against the change in sea state.

On the matter of steering and manoeuvring, the writer is strongly of the opinion that the subject needs rationalizing. At present there is no agreement on what constitutes a good steering ship or a bad, or on what is an easily manoeuvrable ship. No general criteria exist by which standards can be adjudged. There is every case to be made for a detailed and extensive study. It must be that international regulations will call for such criteria during the next ten years.

Designing for economy

Speed

We return to the question of optimum ship speed. It can be proved quite easily that almost any ship will be more economic at lower speed *provided* that the slower vessel can still command the same freight on the open market. This is a big assumption at present but may change as a better understanding of the benefits of lower speed prevails.

Using recognized computer programs for DCF analysis to evaluate the economic worth of different ships,[6] we can establish the effect of installing lower-powered engines giving lower speed and higher earning capacity resulting from less bunkers. A 31 000 dwt bulk carrier as built in 1979 is examined in the various forms in Table 4. Ship 1 is the basis ship of 15 knots service speed with engines developing 10 800 bhp at

Table 4. Economic worth of 31 000 dwt bulk carrier in various forms.

	Ship (1) Basis ship	Ship (2) (1) with mod eng and larger prop	Ship (3) (2) with different eng
Length overall (m)	189.00	189.00	189.00
Length BP (m)	181.00	181.00	181.00
Breadth mld (m)	23.10	23.10	23.10
Depth mld	14.50	14.50	14.50
Block coefficient	0.826	0.826	0.826
Total cargo capacity (m³)	36 850	36 850	37 150
Machinery (Doxford)	Standard 76J4	76J4 modified for optimum performance	76J3 modified for optimum performance
Max continuous rating	12 000 BHP at	7 000 BHP at	7 000 BHP at
BHP (Metric)	123 RPM	100 RPM	100 RPM
Continuous service rating	10 800 at 119 RPM	1 000 at 100 RPM	7 000 at 100 RPM
Speed at CSR and with 10% allowance over trial knots	515.0	13.70	13.70
Engine weight (tonnes)	350	350	279
Deadweight at 10.655 m draft	31 000	31 000	31 050
Payload (tonnes)	28 000	29 000	29 460
Range (miles)	15 500	15 500	15 500
		Larger diameter prop fitted	Larger diameter prop fitted

119 rpm. Ship 2 is the same ship with a modified but similar engine tuned to 7 000 bhp at 100 rpm and with a bigger and more efficient propeller. Speed is now 13.7 knots. Ship 3 is the same ship at the same speed and rpm but with a new engine

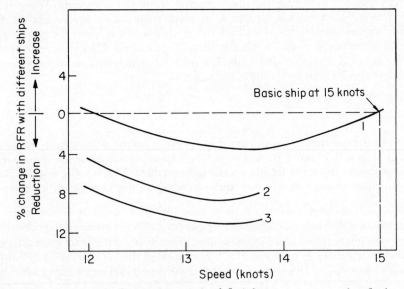

Figure 8. Percentage change in required freight rate (present day fuel cost).

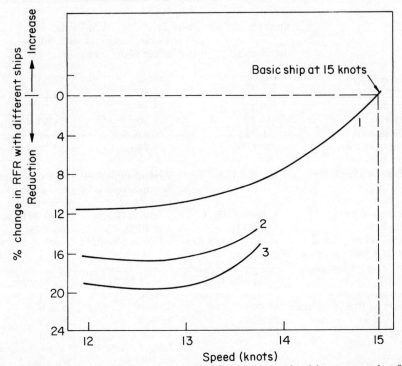

Figure 9. Percentage change in required freight rate (double present day fuel cost).

specifically designed for the lower power. The assumptions used in the calculation of economic worth are given in Appendix II.

When the corresponding 'required freight rate' (RFR) for the cargo has been calculated with net present value of the vessel made zero we can see a measure of relative merit between the ships. Figure 8 shows the reduction in RFR for fuel at present day prices and Figure 9 for fuel at double today's prices. It appears that for this size for ship with fuel at today's price and with 10%/year escalation, the optimum speed is 14 knots rather than the designed 15 knots. If fuel price is twice today's, the optimum is 13 knots. The best economy ship, ie No 3, shows a very real economic advantage of about 8% over the conventional ship, at today's fuel price, *provided* that trading conditions remain the same for each ship.

Accepting that any computer-based analysis, particularly one as simplified as here, is subject to the limitations of the program, we can say that in general, in this time of escalating fuel costs, the ship that is designed to a particular lower speed shows an economic advantage over the conventional vessel simply operated at lower power. This advantage is obtained, it should be noted, without recourse to more complex machinery, and it will obviously be possible to achieve further gain with more sophisticated energy and heat saving devices.

Reduced ship resistance

We can now consider some further approaches at design level to better fuel economy and see how by the 1990s, or even before, there could be savings in power due to closer consideration of the elements that constitute total resistance.

Underwater surface roughness must be improved and it can be. It is generally accepted that a 1% improvement in performance can be expected with a 10 micron reduction in hull roughness. Because an average roughness at present is about 125 and could with care be reduced to at least 100, a 2½% improvement in performance is possible.

Paints will still improve. The current interest in self-polishing paints is symptomatic, and although the degree of efficacy of these is not yet wholly proved and quantified, it is clear that similar compositions will develop further. Because the roughness of some coating systems is known to deteriorate at 75 microns or so per year for the first 6-7 years, and other more expensive epoxy ones at 20 microns per year, there is obviously scope for a paint surface that will give better long life smoothness. Better anti-fouling paints must appear, and cathodic systems with impressed current supplementing the sacrificial systems. Of course, if paints can be avoided altogether this must make sense, and here we have the possibility of better materials making paints unnecessary. Copper–nickel clad hulls to prevent fouling and corrosion could be one answer, although cost and possible erosion at higher water speeds are the present problems.

Air lubrication of the underwater hull is still a possibility and will doubtless be investigated in the coming years.

Better hull forms

The greatest obstacle to improving hull shapes is the cost of model testing. A full programme of experimental tank testing involving methodical variations on just one single hull form can cost up to £100 000 at present. No single shipowner will face costs like this in the development of a design, and few research organizations can fund the number of such exercises needed to provide the range of answers that are needed. There is a great need for the development of a mathematical approach to hydrodynamic performance to the point where the designer can use computer program analysis in his evaluation of the variables open to him.

At present we must still rely on model tests to probe many unknown areas. We still do not know the best hull form for the ballast draughts at which so many bulk cargo vessels run for appeciable periods. For a wide range of typical bulk carriers the ballast voyages constitute 38-48% of the annual distance steamed. Is it better to run light to reduce wetted surface area and accept possibly more adverse resistance and power? Nor do we know the optimum trim in such conditions. Is it better to keep the propeller immersed as far as possible and accept resistance penalties with heavy aft trim, or to let the propeller break surface to a degree? In these same vessels it was found that only 14% of the time was spent above Beaufort Number 5 wind suggesting that the ballast draught conditions should be optimized for the 'good to moderate' weather conditions.

During the decade before the 1990s we must study much more closely the unconventional hull design – the full extent of bulbous bow possibilities; the bulbous stern; the canopied stern designed to ensure better flow aft to the propeller; and the better flow aft to the propeller; and the better determination of power margins to meet expected weather conditions.

Improved propulsive efficiency

It is unlikely that we can improve the conventional propeller design much now, unless metallurgists find considerably stronger materials which will give thinner blade sections and better efficiency. We must adopt a new approach by looking at considerably larger and slower running propellers; contra-rotating propellers; or propellers in ducts or nozzles.

It is basic that the slower the propeller the greater the efficiency, and there are gains available provided the aft end of the ship can be designed appropriately and the power transmission system can be adapted to give the required torque for the lower revolutions per minute. These should be possible, but the associated complications of adverse steering or manoeuvrability must be recognized.

It is generally accepted that the adoption of contra-rotating propellers can give at least 10% improvement in propulsive efficiency. The concept is to leave the wake behind the propeller with minimum rotational momentum and therefore with minimum energy. The difficulties at present are the engineering ones of achieving satisfactory power drive through the bearings and sealings, but these should be overcome in the next ten years. As ever, extra cost is involved but this must be kept continually under review as the overall economics change.

There is still something to learn concerning ducts and nozzles for the larger ships where the accelerated flow can improve propeller efficiency. Large fins forward of and above the propeller are not unknown and several ships have been fitted with them as a cure for propeller-excited vibration. Skilfully designed, these do not necessarily affect the ship's speed appreciably. The writer remains surprised that there is such reluctance to consider fins at the initial design stage; yet operators will go to great lengths to fit them after it is found the ship suffers from vibration in service. It is suggested that the fitting of a well designed fin at the design and building stage can be a simple and prudent way of achieving satisfactory performance on a vessel that might otherwise be suspect regarding aft end flow.

Reduction in lightship weight

There is no merit in propelling unnecessary weight and therefore displacement through the water. Although the main structure of a vessel is controlled by the classification societies and not readily changed, a more careful approach to design could save weight, both in hull steelwork and in outfit items. There will be no dramatic gains but it could be that 2% or 3% reduction in lightship displacement could be achieved, especially if a degree of higher tensile steel is adopted. The metallurgist has not yet really come into his own in ships. They are still built of very convenional materials, but on the matter of energy saving it must be remembered that there is little point in expending more energy in the manufacture of less conventional materials than will be saved in the operation of the ship.

Alternative power sources and fuels

Oil

At present the ships of the world run on oil, being mainly either diesel- or steam-driven, with warships favouring the gas turbine in recent times. The question must therefore centre on the future price of oil and its availability.

As to price, it is obvious it will increase (one estimate is by 300% in real terms by the year 2000); but the bigger unknown is its availability which could be more significant than absolute cost. One distortion, for example, is that the USA, paying an uneconomic cost for its oil, consumes an untoward share of the world's liquid

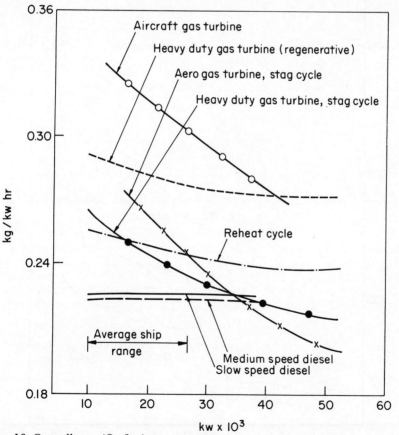

Figure 10. Overall specific fuel consumptions.

Source: R. V. Thompson, Contribution to discussion of R. Lindsay, 'A perspective on oil and other future fuels', *Transactions NE Coast Inst of Engineers and Shipbuilders*, 1979.

hydrocarbons (30% of world available oil each day). It would be well therefore if shipping could find some alternative fuel sooner rather than later; but it is considered that in the 1990s most ships will still be burning oil. Hence the importance of the economies mentioned earlier. Even in the UK fleet in 1979 there were 425 ships, or 25% of the fleet, of less than five years old which might reasonably be expected to be sailing in the 1990s. The reason the marine diesel engine has achieved is present popularity in the propulsion market is shown by Figure 10, the efficiencies are still improving.

There has been much reference in recent times to the deteriorating quality of fuel oil available to ships, because modern refinery techniques take more distillates from each barrel of oil. The residuals left over and which are purchased by shipping

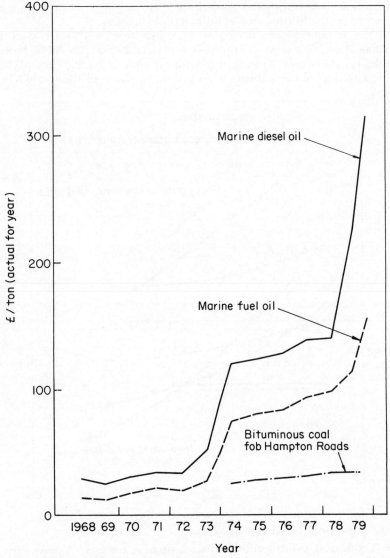

Figure 11. Comparison of coal and oil price.

companies as fuel for diesel or steam engines are then of poorest quality and have deleterious effects on machinery. Much thought is being given to means of coping with it, but it is suggested that within the next few years the position will stabilize so that the supremacy of the diesel will not be challenged on that score.

Coal

Figure 11 shows again the price of marine diesel and residual fuel in recent years, but one particular typical price of coal has been added, although it varies greatly depending on the source. There is an inbuilt reluctance to believe that coal will come back, probably because so many people still remember it as less efficient and unpleasant to handle. Yet the disparity in cost is clear, particularly in those countries such as South Africa and Australia where indigenous coal is cheap and oil is expensive. Reserves of coal throughout the world are vast, those known to be economically viable being some four times as great as reserves of crude. There are difficulties in the UK in altering the relative cost of coal *v* oil as it seems unlikely we can produce cheaper coal. But in Japan there is already a restructuring of energy use away from oil to coal and this could well happen elsewhere, such is the difference in costs.

Coal can either be burned as coal; or it can be used to produce oil; or it can be mixed with oil in a form of slurry or emulsion. It will be relatively easy to design a steamship to burn solid coal because the boiler and turbine are known components and only the method of handling the solid lump needs developing. There have been advances in the handling of coal on land because coal was last used on ships, eg by pneumatic methods, and they could equally well be applied on board ship now. The advent of the fluidized bed boiler, still in its infancy but showing promise, could be a very real help in the more efficient burning of coal on board. It is believed that it would not be practicable to use pulverized coal as is burned in power stations on land because the pulverizing machinery would need to be sited on boadd, occupy space, absorb energy to drive it, and there would still be the dangers of explosion. Then there is the view held by some that even as crude oil is too valuable to burn straight and must have its valuable constituents refined out first, so coal will eventually be seen as too valuable to feed straight into the combustion chamber. Nevertheless it is almost certain that we shall see coal burners in the 1990s even though its lesser heating value means a 30-50% increase in weight of bunkers or 100% increase by volume.

A coal-oil mixture, provided the coal particles can be kept in suspension, would be the most convenient fuel to burn in a boiler, but the proportion of coal would have to be quite high, at least 60%, to make it significantly cheaper than oil. There has been talk recently of endeavouring to run diesel engines on such mixtures, but unless the coal particles can be very finely ground it is difficult to see how damage to the engine can be avoided. The production of oil from coal is an established practice although in a relatively small way, as in South Africa, and it is not ideally suited for the diesel engine. Yet it could be that further research effort will show appreciable economic return in producing synthetic crude in the future.

Other fuels

There are not many alternatives for the 1990s. LNG or LPG will always be too valuable to burn generally at sea. Methanol and hydrogen show promise but will need the customary 20 years of development before they can be handled effectively. The former is manageable and could be burned in boilers either by itself or in mixture with other fuels, but it is not suited as yet to diesel engines. Hydrogen is difficult to store at −252°C, its production is very expensive, and its ignition tendency is a problem.

Wind

Although there have been real improvements in the design of sailing vessels in recent years it appears unlikely that large commercial sailing vessels will be viable in the timespan we are speaking of. There are always variable winds leading to unpredictable voyage times and the difficulties of manoeuvring in ports and restricted waterways. It could be possible, however, that wind-assisted vessels may appear and a figure of an average 10% saving in fuel has been suggested from auxiliary sails on a conventional cargo vessel. More study and development of ducted wind turbines rather than sails could yield benefit although there will always be the problem of the size of the rotors or blades and their encumbrance in the working of cargo.

Nuclear

Even with current technology nuclear-powered ships are economically viable and can be further developed. Their future will depend on acceptance of the concept generally as to safety in operation and disposal of waste. However, there are some 300 nuclear vessels in service and no-one is unduly concerned. Perhaps the fact that they are submarines means that they are not so obvious; but some at least are using the same estuaries that nuclear merchant ships might expect to be debarred from at present. The breeder reactor's success means that nuclear resources are assured for many years. The writer believes therefore that there will be further concentration on the safety aspects of operation and it is possible that by the 1990s nuclear merchant ships could at least be in the planning stages.

Here we close the consideration of the technical solutions. They all end up with a ship somewhat similar in cargo-carrying function to that of today. There is no way avoiding increased cost of transportation although each solution tries to keep it to a minimum. These increased costs can only be passed on to the shipper and eventually the consumer.

THE ORGANIZATIONAL SOLUTION

We now go down the right-hand side of Figure 2 and consider the organizational solution to the cost pressure we considered above. There are not as many features to be examined, and we shall end with a different kind of ship in this case.

Some principles

There are certain basic premises that apply to marine transportation.

(1) The most economically efficient ship is that carrying only one type of cargo. This is obvious with crude oil or grain in bulk, but is equally obvious when we consider the change from the varied cargoes of the traditional cargo liner into a series of containers in a container ship. In this way the ship itself is cheaper to build and its cargoes are more efficiently handled.

(2) The ship must be matched or its cargo as far as possible, eg the roll-on roll-off concept which accepts that over 90% of cargo arrives alongside a ship on wheels; and the cement carriers, liquid gas carriers, chemical carriers etc which are dedicated vessels for their particular cargo. Owners of LNG vessels which have found themselves without a charter have learned the bitter truth on the reverse

side of the coin – there is nothing whatsoever that can be done with these vessels other than carry LNG.

(3) Ship speed will be modest and optimized to the trading conditions pertaining to the service, with the higher-value cargoes still calling for the higher speeds. In this respect it is frequently found that fuel cost is met by the charterer being less sensitive to fuel cost as long as he can settle for a freight rate that ensures profitability. There would seem to be a process of education necessary with charterers to highlight more clearly the advantages of the slower speed ship, and so get him to obviate the pressure on the shipowner to try to design for a normal lower 'economy' speed, but at the same time build in an expensive margin of power to ensure that the ship can command the better freight rates.

(4) The benefits of scale are incontrovertible in marine transportation. Only the environmentalists will prevent tankers reaching their previous or greater size, because structurally they are feasible and economically they are desirable. Otherwise the only limits to size will be the physical and geographical constraints of depth of water and port entry. Even the latter should not be too readily accepted since even ports have been known to be adapted to the vessels using them. Therefore all ships will tend to get bigger.

Rather than increase the speed of the ship, the accent will be on speed of turnround. This is already very apparent with short sea ferries where speed is by and large constant but time is saved on the turnround between sailings, and the aim will be the same on larger vessels, helped by the single type cargoes mentioned in (1) above.

(5) It will always be advantageous to mount the cargo-handling gear on shore and not on the ship, and so reduce the ship's first cost and also the operational cost. However, this depends on the ports to be visited and a knowledge of the ship's likely trading pattern.

Large bulk cargo carriers

Taken together, these generalizations point to larger ships in the major bulk trades (ie oil, grain, coal etc), and to simply constructed ships, relatively slow without cargo-handling gear. They will also apply in principle to ships currently carrying a variety of cargoes, such as chemical carriers. They are somewhat of an exception at present since they tend to be relatively small because of port limitations, and they carry many different types of chemicals and probably three different types of containment system. In ten years time these cargoes will probably begin to be separated out into much bigger parcels of fewer types in any one ship and the ships will become bigger, simpler and relatively cheaper. Otherwise, the only alternative is to treat the cargoes in smaller units and consolidate them as described below.

Minor bulkers and general cargo trades

Vessels of this type have not so far enjoyed the increase in size that brings economies. It is here, therefore, that we could see the radical change in the next ten years. But if the overall grouping of cargoes is to produce ships of a size similar to the major bulk carriers of oil or ore, it can only be done by consolidating a number of smaller units into a large deep-sea vessel or into an integrated multi-unit system incorporating a propulsion vessel. The smaller units could be barges either stowed within or on the parent vessel or combined to form a barge train. It is noteworthy that of all the ship types that have developed into some recognizable form over the past 10-15 years, ie the container ship, the ro-ro, car carrier and so on, only the barge carrier has failed to reach a consensus design. We have the various types shown in Figure 12, and there seems to be no generally accepted size of barge or method of stowing in or on the ship.

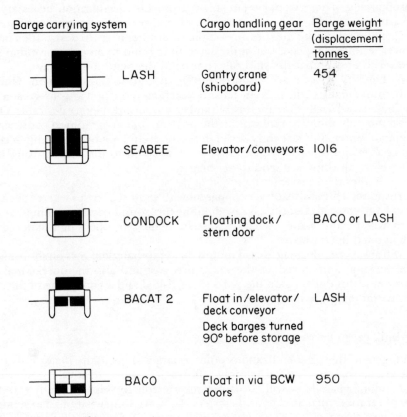

Barge carrying system	Cargo handling gear	Barge weight (displacement tonnes
LASH	Gantry crane (shipboard)	454
SEABEE	Elevator/conveyors	1016
CONDOCK	Floating dock/ stern door	BACO or LASH
BACAT 2	Float in/elevator/ deck conveyor Deck barges turned 90° before storage	LASH
BACO	Float in via BCW doors	950

Figure 12. Types of barge carriers.

However, we could see in the 1990s a firmer approach to a very large barge carrier which would consolidate the coastal barges in such a way that the deep-sea leg becomes as economic as is presently found with the VLCC or other major bulk carrier. The barge will suit whatever cargo is to be carried whether containers, vehicles or liquids, so that specialization will be within the barge unit itself and the parent ship reverts to the modern role of the 'bulk carrier'. The capability of carrying the various cargo types should help to avoid long and unprofitable ballast legs to the voyage.

Hence we see how by organization – or reorganization, it may be possible to recoup some of the heavy penalties resulting from fuel price increase, although it would be expected that every energy-saving device proposed in the technical solutions described above would still be investigated and adopted for the large consolidated vessel.

CONCLUSIONS

(1) The energy and labour cost pressures experienced by ship operators will be accentuated in the 1990s and will be met either with technical solutions or organizational solutions, or both.
(2) The technical solutions will require detailed analysis of many possible areas of energy saving, and the application of technological developments to several spheres of operation; but it will not be possible to avoid higher operating costs altogether and therefore higher freight rates.
(3) There will still be a large diesel-engined world fleet running on oil in the 1990s, but other sources of power will be beginning to make an impact.
(4) The alternative sources will be coal and nuclear power, with a good many coal-burning vessels in operation by then. But because coal sources will be regarded as finite, as oil came to seen in the 1970s, there will be a pragmatic interest developing in nuclear-powered vessels.
(5) The organizational approach will be underway rather like the container revolution in the late 1960s, which was a cargo-organizing event. This could generate a new breed of coastal traffic in barges together with a better defined type of barge-carrying vessel, or a composite barge train. This system will take advantage of economy of size and, together with adoption of the technical aspects already considered, could constitute the transportation system of the period.

RECOMMENDATIONS

The following somewhat random suggestions are gleaned from the various sections of the paper and are advanced as a form of mental preparation for the 1990s:

(1) There must be a greater readiness in maritime circles to accept control of practices, eg navigation and communications. Recent events illustrate the weakness of traditional methods.
(2) An informed dialogue should begin between the involved parties on practical minimum manning levels and the degree of automation associated with them.
(3) Ship operators should take more interest in routeing and accurate navigation with a view to saving on steaming distance.
(4) There should be a better understanding by all parties to marine transportation of the real economies possible, particularly those ensuing from reduced operating speed. Charterers should not insist on an inconveniently high speed as a reserve feature.
(5) Efforts should be made to agree internationally on acceptable criteria for steering and manoeuvring characteristics.
(6) A metallurgical approach to conservation of ship's hulls would be welcome in place of paint protection which is becoming increasingly expensive and demanding of good conditions for application.
(7) Means should be sought to alleviate the high costs of model tank testing either by developing mathematical approaches to resistance and propulsion evaluations or by working to a much smaller scale.

(8) More thought should be given to the fitting of fins to improve aft end flow at the building stage of vessels, rather than treat them as emergency devices if vibration troubles transpire.

(9) The alternatives of solid coal and coal/oil mixtures should be researched quickly in view of the divergent costs and availability of oil and coal.

(10) We should keep nuclear power in mind especially for the ultra large cargo/barge carriers that may be around in ten years time.

Developments in shipping have usually come from the initiative of major shipowners, mainly European and often British. Such has been the run-down among Western shipowners that technical staff have been disbanded and reserves of finance, and possibly of innovation, have been exhausted, except perhaps for the major oil companies. It remains a question of some importance, therefore, where the impetus for new developments will come from. Will it be from the oil companies with the others following, or will it come from the new countries with expanding fleets?

APPENDIX I

Calculation of sensitivity of ships' economic performance of technical and commercial factors

Basis Panamax bulker – particulars and assumptions

Costs in Pounds				%
Summer deadweight	Tons	60 000	Discount rate	12.00
Payload	Tons	55 000	Tax rate	52.00
Load factor	%	55	Capital grant	0.00
Speed	Knots	15	Increment	10.00[a]
Round Trip	Sea miles	11 000	Credit	70.00
			- for 7 years at	8.00

Tons are 1 000 kg Weight saving = extra dwt. No other company profits, ie fully depreciated for tax in first year.

	£	Escalation (%/year growth)		
Crew cost per annum	470 000	9.0	Days in service per annum	348.0
Upkeep cost per annum	450 000	11.0	Days in port per rt	15.0
Fixed cost per annum	240 000	5.0	Shipyard price of ship	12 000 000
Port cost per rt	30 000	7.0	Owners' initial costs	300 000
Cargo handling per ton	0.0	0.0	Residual value of ship	500 000
Fuel cost per ton	73.0	10.0	Shipyard labour cost	2 500
Fuel consumption sea	50.0		Main machinery cost	1 500 000
(Tons/day) port	3.0		Ordered structure weight tons	10 000

Freight rate £8.00 per ton cargo rising at 9.0 per year.
Building account total delivery 2.0 years. reduction due to depreciation and interest.
[a] for changes in cases 2-24.

APPENDIX II

Assumptions for calculation of economic worth

(a) Fixed values

(i)	Load factor	65%
(ii)	Round trip	11 000 sea miles
(iii)	Ship life	15 years
(iv)	Building time	0.8 years
(v)	Discount rate	12%
(vi)	Credit	OECD rates
(vii)	Capital grant	Zero
(viii)	Tax rate	52%
(xi)	Crew costs per annum	£450 000 rising at 9%/year
(x)	Upkeep, maintenance	£390 000 rising at 11%/year
(xi)	Fixed cost, insurance etc	£200 000 rising at 5%/year
(xii)	Port cost per round trip	£15 000 rising at 7%/year
(xiii)	Cargo handling cost/tonne	Zero
(xix)	Owners initial costs	£320 000
(xx)	Days in service per annum	350
(xxi)	Days in port per round trip	20

(b) Variable factors
Due to differing engine configurations.

(i) *Deadweight and payload.* Payload has been calculated for each ship after subtracting fuel and feed water and crew stores and affects from the deadweight.

(ii) *Price.* Changes in shipyard price for each of the modified ships have been included in the calculation.

(iii) *Residual value.* Assumed to be about 23% of first cost. This was on current rates for lightship scrap price.

(iv) *Fuel consumption.* Differences in the ships are only relatively small and it is therefore important to be able to assess as accurately as possible what the daily fuel rate will be. This is particularly important if the main engine is running at part load as the specific fuel consumption (sfc) curve is not flat. Therefore, using the builders speed/power curves and the engine makers sfc curves, the daily main engine fuel rate was calculated for each ship and for each speed. An additional factor for the at sea and in port diesel oil consumption was calculated, in each case corrected to a heavy fuel oil price (current ratio between marine diesel and marine fuel oil is about 2:1). Lubricating oil consumptions are also accounted for.

(c) *Changes postulated to test the sensitivity of each ship's cost/revenue potential*

(i) *Speed.* In order to be able to plot a reasonable length of speed/RFR curve as large a range as possible was taken, consistent with available data. For the three ships this was:

> Ship (1) – 15, 14, 13, 12 knots
> Ship (2) – 13.7, 13, 12 knots
> Ship (3) – 13.7, 13, 12 knots

(ii) *Fuel cost.* Two basic assumptions have been used:

- £85/tonne escalating at 10%/year (av present day price).
- £170/tonne escalating at 10%/year 2× (av present day price).

References and footnotes

1   M. Meek, 'The designer's response', *Philosophical Transactions Royal Society,* 273, 1972.
2   Ocean Transport & Trading Ltd, *Annual Report,* 1978.
3   These scenarios were first propounded in M. B. Casey, 'The shape of ships to come,' paper Seatrade Conference, 'Shipping 2000', 1979.
4   R. Lindsay, 'A perspective on oil and other future fuels', *Transactions NE Coast Inst of Engineers and Shipbuilders,* 1979.
5   J. H. Attwood *et al,* 'How to save fuel in steam tankers', *Marine Engineers Review,* February 1980.
6   *Economic Evaluation of Ship Design,* BSRA Computer Program Notice R101, 1971.

DISCUSSION

Economic implications of ship developments

Slowsteaming

(1) Slowsteaming is being used today for fuel economy reasons, particularly with oil tankers. If these tankers all delivered their cargoes at maximum speed we would have more oil than we could accept and use. But, for economic reasons, the manufacturer or the supplier of a commodity wishes to convert that product into cash as quickly as possible. If we are to be faced in the next and future decades with slower steaming ships, the whole question arises of the economics of converting the product into cash: whether it is shipped on a cif or on an fob basis does not really matter. Slowsteaming may be fine for the shipowner, but what are the implications for the customers at either end, the supplier, and the shipper? Surely we are in an age when we have got to convert products into cash. The world economy is based on this system. We are already seeing this on the passenger side – Townsend–Thorensen are speeding up ferries on the short run between Dover and Calais. The whole point of this is to get the maximum utilization out of a very high capital investment in a particular ship.

(2) In considering the need for slower speeds, it is important to take into account the knotty problem of financing the cargo while in transit. In other words, increasing the voyage time increases the finance costs. This is clearly a major problem in the oil industry at present: a decision always has to be made – particularly near the end of the voyage while ships still have some speed in hand – as to whether to bring the ship in earlier (at higher speed and higher fuel cost) or later (which saves some fuel but costs more in financing the cargo and perhaps in other ship-operating costs).

Ship size

(1) The advocacy of mammoth ships – bigger ships carrying either bulk oil, bulk cargoes, or break-bulk cargo – raises again the question of utilization. In the airline industry, with the advent of jumbo jets load factors are down to about 60% in good cases, with lots of empty seats. When ship operations have to be considered on a year-round basis, it is clear that ship size, as well as ship speed, affects utilization. A vessel may well get a cargo to ship from, for example, the UK to Australia, but it may not get one on the return voyage.

(2) Economy measures concern not merely saving costs for the ship operator. The global costs of ship operation must also be taken into account. Are not the large ships that require large port installations and a considerable amount of dredging to accommodate them – for example in Rotterdam, where the burghers are no longer so enamoured of large ships – putting all such costs onto somebody else's shoulders? Isn't the shipowner therefore casting aside what should properly be his responsibility?

(3) A broader implication raised by the inflexibility of the concept of large ships concerns their effects on the manpower situation and on the supply of trained personnel both for national defence and economic well-being.

Fuel costs

(1) Shipping is the only industry – with the possible exception of the airlines – which has so far come under real economic pressure to adopt fuel economy measures. In general, society has not come to terms at all with economy in fuel – apart from paying more for it. But shipping was already the most economical transport mode relative to other fuel-using systems, and is currently taking all possible steps to become even more economical in most sectors. A possible exception is in certain short-sea ferry trades where speed is still considered to be a prime factor, yet this probably does not increase significantly overall operating costs.

(2) A large amount of fuel can actually be saved in operations. A speed one or two knots slower can result in a big saving in fuel, maybe as much as 50% in some ships.

Ship management

(1) Good housekeeping is most important to economy – what Admiral Sir Frank Mason, when Engineer-in-Chief of the Royal Navy, called 'the importance of ill considered trifles'. Many more savings can be made in existing ships.

(2) A distressingly large number of ships fail to reach their destination – the bigger the ship, the bigger the loss. The problem seems to be one of efficiency of operation – shipboard management and training in efficient bridge procedures.

(3) In regard to the relationship of crew costs of 'other' costs, did crew costs also include management costs? If management costs were categorized as 'other', then by reducing crew costs, management would assume a larger portion of the total.

Technical developments

Hull form

There is an enormous amount of work to be done on improving hull forms. We have not diverged much from the proportions and shapes of the ships of the sail era in the 19th Century. Ship hydrodynamics research needs to follow the lead given by aerodynamics and seek much more economical hull forms, without necessarily aiming for unconventional solutions, most of which do not lend themselves well to cargo- or passenger-carrying.

Alternative fuels

With regard to alternative fuels, we ought to be considering combined cycles of all kinds – coal in gas turbines, coal burning directly in diesel engines, father and son, combined steam and gas turbines etc.

We shall not derive much benefit from the wind propulsion of ships by the 1990s, but work must be started now if wind power is ever to be of any use – what is being called 'environmental power assistance'.

Barge systems

The importance of barge systems has been mentioned. The importance of canal systems should also be emphasized: these systems have been almost totally neglected in the UK because most canals are in disrepair and out-of-date. Commercial canals in the UK do carry a lot of cargo, and in other countries they are extremely important to the economy. The barge system chosen must also be related to the canal systems in which the barges will be used, and not just to the ships which will carry them across the sea.

Automation

Have British shipbuilders fully grasped the nettle of ship automation? Customers are going to Japanese yards where they can have whole automation packages presented to them for consideration, using groups of engine-room simulators in which they can test the packages and train the operators. The UK is falling a long way behind in the range of packages that can be offered.

Navigation

The types of vessels envisaged for the future – highly automated and precisely navigated – are also likely to be among the most hazardous, especially the very large ships whose size greatly restricts the areas and routes which they can navigate. One can imagine all automated ships running along precisely the same route, and there being a large number of end-on or stern-on collisions.

AUTHOR'S RESPONSE

It is interesting to take into account the value of the cargo. I recently made this kind of calculation for an LPG ship and got a totally different shape of curve for optimum speed. It was nothing like as flat as that for bulk carriers; it is almost vertical at a certain speed. All the points discussed have to be taken into account, including the cash effect of the cargo; these are manageable with the programs that we now have available.

I am not sure that ferries are going faster. The ferry is a typical example of savings coming from turn-round in port. It is speeding up turn-round that produces the gain, rather than speeding up the ship. My whole point is that, if anything, one should try to go slower, not speed up the ship; one should get the savings elsewhere. The turn-round time of some of the very large ferries is incredibly fast.

Savings from building big ships are so great that all kinds of things can be done within the context. Space in a ship does not matter so much after such savings, or there would no container ships or ro-ros – they waste so much space within the ship. In discussions on the subject of economy, we must take into account global economic calculations; and it is only on that basis that one can gain an overall picture.

I have concentrated on considerations relating to shipbuilding, and would prefer not to answer in detail questions relating to the commercial side.

Automation is a big problem. I wish we knew better just where we were going on automation. That is one of my pleas today: can we get together on this subject and really decide how much automation we want. As a shipbuilder I just do not know. I know that it is possible with the microprocessor to go along the automated route, but just how much the shipowner wants it and how much it is justified economically, I do not know.

5. UK MERCHANT NAVY MANPOWER NEEDS

THE CASE FOR POLICY CHANGES

Peter Sharpe
(Management and Organization Consultant, Sea Life Programme)

B ritish shipping, or the Merchant Navy, tends to be referred to as if it were a homogeneous industry for whose ills general remedies can be prescribed. Its manpower needs can, similarly, easily be assumed to be ascertainable and capable of being met by planned general policies. These are dangerous fallacies which need to be replaced by more realistic recognition of the immense diversity of the industry and the manpower needs within it. These reflect the technical and commercial transformation of shipping since the second world war. As with similar transformations in other industries, the main consequences involve deeper managerial and operational specialization, and profound effects on employment and personnel policies.

This paper starts, therefore, from the proposition that an apparently meaningful question, 'How many of what sorts of seafarer will the Merchant Navy need in the 1990s?', only provides an opportunity for mainly useless speculation. It presupposes the continuing validity of general formulae for the administration of sea-going manpower.

A possibly more useful question is suggested as the focus for this paper: 'By what means can technical, political and commercial pressures on the operation of UK shipping be matched by appropriate policies for the employment and management of seafaring manpower?'

Nature of the industry

The Merchant Navy is not a single coherent organization with a recognizable centre of authority. No one person or institution is responsible for its future. On both employer and union sides it is essentially more of a loose federation of competing groups held together by coincident needs: shipowners for seafarers, seafarers for jobs.

Since 1964 the number of ships under the UK flag has declined by over 30% and the number of jobs at sea by almost 60%, this latter reduction of course being cushioned in terms of total employment by increases in leave allowances. On a grt per man-on-board basis, the productivity of ships' manpower has more than trebled in this period; on a basis of grt per man-employed it has more than doubled.

Until recently UK manpower had been comparatively cheap alongside other European flags. As these competitors move to different and more cost-effective policies, while sterling remains strong, and as new flags with low-cost manning emerge, the pressure on the UK operator to improve the utilization of his manpower and ships increases inexorably. Survival of the UK merchant fleet at or near its recent position in world rankings is in question.

One factor affecting this survival is the adaptability of the main policies for the engagement, training, and management of UK seafarers. These presently form an employment 'culture' shared by all companies and thus affecting each of them to some degree in their ability to compete. The lack of collective unanimity on the employers' side, stemming from competition in the markets for freights, ships and manpower, is an obstacle to the formulation, not to mention the introduction of, any radical initiatives for collective survival. Employers of one type will disagree with those of another about whether a central labour pool is a necessary, cost-effective and desirable arrangement in today's conditions. Meanwhile all employers remain affected by or dependent on this insecure arrangement for the supply of satisfactory manpower.

Similarly, the arguments of one union which have forced in one type of ship are countered by equally valid but conflicting arguments from a competing union citing an alternative type of ship and trade.

The third power-sharing partner, the Department of Trade (DoT), while doing its best to recognize the arguments for policy exceptions and special cases in the pursuit of cost-effectiveness and/or safety, nevertheless commits the industry as a whole to the larger bureaucratic constraints of international policy makers, which may well further reduce elbow-room for survival at individual company level.

Policy-making inertia inevitably accompanies this confusion of purposes and priorities. It produces adherence to general formulae which are now being, or have already been overtaken by technological and social transformations. Insofar as it is a factor affecting its future survival, the industry is beginning to suffer seriously from manpower policy arthritis.

As a way of approaching answers to the focal question of this paper, an overall map of the industry's manpower system is examined.

Overall employment system

To take employment in the UK Merchant Navy is to enter an interlocking group of systems designed to process the recruit to fill a specified role on board any UK ship. The main systems are those implementing policies of entry, opportunities and training, supply and engagement. These make up a total system which is coherent in the translation of overall policy, given:

(1) the absence of stability in the ship's company; and thus,
(2) a need for centrally established measures of role-competence permitting safe interchangeability of persons to fill roles adequately on *any* ship;
(3) a sufficient flow of acceptable entrants for each role;
(4) the volatile nature of ship and cargo markets, which inclines many employers to offer 'minimum commitment' terms of employment to less skilled seafarers;
(5) that most ships depend on the same on-board role structure for effective and safe operation.

Although an oversimplification, the basic employment subsystems can be regarded as designed to produce fillers-of-roles rather than fillers-of-jobs. Such systems are particularly valued when dependability under stress is called for, because they confer clear lines of authority, which help to reduce uncertainty and chaos in emergencies.

Impermanent shipboard group

The industry's manpower arrangements pivot about a fundamental and long-established need to ensure acceptable work-performance from impermanent work-groups on any ship. In the past impermanence did not necessarily, of itself, impose serious limitations on the ship. When tours of duty were of the order of 9-12 months or longer, such impermanent groups had a reasonable span of time in which to 'shake down' and develop something better than just an acceptable performance. However, greatly increased leave entitlements and tours of duty of about four months are now widespread in every trade. In combination these two factors have almost destroyed the prospects of building a shipboard group's ability to achieve more than acceptable performance; even that may be difficult if the technology or workload of the ship is unusual or complex.

The potential competence of the shipboard group has thus been seriously impaired at the same time as technological and economic pressures for higher performance have increased significantly. This comparatively new problem prompts questions about the rationale of the established employment system.

Basic shipboard role system

This system contains four main role departments: Deck, Engine, Radio and Catering. Vertically it embodies two grades of role: officers and ratings. The industry's subsystems for the entry and induction of recruits precisely mirror these basic departmental and grade distinctions. It is highly unusual and difficult to change departments after entry. It is less unusual, but increasingly difficult, except in the Catering department, to move from rating to officer status.

Opportunity and training systems

The career opportunities for an entrant are automatically defined by his choice of department. The two main career ladders are those of the Deck and Engineering departments. The Radio department is rarely more than one man, basically trained outside the industry and with no career structure within it.

Rating entrants (excluding adults recruited as engine-room ratings) can choose Deck or Catering departments. Excluding the rare exceptions who become officers, deck ratings can progress to the role of AB and eventually Petty Officer or Chief Petty Officer. Catering ratings may in time be appointed as stewards or cooks, and ultimately progress to Catering Officers or Pursers.

Formal teaching of the technical disciplines required to qualify for shipboard roles is concentrated in the Deck and Engine departments. The great bulk of the industry's certification training expenditure, perhaps as much as 90%, is channelled into the Deck and Engine Cadet Schemes. These two departments offer clear career ladders of professional advancement and attractive rewards for success in gaining the next qualification.

In these key departments, until the top is reached, the prime measure of achievement is acquisition of a higher certificate. Such a system can be termed 'status-driven' as distinct from 'performance-driven'. This means that competence in performing the job tends to count for less than acquiring a certificate of competence to fill the role containing that job. This could explain some of the problems of administering appraisal and development schemes in ships. Officers may find it difficult to accept wholeheartedly other measures of competence than certification.

One can also see the difficulty trainee officers have in regarding themselves as part of a particular shipboard team. Bigger returns for effort may be seen to lie in passing the next examination, or in widening experience in another ship. Opportunities to absorb particular non-syllabus skills and techniques are thus in danger of being disregarded by trainees in favour of the topics in which they will be examined.

General trends in educational policy have required the industry increasingly to accept that those entrants passing through its educational establishments should receive broader teaching than that needed to pass DoT examinations alone, so fitting them better for later life should they leave the sea. This and several other pressures within the industry for higher levels of performance and skill in officers have led to the raising of educational entry standards for cadets to achieve acceptable certification pass rates. As a result, together with the almost totally unchanged minimal educational qualifications required of ratings, it has become highly unlikely for any rating without 'O' levels or the equivalent in maths or physics to stand a remote change of becoming an officer.

This qualification gulf has tended to exacerbate division in the ship's complement – labourers and foremen on one side, qualified office-bearers on the other – and to break down the pre-war career model in which good seamen could become officers, and officers were less likely to regard ratings as belonging to a separate caste. Whatever social distinctions existed then have been magnified by this widening difference in entry standards.

For roles on deep-sea ships, Deck and Engine ratings presently have no career structure above the level of senior Petty Officer. By comparison, it is interesting that, in the short-sea sector, the Class 5 Certificate, which specifically provides for rating entrants to aspire to home-trade officer status, has automatically meant establishing a higher level of entry qualification.

If the industry's institutions were to parallel this with similar steps to integrate the foreign-going career structure, the entry standards for ratings would need to be similarly raised, thus helping to close the status gap that has developed in deep-sea ships.

Supply and employment systems

Deck and Engine officers are supplied through the Cadet schemes and selected by companies to become employees of those companies. They will normally remain in employment in this way until gaining their first DoT certificate, but after that they may decide to leave and get experience in other companies, a small minority choosing to be on contract with the Merchant Navy Establishment (MNE) which makes them available for appointment from the MNE Pool to any company. The great majority of qualified officers are nowadays on company contracts and rarely, if ever, transfer via the Pool system. Officers and specialists other than Deck and Engine departments are generally either supplied directly from the domestic labour market, eg electricians and radio engineers, or, in the case of the Catering department, by promotions from rating status, and frequently via the Pool.

Virtually all ratings enter the industry as contractors to the MNE. For many, particularly in the foreign-going tramp trades, the basic contract of employment is the Crew Agreement and the basic means of changing employment is via the Pool. In other trades ratings more frequently hold a Company Service Contract with a shipping company. Many also choose to become company regulars and, although holding no formal contract with the company, rarely register their availability via the MNE Pool.

There are thus several combinations of supply source and forms of employment for seafarers. The dominant characteristics of the major groups, Deck and Engine officers and Deck and Catering ratings are:

- schoolboy entry;
- unsponsored and largely casual engagement for ratings;
- sponsored entry and direct employment of officers.

Recruitment at the earliest age possible offers certain advantages to the employer:

- It enables desired and accepted norms of behaviour in a role-filling culture to be imprinted strongly on impressionable minds. Schoolboys have few yardsticks by which to judge the appropriateness or quality of the industry's conventions, and will thus be more likely to accept them.
- Establishment consequences of today's seafaring systems, such as impermanent friendships and working associations, and the importance of 'fitting-in' to roles, justify and at the same time create an acceptance of transient behaviour – changing ships, companies and trades. This helps those employers who want only to be able to acquire and dispose of labour according to the vicissitudes of the market. Non-commitment is thus legitimated and reinforced.
- The younger the man at entry the younger will he be when qualified, and the more service he is likely to give in return for the cost of his training before inevitable pressures, domestic and social, persuade him to think of leaving the sea.
- The younger at entry, the lower his cost while acquiring operational competence.

These features are also compatible with the roving stereotype of the sailor himself, which still attracts many entrants to what is imagined to be a colourful life of adventure and travel. Lack of attachment, variety of experience and freedom from the sort of ties associated with factory and office work are similarly seen as attractive or advantageous to the young school-leaver.

On the other side of the coin employers have to contend with fecklessness and difficulties in maintaining control of work programmes and operational standards. Also the recruit can soon be discouraged by indifference and irresponsibility in his seniors, and become hardened and disillusioned by the deprivations of seafaring and the lack of fun afforded by hard-worked ships on fast port turn-arounds.

The supply system is entirely consistent with the need to maintain authority and control among random groups of strangers, and attracts and retains those who want or choose to adapt to the characteristics of impermanent work and social groupings.

Some arrangements for employment are unique to this industry. They are dominant for ratings and have an indirectly powerful effect on officers. For a UK rating to sail in a UK-registered ship whose owner or manager is party to National Maritime Board (NMB) Agreements, he must (1) be registered in the MNE Register; (2) have a current Discharge Book (issued by and the property of the DoT); (3) hold a contract of employment, either directly with the employer (company contract) or with the MNE; (4) sign the ship's articles, a crew agreement between him and the ship's master (as agent of the employer), to undertake a voyage in a named capacity (role) in a specific ship with that master.

Compared with the arrangements between other employers and their workers, these seem extraordinarily complicated, especially when in many trades those involved are mainly casual and either unskilled or semi-skilled workers. Such arrangements can greatly complicate the administration of disciplinary and dismissal procedures. Why are they so involved? It is suggested that this administrative superstructure is rooted in the same soil as the opportunity and supply systems. It is entirely consistent with, and the result of, the need to deal with an impermanent shipboard workforce.

Casual workers may be assumed to have a limited sense of commitment to any particular employer, who thus requires recourse to forms of control which will protect the ship and its organization, particularly when it is beyond the direct physical influence of the company's management. What are needed are an on-board authority structure backed by the force of law and means of identifying and keeping track of miscreants. The latter requirement is important to the identification and removal of unsatisfactory individuals. Therefore, because they are casual, some way of 'tagging' individuals and tracking their movements becomes important in a way which applies to few if any other civilian employment relationships. Hence the Discharge Book, the Crew Agreement, the signing-on at the Pool and the MNE Register.

Survival pressures

In the light of the preceding exposition and the focal question of this paper, are there worthwhile arguments for changing the industry's basic philosophy of employment to improve its prospects of resisting and surviving the growing threats to its future? If so, what sorts of change are necessary and what would be their implication?

By focusing the discussion on the work which has to be done aboard the modern ship, it may be possible to identify desirable characteristics about the ship's workers and the ways in which they are employed and managed, which could foster higher levels of efficiency, safety and job satisfaction. The size and effectiveness of the ship's complement, as with any other work-group, is determined by the way in which essential work is divided up between the available manpower, and the methods employed for carrying it out.

When ships wore sails there were few questions which did not answer themselves in this respect, and there was little difference, if any, between jobs and roles. In a traditional industry with an internally mobile workforce these original ways of managing the ship have persisted as dependable and recognizable fixed features in what is otherwise a totally changed and much more diverse industry. It is inferred that they have persisted because transient manning has persisted. From examining the employment systems which facilitate control of such groups it is apparent that they interlock around this fundamental employment principle, and that they generate and sustain a role culture which populates the industry with role-fillers.

This is tantamount to asserting that the division of work on board, and to some extent, the methods employed for its execution, are primarily determined or strongly influenced by this culture, and *not* primarily by the logic of the technology or the priorities of the employer, or even the preferences of the employee. It is also asserted that an impermanent work-group cannot hope to compete with a well trained and integrated team which has developed as a working unit over an appreciable period.

Performance and safety are, in the opinion of the author, only secondarily dependent on qualifications and regulations; these are necessary but are not in themselves sufficient. Performance and safety are held primarily to depend on the integrity of the shipboard team, ie its level of commitment and morale, and thus on the skill with which it is led and motivated. If appreciable gains in cost performance and in the security of the ship and its crew are seriously sought, the integrity of the ship's team has to be enhanced.

From this hypothesis it seems inescapable that this, first and foremost, means the introduction of some foundation of group stability on which higher levels of competence can be reliably built. It might be said to follow automatically that this requires a permanent relationship or bond between the employer and the seafarer for all ranks and all skill groups on board (see Table 1).

Table 1. Illustrative differences between unstable and stable working groups which affect motivation and behaviour.

Unstable	Stable
Insecurity	Security
Roles	Jobs
Ranks	Skill grades
Encapsulation	Interaction
Time-filling	Learning
Responsibility to profession	Accountability to employer
Role emptiness	Job satisfaction
Isolation	Integration
Suppression	Expression
Promotion by service	Promotion by merit + service
Authoritarian power	Man management
Indifference	Commitment
Industry performance standards	Company and team performance standards

Policy control: central v company

Three employment principles seem essential to the achievement of better operational performance:

- direct (as opposed to casual) employment;
- continuity of the ship's complement;
- maximum delegation of decision making from shore to ship.

Although these do not seem penetrating insights, they do in fact mean radical change in the industry's conventions of seafaring employment, and most of the systems which support them. This is because they represent rejection of the age-old model of the impermanent shipboard group on which the present culture is built, and which has become seriously weakened by major reductions in tours of duty aggravated by increases in leave-entitlement. These principles represent a conceptual shift of no great difficulty, but which presents enormous problems of acceptance and implementation if it is to be pursued.

The difficulties are partly illustrated by Figure 1 which shows how the fundamental employment relationships, and thus the control of work-allocation and methods, would have to move away from the central institutions into the ambit of individual companies. Without elaborating on all the implications there is one of great importance. Many excellent and committed seafarers in the industry increasingly have to compensate for and overcome the job–role discrepancy posed by modern ships. Many leave because of the frustrations and job dissatisfaction which arise.

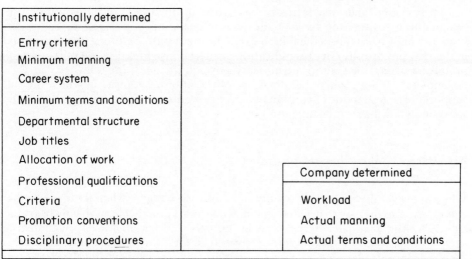

Institutionally determined
Entry criteria
Minimum manning
Career system
Minimum terms and conditions
Departmental structure
Job titles
Allocation of work
Professional qualifications
Criteria
Promotion conventions
Disciplinary procedures

Company determined
Workload
Actual manning
Actual terms and conditions

Company with impermanent shipboard groups filling roles

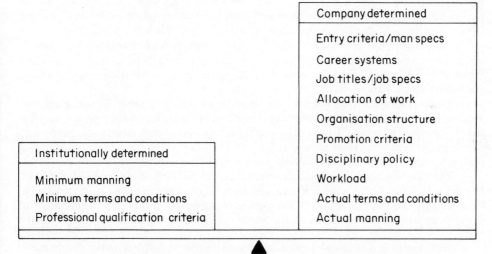

Company determined
Entry criteria/man specs
Career systems
Job titles/job specs
Allocation of work
Organisation structure
Promotion criteria
Disciplinary policy
Workload
Actual terms and conditions
Actual manning

Institutionally determined
Minimum manning
Minimum terms and conditions
Professional qualification criteria

Company with stable shipboard groups filling jobs

Figure 1. Balance of power – institution versus company.

The above change of concept carries two effects: although it would certainly retain more of such men, it would with equal certainty alienate the many who choose or who have come to accept the impermanent model, and who do not seek one demanding greater commitment. These will naturally resist such changes and pose implementation difficulties for both employers and unions. The extent of this change is also illustrated by the differences listed, which are suggested as characterizing the two concepts.

It is evident that new forms of behaviour are involved, and it would be un-reasonable to expect the bulk of the present seafaring population to change so fundamentally in established habits; it would be many years before newcomers raised in the new philosophy could significantly displace those raised in the old, and thus produce a detectable shift in the industry's overall image. If the industry's survival depends on such a change then, because of the interlocking way in which they all support the central mode of employment, the preceding analysis indicates that *all* the subsystems will have to change too.

Are effective policy changes possible?

While many would agree that the only right time to change is when there is no other choice, it is also the case that, where changes take years to yield effect, that is always too late. However, planned interventions at industry and national levels in industrial societies do not have a striking track record. It is not difficult to list failures in areas such as economic planning, social reform, industrial restructuring, local government and town planning. Few industrial strategies have been as successful as that of UK agriculture, although other countries seem to be better preserving their commercial and industrial interests through such interventions.

Should be accept that we are perhaps better suited to *laissez-faire* and should therefore let the future take care of itself? In an industry like UK shipping, which particularly lacks any national focus of authority for strategic planning (*cf* shipbuilding before nationalization) is not the argument against intervention irresistible?

It is suggested that however difficult it may seem, there is at least *some* chance of safeguarding the UK fleet as a national fiscal asset and source of direct employment for over 60 000 people, through some systematic attempt to formulate strategic plans and targets for its survival.

To do nothing invites the fate that has already ravaged other European fleets. What seems lacking is some appropriate machinery or power-forum permitting the development of survival plans between the institutional policy makers – some means of releasing them from their narrow roles of day-to-day haggling and negotiation into policy building focused on achieving a secure, shared future.

The case for a national body specifically and publicly accountable for all UK marine affairs has been powerfully and frequently argued in the past, in particular by Vice-Admiral Sir Ian McGeoch. In my view such a body would have to take maritime manpower policy firmly under its wing as part of securing the future of the Merchant Navy.

This supra-institutional forum seems essential to help destroy the present immobility arising from the tripartite division of power between the employers, unions and government. It would make more probable the emergence of new alliances and joint commitments about the future.

The emergence of better manpower policies will even then take time and require substantial experimentation and development. Protective arrangements to permit such work to be undertaken across a wide spectrum of shipping operations would of course be essential, for both employers and seafarers.

If the top 20 companies which account for some 75% of the ships and jobs in the industry could, under such arrangements, be encouraged publicly to subscribe to the active development of the principles suggested above, the shape of new systems better fitted to today's people and ships might then become visible within five years. Lord

Rochdale specified scores of improvements he felt the industry should attempt; too many, especially in the manpower area, remain neglected. It seems likely that this situation will continue until some active body can be assembled to bring pressure on those with power – ministers, heads of unions and employers' leaders – to help set up an effective policy review and action forum.

By resisting or ignoring the need to change central manpower policies radically, the industry is rejecting the demands of the technological and commercial revolution it has experienced since the second world war. There is little doubt the industry will need committed seafarers for as long as it possesses ships; but how many and with what skills and prospects depends heavily on the extent to which arthritic attitudes and collective inertia towards change can be overcome.

The industry's greatest need is to match its commercial flair and technical ingenuity with greater adaptability and imagination in the utilization of its seafarers. If it cannot let go of some of its manpower traditions voluntarily, there is considerable risk they will take the industry down with its ships.

6. SHIPPING ECONOMICS

With special reference to liner shipping

M. G. Graham
(Economic Adviser to the Board of Overseas Containers Ltd)

Great uncertainty faces the shipping industry during the 1980s. Those involved in management and planning have to spend much time grappling with problems, many of which concern externalities over which we have little or no control. My initial reaction to the invitation to deliver this paper was to say that I was at a loss to say anything meaningful about the 1990s. Events move fast. Let us suppose the year is 1960 and that I am predicting events in the 1970s. Would I have predicted the tanker and shipbuilding boom and slump? Would I have predicted the container revolution and the way it has changed the shape and economics of liner shipping? Would I have predicted the development of shippers' councils and liner codes of conduct and the UNCTAD 40–40–20 principle? The answer must be no. My thinking would have been conditioned by the pleasant decade of the 1950s and perhaps by some unease about the pressure of demand on scarce resources. But the nature and extent of the pressures and upheavals as they unfolded would surely have been missed. I am under no illusion that I can predict what the 1990s will look like. The useful thing is to see what some possibilities may be, whether some seem more probable than others and whether there are broad indications as to how we should react.

Elements such as population growth, a range of growth in world trade and a growing share of the cake for the newly industrialized countries (NICs) – but not much more for the genuinely less developed countries (LDCs) – can be outlined with some degree of credibility, if possible cataclysms are assumed aside. Mr Goodwin has outlined these elements of growth in his paper.

Clearly, energy supply is fundamental. Today there is no basis for predicting that the world will have freed itself, or be in process of freeing itself, from dependence on fossil fuels in 10-15 years' time. The prudent assumption is that nuclear power will have been extended reluctantly, that more coal will be used, that all energy will be used more efficiently, with price forcing real productivity gains to be made, but that the principal OPEC countries will still occupy centre stage. They will be reducing supply and still trying to increase the real price. The USSR will have to become a net importer from willing Middle East sellers, which will do nothing to reduce political tension in the area. China, now a joker in the pack, will have revealed its potential both as producer and user of oil (and indeed of much else) – the extent of which we cannot see in the cards today.

STRUCTURE OF THE LINER TRADES

Liners carry the world's trade in manufactures and high-value produce. Liner services satisfy traders' needs for regular scheduled services (in aggregate) worldwide, for quantities large or small and at known, non-discriminatory tariff rates. It has been accepted for a hundred years that these characteristics require a degree of stability only produced by orderly trading, to which end the shipping conferences were evolved. My basic assumption is that because the system has lasted a century, it will probably last another 20 years, although on bad days it may look as though it might not last that number of months.

There are alternative ways of getting stability. One would be through an oligopoly structure – the 'few' shipping lines selling to the many shippers, in conditions of short-run stability and long-run competition. The economies of scale achievable by large container ships have changed the structure of the liner industry in ways which make an oligopoly set-up possible. The shipping companies are bigger than they used to be and a series of joint fleets, providing even larger organizations, has been formed. In the West such a set-up might be tolerated without conferences, provided the shippers and their councils could talk to the consortia. In the Third World such a system does not look to be acceptable politically.

Alternatively, stability of a kind might be achieved through a system of state-owned fleets, highly regulated as to routes, rates and shares. Most people would probably believe that such a system would be inflexible and lead to diseconomies and high costs. There might be quiet, but the quiet of the tomb for commercial enterprise.

The most likely long-term solution may be that the West, for its intra-Western bloc trade, will continue to use a conference system, disapplying the cargo-sharing provisions of the UN Liner Code; second, that the West's trade with the Third World will apply the Code and be more protected – and less efficient; and third, it remains an open question whether the USA will have moved to close conferences – there are no clear grounds today for saying it will, despite the existance of the Omnibus Bill. Overcapacity will thus still condition economics in important areas, certainly through much of the 1980s.

EFFECT OF PROTECTION ON SHIPPING ECONOMICS

State trading is an instrument of protection. I doubt if ten years will see through the present trends in changes of the centres of industrial growth and export. The stresses are producing a degree of protection. Equally, there is still some will to resist protection becoming too great. An increase, but not a marked increase, in protection of one kind or another may be the best interpretation of the future. The pressures are certainly there in shipping. A second pressure in the 1980s is overtonnaging, due in part to the political pressures just alluded to, in part the aftermath of the oil crisis of the mid-1970s, and in part the result of the rapid penetration of the liner market by container ships. I would expect all this to settle down somewhat in the 1990s. If it were to continue as destructive competition, then further innovation would be prejudiced and protective forces would tend to increase as a form of counter-action. Nevertheless, a degree of flag protection in Third World trades is likely to persist, with 40–40–20 arrangements where we are lucky and 50–50 (60–40?) bilateral deals where we are not.

It is also relevant to consider the degree to which trade will become further regionalized, because greater emphasis on trade within rather than between regional blocs would reduce the distance goods had to be moved, and so reduce the demand for shipping services. The post-war period has seen the emergence of regional groups like the EEC, Lafta, Comecon, the Andean Pact and ASEAN; the motivation has been part economic and part political. These groups have been successful enough to endure, and it is a tenable thesis to consider their future expansion to larger groupings, such as the Far East, incorporating Australasia and China; Europe, incorporating the Mediterranean and North Africa; Latin America as a whole; and the Middle East with the Indian sub-continent. Lower distribution costs would be the fundamental reason for the emergence of such groupings.

The existing blocs work far from perfectly. Many weak developing areas have not been able to build up an adequate industry behind a wall of regional protection and need exports to other major world markets to bolster their economies. Many stronger developing countries (the NICs) have seized opportunities in the large markets of Europe and North America. Indeed, regionalization does not seem to be a major force in trade growth. Even the countries of the EEC, the strongest 'new' free trade area, have retained and developed strong third market connections all over the world. The most likely assumption over the long term is that balance of payments problems, particularly because of the continued energy imbalance, will force nations to seek markets for their exports wherever they can. This is not to say that the pattern of trade will be static, merely that opportunism will require nations to continue to incur the cost of worldwide distribution.

The above is therefore perhaps a rather long digression to establish a neutral point for the future of liner shipping, but the implications of regionalization seem too important to ignore.

TECHNOLOGY AND ECONOMICS

If the 1990s reach a more stable state than the 1980s are likely to, and protective forces are moderate rather than severe, then the climate would be favourable for innovation in the form of technological improvement, but without an impetus to further revolutionary change. In that statement lies the bias of the economist towards putting economics as the motivation for major technological change, rather than scientific advance itself. It is economic need that feeds scientific and technological experiment and provides the fertile soil in which innovation can develop.

This is not to deny that major technological changes have economic con-sequences. Indeed, the really important technological changes are the ones with major economic results. My own chairman pointed out in a recent speech that in shipping the interval between such major changes had been narrowing by a factor of 2.5 on each occasion, and that if the factor held good the next change would occur in 40 years' time. To adapt his thesis but a little, three fundamental changes have occurred:

- weather decks – to withstand ocean conditions and reduce the casualty rates of open ships – leading to the great discovery voyages and the opening up of world trade;
- steamships – reducing, then eliminating, dependence on wind and weather – leading to predictable frequency on routes determined by economics, ie to liner services;
- containers in container/ro-ro ships – leading to the through transport revolution – and all the implications in terms of Physical Distribution Management (PDM) for the traders.

On this thesis another fundamental change would come early in the 21st century. This is certainly credible. The pace of change since the Industrial Revolution has been so great, and the impetus is still being kept up in many fields, although there is nothing one can identify today as a change to come – if not soon, then in the 1990s. One can point to technological changes which, though unlikely to have fundamental economic significance, are still in the category of important improvements – the slow-speed diesel engine now and a nuclear engine perhaps in the 1990s. A safe nuclear engine would certainly be an important innovation: it would bid fair to stabilize marine fuel prices, which in real terms are increasing as shown in Table 1. But a nuclear engine would still be 'another way to boil a kettle', and its ability to allow a ship to steam very long distances without refuelling has no real commercial implication. That virtue is military and already recognized.

Table 1. Index of bunker prices.	
	US$ 'real' bunker index
1973	100.0
1974	254.2
1975	239.2
1976	220.3
1977	247.6
1978	227.8
1979	368.7
1980	488.1
1981	489.8
1982	487.4
1983	486.1
1984	483.6
1985	498.0
1986	512.7
1987	527.9
1988	543.6
1989	559.7
1990	576.3

The silicon chip has moved to the centre of the technological stage and commands attention. It has some significance for shipping in data processing, but the container service operators have already successfully harnessed the computer to cope with the mass of documentation necessary to run a container line service, including satellite transmission where speed is vital. Further electronic improvements will allow operators to dispense with some of the paper altogether. That will be important and is part of a great change in methods of data handling throughout industry and commerce. The chip also has obvious implications for putting people out of work. I do not believe that there will be crewless ships and driverless cranes and straddle carriers. There will be further improvements in productivity, some of which will come from quite simple changes in allocation of jobs arising in a life at sea.

DEGREE OF PENETRATION OF CONTAINER SHIPS

The level of penetration of container ships in world liner trade now is probably around 50% – 'probably', because there is no precise definition of what constitutes liner business and therefore liner cargo. Indeed, in arriving at the figures, we have had to make one or two broad assumptions, especially that the conventional multi-deck fleet is split 50/50 (constantly through time) between tramp and liner services. We have also assumed a container ship overall productivity factor of 2.2 (again a constant *vis-à-vis* breakbulk liners, made up of factors for cellular ships of 3.0, for ro-ros of 2.0 and for combo ships of less than 2.0.

The 50% penetration estimate may seem somewhat low, but it must be remembered that there is a residual 10-15% of liner cargo which is not suitable for containerization (although some of that may still travel on container ships). The effective ceiling is thus something like 85-90% rather than 100%. Given that, the penetration in trades between industrial countries is now high. It is because we are still on the threshold, so to speak, of containerization in developing country trades that the overall percentage is still relatively low. Perhaps one should not speak of even that figure as being low, when it is remembered that it is only 15 years ago that the first commercial international container services appeared.

Estimates for the next ten years (end 1979 to end 1989) are as follows. We estimate demand for liner services to grow at 5.5%/year. However, there is severe overcapacity in liner trades at present, so that effective demand for new liner capacity will grow somewhat more slowly, at 4.5%/year. Container services are beginning to be introduced in developing country trades. Our experience is that once traders feel the benefit of such services, they develop quite quickly. Developing countries nevertheless experience some infrastructure problems with containers and may wish to moderate

Table 2. Fleet size comparison.

Containership fleet	End-1979	End-1989
million dwt	20	50
(or expressed as conventional equivalent)	(44)	(110)
Break-bulk multi-deck fleet		
million dwt	100	73
(of which employed in liner trades)	(50)[a]	(36)

[a] This is statistically greater than 50%, but it is also assumed that there was some underemployment of b/b ships in service in 1979, bringing the b/b fleet back to 50% of the effective liner fleet.

the pace. On balance, we expect that the 1980s will see widespread adoption of container services in these trades and the 50% penetration figure will have increased to about 75% by the end of 1989. Using the 'split' and productivity figures referred to above, this rate of penetration implies a growth in demand for new container ships of 9.5%/year and a net decline in demand for breakbulk liners of -3%/year – 'net', because some new breakbulk ships are bound to be built. The scrapping rate of old breakbulk liners may reach a rate of 5%/year in the second half of the decade, faster than in recent years. The actual fleet sizes at end 1989 compared with end 1979 may then be as shown in Table 2. The above reasoning is shown graphically in Figure 1.

The short point on penetration and the growth of tonnage is that there is a hope that the upheaval of the transitional stage will be over by the 1990s and that the last decade of the century will see a new steady state emerging, with growth in container tonnage more in line with growth in demand for liner services.

ECONOMIC FACTORS DETERMINING CONTAINER SHIP CHARACTERISTICS

What type of vessel will be operating in the 1990s? Because I am suggesting that there will not be further revolutionary changes in design, the 'steady state' of the 1990s will

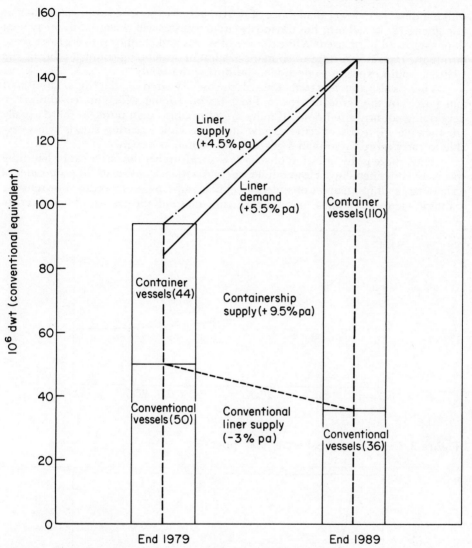

Figure 1. Development of liner demand and supply, 1980-90

be rooted in characteristics observable today. The first question is whether the preeminence of the cellular container ship will continue. Despite the fact that it has been losing ground recently (at end 1975, 67% of the world unit load fleet was cellular and at end 1979, 54%), the cellular ship will predominate, for the simple reason that it is the ship with the highest productivity both in stow and in cargo-handling speed. A fully cellular ship makes the maximum use of ship space available. The cellular construction minimizes lashing, and shore cranes can achieve loading rates of 20-40 box moves an hour. Ro-ros sacrifice use of space for flexibility in type of cargo handled and the handling rate of a large ro-ro is markedly slower than that of a cellular ship. In our experience cellular handling rates can average over 500 freight tons/hour in port, with ro-ro rates only half this rate. The combos also have to make some sacrifices in efficiency to meet the compromise inherent in their dual-purpose design, with handling rates lower than those of ro-ros, in our experience again about half as fast, giving 125 tons/hour, but obviously circumstances will change with the type of ship, cargo and ports used. While the use of ro-ros and combos is likely to increase during the transitional stage of containerization in developing countries during the 1980s, I would expect it to decline again during the 1990s.

There is also a current trend towards the use of geared cellular ships. This is part and parcel of the same desire for flexibility in coping with port conditions in developing country conditions. If there are more ships than ports, as there usually are, then it is more cost effective to gear the ports, while a gearless ship is in any case able to carry more cargo than a geared ship of similar design.

Then there is the question of size. It is a truism that the faster cargo-handling speeds of container ships allowed liner operators to take advantage of economies of scale of larger ships. Curves of scale for cellular ships are of the order shown in the graphs in Figures 2, 3 and 4. It is not surprising that with the passage of time average

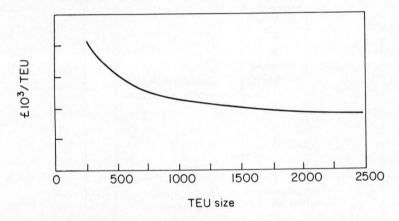

Figure 2. General minimal reefer-ship prices.

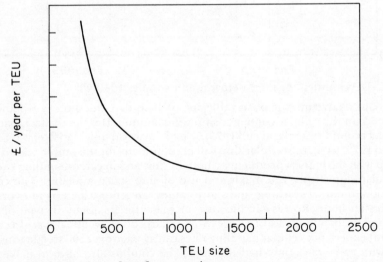

Figure 3. General minimal reefer-operating costs.

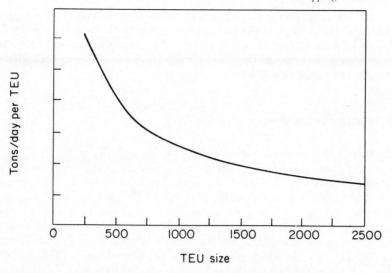

TEU size

Figure 4. General minimal reefer-fuel consumption.

sizes have moved upwards and unit costs have come down in real terms (if fuel prices are deflated by a fuel index rather than a general price index). What has happened is that a great many berths of the first generation were of the order of 700 ft long. This accommodated a 1 500 TEU ship, now rising to ± 1 800 TEU as further ship design improvements are made with time. Then there have been a limited number of ships built to Panamax limits, up to 2 500 TEQ taking even greater advantage of scale.

The reason why the numbers have been limited is that size of this order begins to bring certain inflexibilities. A fleet of such ships must be sure that it has enough cargo to maintain an economic load factor and of course berthing facilities giving about 1 000 ft in length, supporting large cranes both as to height and reach and drawing 40 ft or more of water. If the cargo is not there, it is more difficult to redeploy single large units than smaller ships.

An alternative is of course to add wayport calls. This has been done successfully, but the more calls that are added, the greater the opportunity cost of the time delay involved; for a big ship that opportunity cost is obviously bigger than for a small one. Panamax ships have been successful in fleets like Trio, Scandutch and SAECS, but remain a minority of the world fleet. With much competition in the Atlantic and Pacific, for example, the optimum size of ship, given the amount of cargo and the relatively short voyage times (increasing the proportion of time spent in port), is in the 1 250-1 500-1 800 TEQ ranges.

As to speed, the strongly rising price of oil and the development of the slow-speed diesel has meant that new container ships will now be motorships, even up to Panamax limits; and indeed that it is economic to re-engine large ships with diesels – and this is being done. The trend of the 1960s and 1970s towards faster ships has been halted, and speeds plus or minus 20 knots are becoming the new norm.

If, as predicted above, the 1990s produce more of a steady state than is likely in the 1980s, then the typical cargo liner of the 1990s will be a gearless, cellular motorship, of between 1 500-2 000 TEQ operating at about 20 knots. All such figures assume that present influences work themselves through the system so that the system as a whole comes closer to what we can judge today looks like the optimum. In real life new factors always emerge, which are unknown today, to disturb this hypothetical steady state and to limit the usefulness of our predictions. For instance, a breakthrough in nuclear propulsion or acceptance of certain nuclear standards under great pressure from oil prices and supply, would bring new criteria for optimum speed and perhaps have secondary effects on optimum size. One cannot tell if this will be so or what the criteria will be.

UK SHIPPING IN THE 1990s

Recently there has been the observed tendency, already alluded to, for more cargo to be reserved in one way or another for the flags of the nations which generate the cargo. Clearly, this favours shipowners of countries with strong growth. I do not attempt a forecast of the UK's economic position in the 1990s after a decade as a major oil producer but facing declining oil production. I would only like to make one point concerning it. People are talking of the UK ceasing to be a manufacturing nation and relying on invisible exports. The arithmetic of such a premise simply does not add up. The last year for which a full breakdown is available is 1978, for which the profile of the UK trade balance looks broadly similar to that of the three previous years. To put the case starkly, invisible exports would have to be equivalent to the value of manufacturing output less exports (which would no longer be produced) plus imports (except that part going into output for exports). If one takes a crude look at the figures without any attempt to assess secondary effects of such a radical change in the trade balance, the results are as shown in Table 3. Net invisible earnings, at £2.2 billion (10^9), look even smaller against the £116.7 billion, namely 1.9%.

Table 3. UK trade balance 1978.

	£ billion(10^9)
Manufacturing output	121.3
plus manufacturing imports	26.1
	147.4
less manufacturing exports	30.7
	116.7
to be paid for by invisible exports	
Invisible exports	18.3
less those on shipping account	3.2
	15.1

Therefore invisibles need to be multiplied 7.7 times to cover the contribution of the vanishing manufactures

---

The discrepancy is so great that I conclude that there is no comfort to be gained from looking forward to an era in which manufacturing in the UK has become obsolete. I assume that realization of this fact will eventually – some time in the 1980s – produce the political will to improve the UK's industrial performance. A fundamental decadence would stop this happening, but, although I see the West as a whole conceding shares of trade to a vigorous East, the UK does not seem to be fundamentally less stable as a society than other countries in the West; so I have set aside fears of a fundamental decline. The whole of this point is a long way from shipping economics, but it is of great importance for the future of British shipping, as of much else that is British. There are thus grounds for saying that in the 1990s the UK will be economically stronger relative to other traditional industrial nations than it is today. This would be a plus for UK shipping.

A firmer prediction is that the tendency to place shipping under the national flag will not be taken as far within the OECD group as elsewhere. Although the OECD will concede shares of world trade in the next two decades, it will remain the largest trading bloc, thus giving elbow-room for the enterprising operators. The British, and also the Scandinavians and the Dutch, will all be strong defenders of the cross-trading interest. Together with the Greeks they will also be defending this interest in tanker and bulk trades, as well as in the liner market.

The container service market is a quality market. To date British enterprise has kept the UK flag in the forefront of 'the revolution'. At end-1979 the UK flag came second to the US flag with 17.5% of the world cellular fleet compared to 20%. Japan and West Germany followed with 11.5% and 10.5% respectively, and then there was a significant gap. In terms of companies OCL was third in the world and ACT fifth (still in terms of capacity). A decade from now, some Asian countries will have closed the gap, but I doubt if any one will have overtaken the 'Big Four' countries. Perhaps a touch of chauvinism may be forgiven at Greenwich. My last prediction is that the British container operators will keep the UK in the Big Four.

7. THE PORTS OF GREAT BRITAIN

K. A. Heathcote (Joint Secretary, National Ports Council)

Thispaper is concerned with the ports of mainland Great Britain. From the port point of view, the most important feature of Great Britain is that it is an island and therefore all its overseas trade has to pass through one of its ports. In terms of value of trade the most important port is an airport – Heathrow; but in terms of weight 99% of UK overseas trade goes through sea ports, and until such time as the Channel Tunnel is built overseas trade must go through one port or another, whether it is deep-sea traffic, near-sea traffic or transshipped.

Some part of domestic trade – in particular that with Northern Ireland – must travel by sea and therefore move through ports. Traffic from one port to another along the coast is part of the UK internal transport network. Traffic which comes from the sea itself – fish or gravel – uses ports. The principal activity of the ports is, however, the overseas trade of the country.

DEVELOPMENTS IN UK TRADE AND TRAFFIC

To give some idea of proportions, UK traffic can be divided simply between overseas trade and coastal trade – including trade with Northern Ireland – and between fuels, overwhelmingly oil and its derivatives, and other traffics.

The traffic of the ports of Great Britain in 1978 was: (1) foreign 243 million tonnes; and (2) coastwise 110 million tonnes. Of these figures fuels, predominantly petroleum, accounted for: (1) foreign 132 million tonnes; (2) coastwise 96 million tonnes.

The majority of the non-foreign trade of UK ports is therefore fuels, above all petroleum (even though because Northern Irish trade is counted as coastwise, that does not apply to the Northern Irish trade); but the (bigger) overseas trade is mainly non-fuel traffic.

Another way of looking at this is to consider the relative importance of different types of transport for inland transport activity as shown by the Ministry of Transport's statistics.[1] In round terms coastal shipping accounted for 14% of inland traffic compared to 68% by road. Rail, incidentally, accounted for 16% and British Waterways for less than one-tenth of 1%.

However, there is no alternative for most overseas traffic of this country but to travel by sea, and therefore through one or other port. A second point to be made follows naturally from this. UK ports fundamentally serve the UK economy. There is a little transshipment or entrepôt traffic, but for practical purposes the trade of the ports is the trade of the country, and ports are merely part of the infrastructure whereby the trade of the country is sustained. It is the ports which are generated by the economic activity, however much it might be the other way round in an underdeveloped country.

It is important to consider what now are and what will be the most important areas with which this country trades. Since 1965 the National Ports Council (NPC) –

due to be abolished '– has maintained a series of port statistics, and has developed a unique series of forecasts of the country's trade by weight and by commodity.

Table 1 is a summary analysis of UK foreign trade in 1968, 1978 and the NPC forecast for 1988 in main commodities. From this Table it appears that, thanks to the

Table 1. UK foreign trade 1968, 1978, 1988 by commodity (10^3 net tonnes).

	Imports			Exports		
	1968	*1978*	*1988*	*1968*	*1978*	*1988*
Unmilled cereals	8 186	7 081	6 000	684	2 424	740
Sugar and sugar preps	2 578	2 313	1 770	–	–	–
Animal feeding stuffs	1 860	1 834	1 200	–	–	–
Oil seeds and nuts	680	1 564	2 100	–	–	–
Wood lumber and cork	5 951	4 568	4 350	–	–	–
Pulp and waste paper	3 595	2 229	1 900	–	–	–
Crude fertilizers	1 942	1 805	2 300	–	–	–
Crude minerals	2 845	3 599	4 650	4 491	10 254	11 550
Iron ore and pyrites	17 896	15 678	18 000	} 956	} 1 734	} 1 500
Other ores and scrap	2 070	2 206	2 100			
Animal and vegetable oils and fats	847	905	1 050	–	–	–
Chemical fertilizers	1 580	1 449	1 440	492	779	950
Other non-fuels	23 397	29 729	38 250	17 224	16 258	30 440
Total non-fuels	73 425	74 961	85 110	23 847	31 450	45 180
Crude petroleum	83 014	65 459	50 000	3 614	23 139	30 000
Petroleum products	23 414	18 395	11 000	334	14 763	25 000
Coal, coke, briquettes	71	2 600	8 400	14 259	3 316	3 000
Total fuel	106 499	86 453	69 400	18 206	41 218	58 000
Total traffic	**179 924**	**161 414**	**154 510**	**42 053**	**72 668**	**103 180**

North Sea, exports of petroleum and its products will increase and imports of petroleum and its products decrease. Imports of coal and its relations will also increase however, and exports decrease – despite the UK's history as a coal-exporting country – and, even more significant, exports of non-fuels will increase only a little more rapidly than imports. The stability of the iron ore import figure reflects the decline of the steel industry, and the decline of the sugar figures is based on the decline of the cane-based industries. But above all the Table shows that the rate of growth of exports has fallen off more quickly in tonnage terms than the rate of growth of imports. While UK trade is growing, it is growing slowly – and at a slower rate.

Table 2 illustrates perhaps the most important change affecting UK ports since the second world war, again by the years 1968 and 1978 on a historical basis and 1988 on a forecast basis. These figures show that deep-sea trade in tonnage terms is stable or declining and near- and short-sea trade expanding. In 1968, for example, trade with Australasia was much greater than that with West Germany; but by 1988 we expect trade with Australasia to have continued to decline – to 20% less than it was in tonnage terms in 1968 – and exceeded by a factor of almost 250% by trade with West Germany. In 1968 trade with Africa was over double trade with the Netherlands, in 1988 we expect it to be identical. In 1988 we foresee trade with the USA as being slightly less than that with Belgium and Luxembourg. Very simply, the UK now trades preponderantly

Table 2. UK foreign trade other than fuels, 1968, 1978, 1988 by country (10^3 net tonnes).

	1968			1978			1988		
	Imports	*Exports*	*Total*	*Imports*	*Exports*	*Total*	*Imports*	*Exports*	*Total*
Irish Rep	1 893	1 236	3 129	2 398	2 886	5 284	2 980	2 970	5 950
Persian Gulf	43	662	705	50	1 952	2 002	180	1 940	2 120
India	697	198	895	309	313	622	300	180	480
Africa	9 185	1 867	11 052	6 484	3 296	9 780	8 030	3 120	11 150
Japan	314	152	466	615	241	856	930	320	1 250
Australasia	3 383	1 118	4 501	3 200	698	3 898	2 950	720	3 670
Canada	8 788	666	9 454	7 830	562	8 392	8 270	470	8 740
USA	5 242	2 546	7 788	6 472	2 275	8 747	5 770	2 180	7 950
South and Central America and West Indies	5 467	1 219	6 686	7 363	1 201	8 564	7 120	1 030	8 150
West Germany	1 501	1 761	3 262	4 269	3 374	7 643	4 820	4 570	9 390
Netherlands	3 507	1 246	4 753	4 025	4 591	8 616	5 930	5 220	11 150
Belgium/Luxemburg	1 083	764	1 847	2 451	4 176	6 627	3 510	4 570	8 080
France	2 145	1 458	3 603	4 634	3 697	8 331	5 610	4 550	10 160
Italy	924	1 258	2 182	2 165	1 614	3 779	2 970	1 870	4 840
Denmark	1 142	667	1 809	1 159	881	2 040	1 210	1 000	2 210
Rest of Scandinavia	15 085	2 630	17 715	11 004	2 843	13 847	11 890	3 780	15 670
Baltic	5 053	422	5 475	2 942	1 523	4 465	3 470	930	4 400
Spain and Portugal	2 071	1 019	3 090	2 230	1 738	3 968	2 860	2 090	4 950
Other Europe and Med	4 379	1 593	5 972	3 536	2 180	5 716	4 060	2 500	6 560
Other Countries	1 524	1 363	2 887	1 825	1 408	3 233	2 250	1 170	3 420
Total	73 425	23 847	97 272	74 961	41 450	116 411	85 110	45 180	130 290

with Europe and Scandinavia, and we expect this pattern to continue and intensify. The deep-sea trades are becoming, relatively, less important and this carries with it a whole series of consequences for ports (see Table 3).

Table 3. UK conventional traffic as percent of total non-bulk traffic (inwards and outwards).

	1975	1980
Total near continent	19.4	14.7
Scandinavia and Baltic (incl Denmark)	49.8	39.2
Irish Republic	1.7	2.7
Iberia and Mediterranean	48.4	33.0
Total short sea	49.2	36.9
Canada and USA	20.8	16.9
South and Central America and W Indies	58.8	43.7
Australasia	40.3	9.9
Far East	41.5	18.8
Africa	77.1	38.2
Persian Gulf and Indian Ocean	76.1	51.3
Total deep sea	48.4	26.7

Source: National Ports Council, *Bulletin*, No 11, Tables 6 and 7 (NPC estimates).

PORTS AND CARGO SYSTEMS

The most immediately visible consequence is that those ports geographically well sited for trade with north-west Europe and Scandinavia have been very successful. It does not matter whether Dover on some statistical basis is the 'most important' general cargo port. What is important is that it is an enormously important general cargo port, with the new A2 extension built directly to it, coming down off the cliffs on a viaduct into the port itself. Felixstowe, Harwich and Ipswich on Harwich Haven have all grown remarkably – even much humbler places, like Ramsgate and Folkestone, King's Lynn and Montrose have all done very well indeed.

But part of this activity has been because of the fact that a lot of traffic which used to go to, say, Preston from Scandinavia now goes to the east coast and is hauled overland to Lancashire markets. In a rough and ready way, (increased) trade with Europe and Scandinavia is conducted through the ports that face those countries to an even greater degree than before.

This is a very rough and ready statement – iron ore from Narvik for the South Wales steel industry would still go to South Wales – 'would', because it would obviously be more logical if it went to the Tees or the Humber and were consumed in the British Steel Corporation (BSC) plants fed by Redcar and Killingholme. 'More logical', because one ship would be able to carry more ore from Narvik to Redcar in a year than to Port Talbot and, all things being equal, transport costs would be lower. But this discussion brings us into the area of cargo systems.

We tend to think of cargo systems in terms of cargo-handling systems; the use of the big homogeneous bulk carrier, of the container ship, of the ro/ro vessel requiring complementary port facilities and enabling individual terminals to handle tonnages vastly in excess of their predecessors.

I propose, however, to use the term cargo system to describe something which is far more deep-seated and in which particular technical devices – the VLCC or the ro/ro vessel – play a vital but not entirely dominant role, promoting new possibilities but themselves promoted by them.

In general, ships of all sorts and classes, containers etc, are increasingly part of cargo systems designed to control the movement of cargo from sources to destination, more than from port to port, and where the decision maker can be either a consignee, a consignor or a transport system operator.

A consignee-dominated system

A well known example is the control exercised by the big oil companies over integrated production, transport, refining and sales systems. The enormous growth in the consumption of oil since the second world war provided the circumstances for such major developments as the giant oil tanker, whose ultimate justification is the need to move as cheaply as possible massive amounts of cargo over long distances to individually large consumption points, namely the big refineries; or, indeed, for the new 'oil port', of which the best known UK example is Milford Haven, which since 1957 has become the site of four refineries plus a remote terminal connected by a 68 mile pipeline to a previously existing refinery. There are, however, parallels to Milford Haven elsewhere in Europe: Wilhelmshaven in West Germany, or the giant tanker terminal built at Cap D' Antifer, connected by pipelines to refineries deep in Europe.

Yet another example of the dominance of the cargo system in the largest sense of the word is how the crude oil for the long-established oil refinery at Stanlow was first received in the Manchester Ship Canal, then at a new dock at Eastham, then at new landing stages in the River Mersey, and finally at a terminal off Anglesey connected by a 100 mile pipeline to the refinery. If the planners had known about North Sea oil then they might not have proceeded with Anglesey; this reflects the dominance of the system, the moving of traffic from port to port to fit in with the overriding requirements of delivering, profitably, refined petroleum in the market place. Oil is an example of the consignee-dominated system. Even though the oil companies are producers as well, OPEC has ensured that the traditional oil industry is market-centred, and from our point of view a consignee cargo system.

The consignor system

The best example of the alternative, the consignor system, in terms of effects on UK ports, used to be coal, because at least 15 ports were literally built for coal shipment. What this means in fact is exemplified by Sunderland, a port built out artificially below a cliff into the hostile North Sea, to serve the needs of collieries nearby. But the coal trade was consignor-based in more than the simple requirements of moving coal from as near as possible to the coalmine. The Durham coal owners and the Newcastle coal merchants had long established powerful and effective confederations, mini-OPECs of their day.

Nowadays the consignor abroad is playing an increasingly important role. Outspan, for instance, do not merely coordinate the shipment of their citrus fruit from South Africa: they ensure that it is delivered as efficiently and as cheaply as possible to consignees, and that can produce novel results. Oranges for south Lancashire come in through South Wales on chartered citrus fruit carriers: every item of alternative through costs has been appraised.

Another example is the way in which the big Scandinavian forest products manufacturers have developed systems of shipment on specialized carriers to concentrated discharge points, related to their local markets and used as storage points by the shipper abroad. Thus the biggest Swedish firm, SCA, deliver to one port only, Tilbury, in specialized ships to a specialized terminal, and sell to the whole UK from that terminal.

The transport operator cargo system

These big movements do not take place with the consignee or the consignor in isolation. SCA operate in a market in which the big receivers are trying to play-off Swedes against Finns against Russians against South Africans against Malaysians against Canadians. The receivers will try and buy in the cheapest market. The object of SCA, by their elaborate system, is to ensure that they are, for the part of the market they are interested in, the cheapest source; but by and large big seller is matched by big buyer.

In the citrus fruit trade mentioned above, Outspan will be dealing with Marks and Spencer or Sainsburys, not middle-men. There are all sorts of permutations possible – Geests do not themselves own the West Indies banana plantations they market, for example; and this third element of the cargo system operator is the third and equally diverse area of giant cargo system with which we have become accustomed. The ocean-going container consortia offer as far as possible a door-to-door service. In the short-sea, as well as container operators like British Rail or Bell Line, there are international hauliers like Pandoro for whom the ships that carry the lorries are just part of the transport system. Other big haulage/forwarding firms use third-parties ferries.

These international cargo systems are spreading steadily – eg as producer countries take a firmer grip of their products and try to extract every part of added value out of them – and depend on modern high-speed documentation and data transfer, itself the key to the efficiency of such sales organizations as Tesco or Sainsburys; and they are all dedicated to getting the cost of transport down to an irreducible minimum.

Cost reduction

The search for lower transport costs always includes something very familiar – the need to employ fewer men. For example, the route from Loch Ryan to Larne, the shortest sea route to Ireland, has done well because the ships can be worked harder and at the end of the day fewer man-hours are required to move the same tonnage in comparison with eg Liverpool to Dublin.

For the ports, the search for minimum cost means in practice minimum number of ports of call and wherever possible minimum steaming time. For bulk trades the traffic goes to the market, but even then the terminal may be 100 miles away from the market (in the case of oil for Stanlow) and two or three times that much (in the case of forest products from Tilbury to the north). The most dramatic and most glamorous example is the transference of deep-sea general cargo into unit systems, above all containers, and their concentration on still fewer ports. There were never many important deep-sea general cargo ports in the UK: Liverpool and London were dominant, but that relative importance has changed. Because of developments such as containers Southampton has become much more important in deep-sea general cargo trades, and London and Liverpool much less important.

UK PORT AND SHIPPING ACTIVITY: FACTORS OF CHANGE

The real question is perhaps whether this process has stopped. We have already seen that relatively the deep-sea trades are less important and will become even less important; it is important to emphasize 'relatively' because clearly they will remain large and valuable. But discussions about increasing trade with Europe and Scandinavia must account for the fact that the UK has passed the point of talking about going into Europe and is now effectively a part of Europe; the UK will become even more closely knit into this grouping in the future.

If this is an accurate reflection of the position, then demographic factors are clearly important. The UK has a population of 50 million whereas continental Europe has 250 million. The same kind of disparity applies to the individual regions of the UK. London has a population of about 10 million, and the North West about 6 million, which are individually much smaller than the populations of the 'Golden Triangle' of the Low Countries and Lower Rhine.

Shipping patterns have always been based on economic activity, and we became accustomed to one period appearance of this. Even between the wars this country accounted for about a quarter of total world seaborne trade, and it was a great deal more than that before 1914. Thus, if there was anywhere for a ship to go to for business at that time it was to the UK, and in the UK it was to the areas of principal activity. Nowadays things have changed: looking at Europe as a whole it is difficult to avoid the conclusion that one should now rationally think in terms of four types of port and shipping activity related to Britain.

(1)   Internal traffic, ie trade between the UK and Scandinavia, Europe and Ireland, with the North Sea as a sort of European inland sea.
(2)   Major bulk movements either to big production centres, steelworks or oil refineries, or to distribution centres like the SCA terminal. Where the traffic to the individual point is big enough this will be whole-shipload traffic.
(3)   Part-shipload traffic where part-cargoes are discharged in two or three consecutive ports.
(4)   There will be concentration movements, fed by appropriated or general purpose ferries (Category 1 above).

This could be a description of how traffic was formerly organized in the UK. In the future it would seem logically to be how it will be organized in Europe, with the UK as a part; and the less important deep-sea trade is as part of the total activity, the greater the need to achieve maximum economies, and more it may be that fewer direct calls in the UK will be made by ocean general cargo ships.

Everything ultimately depends, as before, on the amount of cargo to be moved. In part this will be affected by world trade activity, in part in less obvious ways. If, for example, goods are manufactured under licence in the UK rather than imported, that element of visible trade will largely be replaced by invisible trade. But it seems more reasonable to consider the future levels of economic activity, if we believe that port activity is primarily and often solely related to the port's own regional hinterland. For the UK, this has hitherto been a matter for speculation and argument, into which subjects like transshipment and competition between ports both in the UK and within Europe have been introduced.

In 1980, for the first time, there are reliable statistics derived from a survey, based on Customs data, of the internal source or destination of overseas trade, by commodity and by county. This information is still being analysed, but the first general cut is set out in Tables 4 - 11.

It is clear that regional ports command a majority of the trade of their region despite the effects of trade shifts etc discussed above. Let us take one example, the one nearest to Greenwich. Tables 4 - 11 refer to 'Thames and Kent' as the port area and

Table 4. Foreign imports of traffic other than fuels, UK seaports, 1978 – all trading areas; UK port area by inland region of final destination (10³ tonnes).

UK port area	Greater London	South east (excluding London)	South West	Wales	West Midlands	North West	Scotland	North	Yorks and Humber	East Midlands	East Anglia	Northern Ireland	Total Specified	Region not Specified	Total
Thames & Kent	5 389	3 008	396	185	751	810	810	199	425	613	261	11	12 226	2 774	15 000
Sussex & Hants	523	870	162	200	204	234	61	78	107	111	71	10	2 631	986	3 617
West Country	48	55	315	31	40	30	14	8	22	10	9	–	581	186	767
Bristol Channel	169	195	1 243	4 684	188	253	20	43	134	45	23	21	7 019	1 556	8 575
West & North Wales	39	27	19	335	10	71	7	3	19	14	3	–	546	29	575
Lancs & Cumbria	183	129	123	1 288	512	4 808	238	832	354	149	56	24	8 496	1 979	10 475
Scotland	51	41	22	4	10	65	5 463	19	41	8	3	4	5 730	439	6 169
North East	61	52	39	6	23	420	118	8 649	195	75	17	10	4 664	1 845	6 509
Humber	170	80	48	89	779	922	138	259	7 756	471	43	5	10 753	1 673	12 426
Wash & Northern East Anglia	78	164	51	27	342	134	42	32	93	248	297	2	1 510	506	2 016
Haven ports	770	874	175	83	267	489	70	88	163	295	237	6	3 818	753	4 571
Northern Ireland	–	–	–	2	–	5	–	–	1	–	–	179	1 187	406	1 593
Total UK Seaports	7 482	5 494	2 591	6 935	2 925	8 240	6 346	5 209	9 309	2 040	1 318	1 272	59 163	13 132	72 295

Table 5. Foreign exports of traffic other than fuels, UK seaports, 1978 – all trading areas; UK port by inland region of origin (10³ tonnes).

UK port area	Greater London	South east (excluding London)	South West	Wales	West Midlands	North West	Scotland	North	Yorks and Humber	East Midlands	East Anglia	Northern Ireland	Total Specified	Region not Specified	Total
Thames & Kent	953	2 985	280	278	474	505	260	164	419	287	149	25	6 778	734	7 512
Sussex & Hants	178	424	118	88	193	211	158	118	155	90	56	19	1 807	249	2 056
West Country	9	53	2 672	13	30	26	18	5	27	5	6	2	2866	133	2 999
Bristol Channel	57	118	223	1 044	101	39	18	13	31	51	12	1	1 707	541	2 248
West & North Wales	25	34	9	782	19	47	11	9	14	16	7	2	974	38	1 012
Lancs & Cumbria	120	157	70	252	391	2 091	211	356	512	241	56	30	4 488	337	4 825
Scotland	30	16	8	5	37	79	1 370	57	46	23	3	3	1 677	288	1 965
North East	23	69	41	44	58	113	113	2 054	326	68	23	10	2 941	236	3 177
Humber	38	79	44	58	223	448	165	233	1 636	311	25	12	3 273	457	3 730
Wash & Northern East Anglia	25	81	20	23	52	79	16	20	44	119	249	1	730	605	1 335
Haven ports	302	478	173	170	345	333	134	78	205	186	209	8	2 621	250	2 871
Northern Ireland	1	–	–	1	–	–	1	–	–	2	–	154	159	35	194
Total UK Seaports	1 760	4 494	3 657	2 755	1 923	3 972	2 473	3 108	3 414	1 400	797	267	30 019	3 904	33 923

Table 6. Foreign imports of traffic other than fuels, UK seaports, 1978 – near and short sea trading areas; UK port area by inland region of final destination (10^3 tonnes).

UK port area	Greater London	South east (excluding London)	South West	Wales	West Midlands	North West	Scotland	North	Yorks and Humber	East Midlands	East Anglia	Northern Ireland	Total Specified	Region not Specified	Total
Thames & Kent	2 504	2 024	267	146	666	560	115	109	284	286	202	9	7 172	1 662	8 834
Sussex & Hants	291	608	114	24	115	77	24	63	36	49	32	2	1 435	495	1 930
West Country	48	55	275	31	40	30	14	8	22	10	9	1	543	156	699
Bristol Channel	20	50	639	1 053	81	46	8	3	12	15	6	8	1 941	474	2 415
West & North Wales	34	23	18	113	7	65	–	3	19	12	3	–	297	27	324
Lancs & Cumbria	72	49	28	238	161	1 676	94	700	110	34	15	2	3 179	1 108	4 287
Scotland	39	23	10	–	3	25	2 309	11	8	1	–		2 429	253	2 682
North East	58	49	26	6	20	379	108	1 662	176	67	17	7	2 575	1 006	3 581
Humber	100	59	37	84	635	844	126	238	2 808	375	40	5	5 351	1 447	6 798
Wash & Northern East Anglia	76	160	49	27	339	134	42	32	92	238	272	2	1 463	473	1 936
Haven ports	696	739	156	70	242	442	65	73	125	246	483	6	3 343	630	3 973
Northern Ireland	–	–	–	2	–	5	–	–	1	–	–	814	822	283	1 105
Total UK Seaports	3 940	3 838	1 617	1 794	2 308	4 281	2 904	2 900	3 691	1 334	1 078	855	30 545	8 014	38 559

Table 7. Foreign exports of traffic other than fuels, UK seaports, 1978 – near and short sea trading areas; UK port area by inland region of origin (10³ tonnes).

UK port area	Greater London	South east (excluding London)	South West	Wales	West Midlands	North West	Scotland	North	Yorks and Humber	East Midlands	East Anglia	Northern Ireland	Total Specified	Region not Specified	Total
Thames & Kent	603	851	197	175	288	291	164	69	253	152	77	17	3 135	643	3 778
Sussex & Hants	29	263	62	44	88	50	43	27	57	26	12	5	704	216	920
West Country	8	49	2 612	13	28	21	15	5	27	5	6	2	2 790	132	2 922
Bristol Channel	32	86	189	561	49	21	6	8	20	37	10	–	1 015	459	1 474
West & North Wales	25	34	8	753	18	39	9	6	11	15	7	1	924	22	946
Lancs & Cumbria	50	47	22	139	122	1 212	48	1 138	195	68	13	4	2 060	264	2 324
Scotland	12	–	–	1	–	7	947	28	6	–	–	–	1 000	243	1 243
North East	11	33	31	13	8	41	75	1 581	85	13	11	7	1 908	214	2 122
Humber	19	30	36	44	158	359	127	184	1 167	245	13	10	2 393	430	2 823
Wash & Northern East Anglia	24	79	17	23	48	71	16	19	40	112	248	1	698	605	1 303
Haven ports	209	346	141	142	248	259	93	50	133	131	175	3	1 931	200	2 131
Northern Ireland	1	–	–	–	–	–	1	–	–	2	–	151	155	35	190
Total UK Seaports	1 023	1 819	3 312	1 906	1 055	2 372	1 540	2 014	1 993	806	573	200	18 712	3 463	22 175

Table 8. Foreign imports of traffic other than fuels, UK seaports, 1978 – deep sea trading areas; UK port area by inland region of final destination (10 tonnes).

UK port area	Greater London	South east (excluding London)	South West	Wales	West Midlands	North West	Scotland	North	Yorks and Humber	East Midlands	East Anglia	Northern Ireland	Total Specified	Region not Specified	Total
Thames & Kent	2 885	984	129	39	85	250	65	90	141	327	59	2	5 056	1 112	6 168
Sussex & Hants	232	262	48	176	89	157	37	15	71	62	39	8	1 196	491	1 687
West Country	–	–	40	–	–	–	–	–	–	–	–	–	40	30	70
Bristol Channel	149	145	604	3 631	107	207	12	40	122	30	17	13	5 077	1 082	6 159
West & North Wales	5	4	1	222	3	6	7	–	–	2	–	–	250	2	252
Lancs & Cumbria	111	80	95	1 050	151	3 132	144	132	244	115	41	22	5 317	871	6 188
Scotland	12	18	12	4	7	40	3 154	8	33	7	3	4	3 302	186	3 488
North East	3	3	13	–	3	41	10	1 987	19	8	–	3	2 090	839	2 929
Humber	70	21	11	5	144	78	7	21	4 948	96	3	–	5 404	226	5 630
Wash & Northern East Anglia	2	4	2	–	3	–	–	–	1	10	25	–	47	33	80
Haven ports	74	135	19	13	25	47	5	15	38	49	54	–	474	123	597
Northern Ireland	–	–	–	–	–	–	–	–	–	–	–	365	365	123	488
Total UK Seaports	3 542	1 656	976	5 141	617	3 959	3 442	2 309	5 618	706	240	417	28 620	5 118	33 741

Table 9. Foreign exports of traffic other than fuels, UK seaports, 1978 – deep sea trading areas; UK port area by inland region of origin (10³ tonnes).

UK port area	Greater London	South east (excluding London)	South West	Wales	West Midlands	North West	Scotland	North	Yorks and Humber	East Midlands	East Anglia	Northern Ireland	Total Specified	Region not Specified	Total
Thames & Kent	350	2 134	83	103	186	214	96	95	166	135	72	8	3 643	91	3 734
Sussex & Hants	149	161	56	44	105	161	115	91	98	64	44	14	1 103	33	1 136
West Country	1	4	60	–	2	5	3	–	–	–	–	1	77	–	77
Bristol Channel	25	32	34	483	52	18	12	5	11	14	2	1	692	82	774
West & North Wales	–	–	1	29	1	8	2	3	3	1	–	1	50	16	66
Lancs & Cumbria	70	110	48	113	269	878	163	218	317	173	43	26	2 428	73	2 501
Scotland	18	16	8	4	37	72	423	29	40	23	3	3	677	45	722
North East	12	36	10	31	50	72	38	473	241	55	12	3	1 033	22	1 055
Humber	19	49	8	14	65	89	38	49	469	66	12	2	880	27	907
Wash & Northern East Anglia	1	2	3	–	4	8	–	1	4	7	1	–	32	–	32
Haven ports	93	132	32	28	97	74	41	28	72	55	34	5	690	50	740
Northern Ireland	–	–	–	–	–	–	–	–	–	–	–	3	4	–	4
Total UK Seaports	737	2 675	345	849	868	1 600	933	993	1 421	594	224	67	11 307	441	11 748

Table 10. Foreign imports of traffic other than fuels, UK seaports, 1978 – all trading areas; UK port area by mode of inland transport from port (10^3tonnes).

UK port area	Road	Rail	Inland waterway	Sea	Other	Total specified	Mode not specified	Total
Thames & Kent	9 805	600	1 041	136	2 988	14 569	431	15 000
Sussex & Hants	2 547	373	–	7	651	3 579	38	3 617
West Country	640	26	–	–	98	763	4	767
Bristol Channel	2 645	567	–	8	5 254	8 476	99	8 575
West & North Wales	277	66	–	–	231	574	1	575
Lancs & Cumbria	5 482	1 381	304	97	2 992	10 257	218	10 475
Scotland	3 573	1 178	–	26	1 343	6 120	49	6 169
North East	2 259	1 622	–	3	2 404	6 288	221	6 509
Humber	5 713	4 572	137	2	1 899	12 322	104	12 426
Wash & Northern East Anglia	1 639	85	–	–	274	1 998	18	2 016
Haven Ports	3 641	557	–	–	289	4 488	83	4 571
Northern Ireland	1 127	6	–	18	400	1 550	43	1 593
Total UK Seaports	39 352	11 032	1 482	297	18 823	70 986	1 309	72 295

Table 11. Foreign exports of traffic other than fuels, UK seaports, 1978 – all trading areas; UK port area by mode of inland transport from port (10 tonnes).

	Mode of inland transport from port							
UK port area	Road	Rail	Inland waterway	Sea	Other	Total specified	Mode not specified	Total
Thames & Kent	4 953	382	140	47	1 909	7 431	81	7 512
Sussex & Hants	1 590	312	–	5	115	2 023	33	2 056
West Country	2 456	397	–	65	67	2 986	13	2 999
Bristol Channel	1 606	360	–	3	267	2 236	12	2 248
West & North Wales	222	55	–	16	716	1 009	3	1 012
Lancs & Cumbria	3 821	237	40	82	594	4 774	51	4 825
Scotland	1 447	65	3	63	302	1 880	85	1 965
North East	1 781	475	22	12	830	3 120	57	3 177
Humber	3 121	288	12	8	287	3 716	14	3 730
Wash & Northern East Anglia	1 125	41	2	2	145	1 315	20	1 335
Haven Ports	2 261	465	–	95	25	2 847	24	2 871
Northern Ireland	182		–	2	6	190	4	194
Total UK seaports	24 565	3 078	219	399	5 264	33 525	398	33 923

demonstrate conclusively that the ports of this area dominate the traffic of the relevant economic region.

Tables 12 - 15 are analysed more closely to relate only to three ports – London, Felixstowe and Medway. Again it is clear from these figures that London still dominates the trade of Greater London and to a lesser extent of the South East.

These figures are important partly because they accurately tell us what was previously guessed at, and because they underline two facts which were emphasized above. The UK is an island; therefore whether trade is trans-shipped or whatever happens to it in terms of transport mode, it always finishes up passing through a port. Accepting this, and not being concerned here by

Table 12. Foreign traffic, UK seaports, 1978 – all non-fuel commodities, inland region by port (10^3 tonnes).

Imports	Inland region	London	Felixstowe	Medway	Other ports[a]	Total
	Greater London	4 288	351	278	2 603	7 520
	South East exc London	1 776	406	601	2 742	5 525
	South West	216	86	89	2 206	2 597
	West Midlands	357	116	152	2 310	2 935
	North West	406	207	79	7 585	8 277
	North	105	42	22	5 047	5 216
	Yorkshire & Humberside	212	85	25	9 002	9 324
	East Midlands	375	155	52	1 468	2 050
	East Anglia	142	174	27	980	1 323
	Wales	90	37	25	6 769	6 948
	Scotland	86	31	14	6 241	6 372
	Northern Ireland	2	1	1	2 086	2 090
	Total specified	8 055	1 692	1 365	49 067	60 179
	Various regions	1 090	129	387	6 638	8 244
	Not specified	552	162	118	4 169	5 001
	Total	**9 697**	**1 983**	**1 870**	**59 874**	**73 424**

Exports		London	Felixstowe	Medway	Other ports[a]	Total
	Greater London	717	154	34	886	1 791
	South East exc London	2 324	233	254	1 727	4 538
	South West	101	92	20	3 455	3 668
	West Midlands	230	164	19	1 539	1 952
	North West	242	130	15	3 693	4 080
	North	96	47	16	2 995	3 154
	Yorkshire & Humberside	163	121	28	3 170	3 482
	East Midlands	151	110	15	1 155	1 431
	East Anglia	82	107	2	610	801
	Wales	137	79	31	2 522	2 769
	Scotland	110	68	17	2 341	2 536
	Northern Ireland	9	5	–	916	930
	Total specified	4 361	1 312	451	25 007	31 131
	Various regions	293	28	75	2 379	2 775
	Not specified	108	58	21	1 077	1 264
	Total	**4 762**	**1 398**	**547**	**28 463**	**35 170**

[a] Includes Irish Land Boundary.

the size of ship, or even by the type of ship, but merely by whether or not the nation's interests are being served, then we see, unsurprisingly, that the UK has a large collection of ports whose baseload is regional and which attract other traffic significantly in relation to their geographical situation in terms of destination country.

This suggests that much that has been said about competition between ports is nonsense. The unsurprising conclusion is that the port which can most vigorously

Table 13. Foreign traffic, UK seaports, 1978 – non-fuel 'bulk' commodities, inland region by port by port (10^3 tonnes).

Imports	Inland region	London	Felixstowe	Medway	Other ports[a]	Total
	Greater London	2 460	12	14	234	2 720
	South East exc London	267	24	57	386	734
	South West	–	–	1	1 126	1 127
	West Midlands	22	2	6	250	280
	North West	9	–	3	2 898	2 910
	North	19	–	–	3 539	3 558
	Yorkshire & Humberside	14	17	–	6 348	6 379
	East Midlands	192	6	–	239	437
	East Anglia	8	5	–	142	155
	Wales	11	–	–	5 776	5 787
	Scotland	–	–	–	4 162	4 162
	Northern Ireland	–	–	–	1 084	1 084
	Total specified	3 002	65	82	26 185	29 334
	Various regions	403	5	11	3 365	3 784
	Not specified	105	15	8	2 168	2 296
	Total	**3 510**	**85**	**101**	**31 718**	**35 414**

Exports	Inland region	London	Felixstowe	Medway	Other ports[a]	Total
	Greater London	161	6	1	58	226
	South East exc London	28	10	44	160	242
	South West	23	3	1	2 681	2 708
	West Midlands	9	5	–	49	63
	North West	8	7	–	617	632
	North	–	3	6	548	557
	Yorkshire & Humberside	4	6	–	134	144
	East Midlands	3	4	2	133	142
	East Anglia	2	13	–	217	232
	Wales	–	1	–	646	647
	Scotland	6	–	11	408	425
	Northern Ireland	–	–	–	200	200
	Total specified	242	59	64	5 852	6 217
	Various regions	260	3	70	1 947	2 280
	Not specified	45	8	7	641	701
	Total	**547**	**70**	**141**	**8 440**	**9 198**

[a] Includes Irish Land Boundary.

compete with another port is one which is immediately alongside it. The figures shown relate to port areas as conceived in economic terms, and do not relate to port authorities which are entirely artificial administrative entities.

An illustration of this is the Port of London Authority (PLA), which is the conservancy authority for the River Thames below Teddington and also owns a series of docks systems. A few years ago there were five docks systems. Following the

Table 14. Foreign traffic, UK seaports, 1978 – non-fuel 'partially bulk' commodities, inland region by port (10^3 tonnes).

Imports Inland region	London	Felixstowe	Medway	Other ports[a]	Total
Greater London	1 302	165	105	633	2 205
South East exc London	1 173	213	488	1 025	2 899
South West	180	44	81	654	959
West Midlands	292	56	140	1 236	1 724
North West	326	112	66	2 796	3 300
North	74	19	19	1 220	1 332
Yorkshire & Humberside	121	29	19	1 760	1 929
East Midlands	98	67	42	689	896
East Anglia	86	75	13	480	654
Wales	67	19	19	702	807
Scotland	70	11	13	1 469	1 536
Northern Ireland	2	1	–	624	627
Total specified	3 791	812	1 003	13 289	18 895
Various regions	464	49	94	1 597	2 204
Not specified	273	77	74	983	1 407
Total	4 528	938	1 171	15 869	22 506

Exports	London	Felixstowe	Medway	Other ports[a]	Total
Greater London	137	38	8	190	373
South East exc London	1 828	66	187	563	2 644
South West	22	21	4	240	287
West Midlands	63	37	10	475	585
North West	123	42	5	1 753	1 923
North	32	18	6	1 987	2 043
Yorkshire & Humberside	70	45	3	1 998	2 116
East Midlands	44	25	–	419	488
East Anglia	12	12	–	118	142
Wales	73	26	22	1 528	1 649
Scotland	16	7	1	640	664
Northern Ireland	–	–	–	246	246
Total specified	2 419	335	245	10 162	13 161
Various regions	6	6	1	64	77
Not specified	18	9	11	150	188
Total	2 443	350	257	10 376	13 426

[a] Includes Irish Land Boundary.

determination to close the India and Millwall system on the Isle of Dogs there will be two – the Royals and Tilbury; but when, in statistics like those in Table 11, we talk of the Port of London we refer not merely to the facilities owned and operated by the Authority but also to those other facilities reached through the waters controlled by the Authority. Most notably such facilities include the refinery terminals of Canvey Island; but even now after so many other closures there is still a large and thriving

Table 15. Foreign traffic, UK seaports, 1978 – non-fuel 'general cargo' commodities, inland region by port (10^3 tonnes).

Imports	Inland region	London	Felixstowe	Medway	Other ports[a]	Total
	Greater London	526	174	159	1 735	2 594
	South East exc London	336	170	56	1 330	1 892
	South West	37	42	7	426	512
	West Midlands	44	59	6	822	931
	North West	71	96	9	1 891	2 067
	North	12	23	3	287	325
	Yorkshire & Humberside	77	39	7	893	1 016
	East Midlands	84	82	10	540	716
	East Anglia	48	94	15	357	514
	Wales	12	18	6	318	354
	Scotland	16	20	1	610	647
	Northern Ireland	–	–	1	378	379
	Total specified	1 262	816	281	9 590	11 949
	Various regions	223	76	281	1 676	2 256
	Not specified	174	69	36	1 019	1 298
	Total	**1 659**	**961**	**598**	**12 285**	**15 503**

Exports		London	Felixstowe	Medway	Other ports[a]	Total
	Greater London	419	110	26	636	1 191
	South East exc London	469	157	23	1 003	1 652
	South West	57	68	16	532	673
	West Midlands	158	122	9	1 015	1 304
	North West	112	82	10	1 322	1 526
	North	64	26	4	460	554
	Yorkshire & Humberside	89	70	26	1 037	1 222
	East Midlands	104	81	13	603	801
	East Anglia	68	82	2	275	427
	Wales	64	52	9	348	437
	Scotland	89	60	5	1 292	1 446
	Northern Ireland	9	5	–	469	483
	Total specified	1 701	916	141	8 995	11 763
	Various regions	27	20	5	366	418
	Not specified	45	41	3	286	375
	Total	**1 773**	**977**	**149**	**9 647**	**12 546**

[a] Includes Irish Land Boundary.

collection of private wharves within the port of London, although outside the docks owned by the PLA.

About a mile upstream from Greenwich College is a private wharf, part of which literally surrounds part of the old Deptford naval base and which includes the ro-ro facility farthest up the River Thames. A mile or so downstream from Greenwich is the

Victoria Deep Water Terminal, a short-sea container terminal. On the Isle of Dogs, itself virtually opposite the College, is a wharf specializing in the import of steel. None of these three wharves will be closed when the India and Millwall systems go. As far as statistics, and indeed reality, are concerned they are part of the Port of London. The dockers employed there are just as much registered dockworkers as ever the men within the docks are. Two points are perhaps worth making: first, that the media understandably but irritatingly too readily assume that all the useful activity of the Port of London is carried on within the PLA's dock systems; and second, that common sense suggests that the most vigorous competition for the PLA's docks in fact comes from such wharves within the 'port', rather than from, eg, Antwerp, where UK traffic can neither begin nor finish; or from Felixstowe which now has a much smaller share of London's traffic than London, in the broad sense of the port.

The conclusion concerning port competition is reinforced by other examples shown in the Tables. The most vigorous competitors of Liverpool are the other ports of the North West; the strongest competitors of the Tyne are the other ports of the North East. Why then has the general policy been for many years to promote local amalgamations, which surely must of their nature reduce the effect of competition? After all, the PLA itself was set up in 1908 to replace five apparently unsuccessful local bodies which we would now see as competing bodies. Is competition not a good thing in the ports' area?

It is unlikely that policy is even related to practice as conveniently as that. What may be more realistic is to consider what might be meant by competition in this context. Clearly the ro-ro facilities at Deptford are not competing with Tilbury for OCL's Australasian traffic. More interesting is that, while it can be accepted that the deep-sea container traffic has migrated to Southampton, or via ferry connections to Europe, the departure of the traffic of the Deptford wharf from the Thames cannot be foreseen, because it is based on the activity of Fleet Street; ie this wharf primarily, but not exclusively, handles newsprint. It is in fact unglamorous but permanent, whereas the big container ships are much more glamorous but, quite possibly, much less permanent.

TECHNOLOGY, PORT CHANGE AND THE FUTURE

Technology is the most familiar aspect of port change. From the point of view of the port this technology (which extends beyond the ship) means there is less and less to be done at the port, and in the broadest sense ports become smaller. The most extreme example of this is the single point mooring buoys of Anglesey or at Tetney in the Humber, or the oil-loading tower at Scapa Flow. All that is visible on the sea is a buoy, however large, and some hoses and mooring lines. The same principle holds good throughout the gamut of modern port facilities. A floating ro-ro pontoon, for example, such as used at Zeebrugge or indeed at Deptford, is intrinsically mobile and, when moored against a quay, can enable a berth to handle anything up to ten times the traffic that a traditional conventional berth could do, and with far fewer men. It goes beyond this, however, because the comprehensive cargo system described above, aided by the refrigerated container or refrigerated lorry, abolishes to a large extent the need for cold-stores and warehousing at ports. This can have secondary effects on related industries, eg the modern equivalent of the butter-packaging area around Tooley Street, London (now largely derelict) is at Leek, N Staffordshire.

Traffics that used to move as general cargo now move in specialized ships to specialized terminals – the most familiar aspect of the changes that have overtaken the ports. Least port is best port; but the consequent decline in demand for men is erratic.

The most discussed feature of the port at present is the Registered Dockworkers Scheme. Ten years ago the industry employed about 120 000 people of whom half were Registered Dockworkers (Table 16). The figure has halved and this process continues. Any benefits derived from closing the West India and Millwall docks are not associated with resale value, but entirely associated with the possibility created of

Table 16. Total number of employees in UK port transport industry (10^3).

	10 Jan 1968	10 May 1979
Dockworkers		
Scheme	56	27
Non-scheme	–	9
Other employees	–	33
Total	**109**	**70**

severing employees and, by saving on the wage bill, with the aim for the PLA to become more prosperous. Some years ago a port dealt with fluctuations in labour and a shipping line dealt with fluctuations in demand in the same way – they paid their men off. Nowadays, it is far from being so simple. Few employers who lose a man try very hard to replace him; ships and cargo systems are now largely devoted to keeping the labour content down, and in general the same is true of ports.

It is not the Dock Labour Scheme which has caused the current problems: ports which fomerly employed few people and have been built up from such a position have done well, whereas ports with a large workforce and which have been confronted with a series of changes have done worse, and will continue to do worse. The lack of consistency between one port and another causes much of the problem. Things would be simpler if both reduction and the decline in traffic were consistent. The shift of UK trade towards Europe and the development of large-scale cargo systems have caused redistribution of trade between ports accompanied by redundancy on both counts. However, the traffic lost by London is not so much baseload traffic as the traffic formerly attracted by that port's role at a particular time and (as we would now judge) at a temporary stage of technological development, by trade patterns and the relative importance of the UK in world trade activity.

The predominantly local (or rather regional) traffic which remains to London is itself substantial, and this seems much harder to shift. Within that regional role the biggest competitors are the ports which are nearest. Wharves at Deptford or East Greenwich are the main competition for the market of the Port of London, not the ports involved in the developing rearrangement of economic life. The UK is part of Europe, and the marginal traffic (which is increasingly deep-sea general cargo traffic) is more likely to be distributed to the main European ports near the major industrial population areas rather than elsewhere.

The steady decline of the UK from the dominant element in world trade to (however important) a minority element, from being a country primarily trading with the greater world to part of Europe primarily trading with its colleagues in Greater Europe, is hard to accept. It is easier, in some respects, but even more difficult in others, to accept the port industry's transition from a large to a small employer. In the cases of the biggest ports, even fewer men are now employed than those ports' fair share of national decline would seem to justify.

The corollary of the importance of baseload regional traffic for UK ports is that a port can only bid for mobile traffic outside the region. Such traffic is greatly influenced not merely by whatever price the port charges for its service but also by considerations of overall ship economics and transport economics. The task of marketing a port is highly specialized: today specialization is considered the answer, with readiness to turn away traffic, however traditional and attractive, if it will not pay.

None of the above considerations will be surprising to shipowners; but a final and fair conclusion must consider whether it matters to UK ports what flag is flown by the ships that use them. It is clear from the above that if traffic does not pay, then it is not worth having; and that it does not matter whether a port's trade is carried in big or small ships so long as the port is thriving and useful. It is true than when Lines have used a port for a long period there may be a reluctance to leave because of established systems back-up and a clearly understood relationship to the market. This kind of legitimate shared interest is not confined to UK shipowners. Long-established foreign shipowners are in the same position, the modern consortium is often multinational, and it is difficult, as a member of Europe, to see why German shipowners or Belgian shipowners should be regarded as intrinsically different from UK shipowners when there is no evidence that the latter allow sentiment to sway them. Shipowners can certainly no longer afford the luxury of sentiment; and neither can the ports.

There is a more profound, and perhaps emotional aspect. In the UK's two traditional major ports, London and Liverpool, the most important employers of dockworkers used to be shipowners, who were more concerned with turning their ships around than anything else, and pursued often unfortunate industrial relations policies. More recently, however, there has been a wholesale disengagement by shipowners from the employment of dockers and, particularly in Liverpool, the port has been left to deal with the situation and pay some of the costs – not an inconsiderable proportion of the shipowners' search for economical operation. Perhaps coincidentally, probably the most successful part of the Port of London as a whole is the wharves in that they have the best industrial relations and the most sensible contracts: the wharves are precisely the element of that port where the shipowners have had least influence.

My message is that the UK ports have no more special relationship with the UK Merchant Marine than is afforded by the fact that both are economic activities based in the same country. They are in different businesses seeking different objectives. Ports cannot move, whereas ships can – from port to port, from country to country, and from owner to owner.

Reference

1   See the National Ports Council Report to the Secretary of State for Transport, 1978, Appendix 2.

DISCUSSION

Nature of growth in UK port activity

One implication of the future given on the trade handled by UK ports is that the bulk of the British shipping fleet is engaged in trades quite different from those where growth rate can be anticipated through British ports. Does the author expect, therefore, that such growth will take place mainly, if not entirely, in the development of ferry services to the Continent – ro-ros and so on – and that the nature of the UK shipping industry will then become much more divided that it is at present between long-haulage and short-haulage business?

Author's response. I was careful not to discuss the UK Merchant Marine as such. It does seem that the ports' interests are not the same as those of the merchant fleet because of the absence of cross trades. I do not think that the port operators are interested from an economic point of view in the flag flown by the ship. I believe that P & O, for example, has a heavy involvement in the near-sea general cargo trades, and that SEABRIDGE, for example, would send a ship out to load iron ore at Narvik as readily as it would to any other iron ore loading port in the world. For descriptive and forecasting purposes, this is how the trade of the UK operates. The British Merchant Marine is engaged in offering services to carry anybody's business from anywhere to anywhere, and that is how it makes its money. For these reasons my paper seems to be slightly out of line with the main thrust of the others given in the course of today's proceedings.

The SOLAS Convention

The 1974 International Safety of Life at Sea (SOLAS) Convention states that a port state has jurisdiction over the safety of ships using that port. How would the author see the port industry in the UK undertaking a surveillance role to ensure that ships using the port are in a seaworthy and cargoworthy condition, or does he think that this is bad legislation?

Author's response. Ever since the 1847 Clauses Acts which enable particular clauses to be incorporated in port legislation, the power of a harbourmaster has existed to control whether he will allow a ship to berth, where he will require it to go, and generally to ensure that it is only let near a berth if in his view it is in a satisfactory state. But this is a separate line of activity from the economic one. Hardly surprisingly, the ports perform two entirely separate functions, which is one reason why they must all operate under statute. From one point of view they are regulatory bodies of part of the coastline and the waters round the coastline; from another they are concerned with the handling of cargo. For example, down the River Thames from the Royal Naval College there is a private wharf which handles cargo. There is no intrinsic difference between that and those parts of the Port of London Authority (PLA) that handle cargo. The PLA has the additional dimension that it is also concerned with the regulation, as part of the general law of the UK, of the behaviour of people and of ships within part of the municipal territory. The two things are quite readily distinguished. In fact, in some ports they are distinguished organizationally. A conservancy body may do one thing and dock companies the other.

Operating costs and transshipment

The operator wishing to operate very large ships must pay for the necessary berth facilities. This is a trade-off that any operator planning services must make. He has certain economies of scale from which to benefit on the one hand, and he has certain costs and inflexibilities on the other. One of these costs is the cost of dredging-out and having a strong quay-face long enough and strong enough to support a very high crane with a big outreach. In theory, in a trade like that from the Middle East, the cargo is sufficient to warrant the use of very large ships; but on the whole the risks involved with continued employment in that trade and the difficulty of finding alternative employment for very large ships, is such that the reallotment size for that trade is somewhat smaller.

However, in the UK we are in a situation where the port that has now developed as the most convenient deep-sea port with the best facilities and the best topography – Southampton – is getting into a position where the investment has been made and the operators and the port authorities have made their contributions, but operating costs are becoming so high that transshipment figures will go up if something is not done about this problem. It is a very serious situation indeed.

Author's response. Transshipment should be the least-cost route where it is used. The least-cost route ought to be the best one for the country's economy, and there is thus nothing intrinsically wrong with transshipment.

UK coastwise trading

What is the author's view of the possible future redevelopment of coastwise shipping? The great increase in short-sea shipping is due to the fact that, because Britain is an island, any increase in the market has to be met by shipping. Coastwise shipping around the British Isles competes with road and rail and has certainly diminished to almost nothing. This could possibly change if the fuel economy advantages of shipping were in some way to reassert themselves as the cost of fuel goes up. That would mean that a large number of very small ports – harbours really – might have to be reprovided with the modern facilities of the mini-container or ro-ro kind. Is there any possibility of that occurring, and what sort of increase in the price of fuel would have to take place before it would become economic in a competitive sense to use ships for coastwise trading instead of road or rail?

Author's response. I believe that there has been a growth in what might be described as the triangular trades with three ports, two in the UK and one on the Continent, forming part of a system. It is difficult to predict the development of such trading in respect of bulk materials, apart from oil, where obviously there will be an enormous growth in technical coasting because of the North Sea oil movements from the Shetlands and Orkneys, and from the Firth of Forth to the refineries. Coal used to be the staple commodity in such trade, but given the tendency to burn on the coalfields, one would not have thought there was much prospect for such trade in the future; grain, possibly, but that is a stable market – it is difficult to predict with regard to general cargo. It is difficult to even guess, except to the extent that, thanks to the operation of the tax system, the relative increase in the cost of fuel for land vehicles has been much less than the increase in the cost of fuel for sea vehicles. In the 1990s – which I have assiduously avoided – maybe such trades might develop, but I do not believe they are in prospect fo the 1980s.

Air–sea transshipment

One of the most interesting elements in the original plans for Maplin was that there would be, or there was the intention for there to be a transcontinental airport and a transcontinental seaport in the same place. Is there any validity in the concept of air-sea transshipment in that area of the UK?

Author's response. Long-distance air freight suffered a slight setback when containers started because the reliability of delivery improved and the cost became lower. But in a general way of business, London Airport is already the most important port in the UK from the point of view of value, but it tends to handle very high-value goods. It is somewhat difficult to evisage the sort of movement which would involve a deep-sea movement to London and a short air-flip across to the Continent or vice versa. Second, while the authorities seem to change their minds every five years, at present the Third London Airport is scheduled for Stansted. Provided the promised roads are built, it is not necessary to build Maplin to enable transfers to be arranged quite conveniently between, for example, Stansted, London, Gatwick and the Tilbury Docks or London Wharfs. It should be possible to achieve whatever advantages of transshipment exist without putting in additional infrastructure.

The 'superport' concept

25 years ago, the Dutch government and the authorities in Rotterdam saw the potential for improving the Dutch industrial economy – so necessary as a result of loss of their East Indies economies – a massive industrial development based on oil refining and other bulk handling in Rotterdam to create Europort. Later this idea was considered as being possibly of importance for the UK. Reports were written, but very little action was taken. The French government saw the possibilities and has been actively investing in the same general principles in the South of France, and in Northern France also to some extent. Developing countries – particularly those in the Middle East – saw port development as the initiator of modernization and industrial development, perhaps to an alarming extent but, nevertheless, very successfully, and such developments are still taking place. Has the moment for this concept – where ports are not merely responding to trade but are initiating it, and are not merely responding to the ships but are providing new opportunities for the shipping world – has the time for this now passed?

Author's response. An excellent report was written on this subject in the UK in 1963. The idea then was to build an optimum environment for primary, secondary, tertiary etc, industry. The idea was vitiated to some extent by the actions of OPEC, as were the French super ports. One of the things I am hoping that the Study Groups will discuss is the idea in the UK government's 1980 Budget of developing a free area near a port. Admittedly, this referred to the Docklands Area, with a great deal more than the port involved, but the port is obviously a contributing element. I should very much like to hear the views of the Study Groups on whether this can be seen as a pilot project for something on a much larger and more purposeful scale, but probably in the future more directed towards manufacturing industry, rather than primary industry. As things now stand, we would do well to leave considerations about primary industry to others.

UK coal economy – indigenous production and imports

With regard to the possibilities of coal for land usage as opposed to marine usage, it is probable that coal will replace oil. Some move has to be made to overcome the vast increases in oil prices. Power stations are increasingly making use of coal, and for domestic use, and for many other uses, coal is becoming a possible fuel. Taking the total current output of the UK National Coal Board (NCB), with its forecasts for the future, it seems likely, indeed almost certain, that not enough coal can be mined indigenously to meet UK needs. There are problems too in that UK coal reserves – although massive in total volume and at present rate of use sufficient for about 300 years – are located at large depths. More and more UK coal is now down deeper than about 2 000 ft, whereas overseas there are large amounts of coal, as in Australia, that are almost open-cast. Consequently, Australian coal can now be bought in the UK cheaper than coal from the NCB; the price differences are also quite large. One suspects that the differences will remain and perhaps grow, provided that the shipping is sensibly done, ie in terms of the very large colliers. Unfortunately, at present 100 000 tonnes or larger colliers cannot be received in the UK, at least not directly: they would have to transship. This in turn adds about 15% to the cost of coal. Because of land usage of coal, there is a growing need for a coal import trade, which is likely to expand, and that trade will be fostered and will demand far larger port facilities in the UK than are now available. This is a very long-term, expensive matter. It is one that the different electricity utilities in the UK are thinking about, but there seem to be no firm plans. Ought we not to be thinking seriously about quite large coal ports in the UK capable of taking 70 000 - 150 000 tonne vessels?

Author's response. There are four coal ports capable of handling coal carriers of 100 000 tonnes or more. These are the British Steel Corporation iron ore wharves which are equipped with alternative grabs, conveyors and stockyards for coal. Since they will be operated greatly under-capacity on iron ore alone, there is an immense reserve of capacity there to import coal in large ships – if this is desired,

Rejoinder. The point about coal, more than oil, is that, rather like landing gravel, coal has to be landed where it is needed; otherwise extra transport costs will be incurred. The author's point probably applies only to coking coal in the steel industry, and not to coal for other uses.

Author's rejoinder. One must work on the supposition that the main user, the Central Electricity Generating Board, will carry out some switching. The Immingham berth would be well placed to supplement or replace the Midlands field for the Trent station. The Port Talbot receiver could serve Didcot. The distance from Didcot to Port Talbot is no greater than from Didcot to any major coalfield. Admittedly, to deal with Fiddler's Ferry something else would have to be done. The Tees facility could equally cover the Trent field. The one site that is rather out on a limb is Hunterston where there is nothing really burning on a large scale. Even so, given Killingholme on the Humber, Port Talbot and Redcar, I would think in terms of a 15-20 million tonnes/year capacity between them.

8. ORGANIZATION OF SEA TRAFFIC: NOTIONS FOR THE NINETIES

R. B. Richardson FRIN
(Formerly Harbour Master, Port of London)

T he notes on the present position circulated by the Forum certainly highlight the dramatic situation now confronting international shipping. By no possible stretch of imagination can it be held that the whole of this new structure of sea transportation, and its revolutionary impact across the whole spectrum of the commercial operation, can hope to go forward effectively using precisely the same old, well tried modes of conduct and operation such as have been applied to the old order for well over a century.

Yet there seem to be large sections of the hierarchy of shipping both afloat and ashore who still point to the total immutability, in their belief, of many cherished aspects of sea transport practices. The good order and conformity of movement – at sea and in harbours – is a case in point. Increasingly, the efficiency of given operations includes the efficiency of given operations includes the efficiency of movement and its modern complement, the advancement of safety. Despite this, one finds massive institutional resistance to the procedures for these, in many conventional corners.

How can cries of 'change for change's sake', and that sort of attitude, be levelled any longer as defence against needed adjustments to certain old philosophies, when the impact of new applications has already altered circumstance almost beyond recognition in many cases. So it is, I believe, in the persistence of the traditionalists in some countries – including the UK – to keep on expressing majestic indifference to the possibilities of change in matters concerning the efficiency of sea movement disciplines.

If this is allowed to continue as a stopper on rational advance, then there is a very real danger that new movement disciplines may be imposed instead by some emerging maritime nations, with the risk of these not being fully thought through. Their interests are not traditional in any maritime sense, but they still use the City of London for financial and marketing operations, and look this way for a lead in many things.

It is possible that the international community could well accept a new Code of Sea Conduct or somesuch, if this was initiated here, so long as this was sufficiently modern in outlook. I have therefore set down some proposals, and supporting reasons, so that a more meaningful start can be made to lay a solid basis on which the movement disciplines of the 1990s can be built. All we have so far is a patchwork of random, disjointed moves, born of a strange mix of fear and caution, as the impact of modern communications has invaded marine affairs since the early 1960s. We must, for we owe it to society, bequeath a better legacy to the future.

THE BACKGROUND

We are now witnessing the beginning of a tremendous acquisition by nations of vast sea areas, in extension of their territorial waters, as a result of the Law of the Sea

Conferences. Some of these have already been proclaimed unilaterally. There is therefore an immediacy in the present situation, which clearly calls for some acknowledgment of the fact that, unlike the rules for air space, there is no agreed international doctrine, and hence no rules, for organizing the structures of regulation in these new sea spaces so far as the conduct of traffic is concerned, although political outcry is calling increasingly for remedies.

The novelty of the present situation presents a unique moment, which may easily pass by, for the introduction of considerable advances in the conduct of sea traffic, in the simultaneous interests of society in general, the economics of its transport systems, and the protection of its environment. It emphasizes the new global trend towards massive increases of regulatory measures, hitherto resisted by shipping interests but now being demanded by international consensus. The resistance to supervision of movement is not likely to continue effectively, as already Ship Movement Services are proliferating in critical areas and orderly proceedings are seen as the comrade of efficiency and safety. More and more, with a growing population of ships, is this likely to be so. Such measures clearly involve some degree of organization and procedure, often in conjunction with communications or electronics in support, which may not always please the old institutions.

The philosophy needed for orderly and acceptable traffic management must bring about the marriage of the logic of the ship (and all the attendant regulations relating to its hull equipment and personnel), and the logic of the cargo (and all the attendant contractual obligations between the shipowner, charterer, underwriters, consignors and consignees), so that the ship itself can operate efficiently within a framework of proliferating offshore zonal legislation. Many believe these problems should be solved by traffic-oriented rather than ship-oriented schemes. But at present there are widely differing opinions between nations regarding the functions, procedures and general operating format of traffic separation or routeing schemes, movement control or information services. These have each arisen in response to a specific localized requirement and follow no basic rationale or common ground.

There is no basic international convention or doctrine applying to the conduct of marine traffic generally, other than the Collision Regulations of the Safety of Life at Sea Conventions; the tendency to perpetuate non-standard procedures is thus left wide open. It will not be good enough for all to draft their own different regulations, nor will it be sufficient for nations to proceed individually in perpetuating their own vague national approach to the problem which can no longer be regarded as theirs alone. There must surely be a sufficiency of undisputed assumptions of doctrine, which could be held as agreeable to all administrations and hence applicable in part or wholly to any schemes introduced under their jurisdiction. These assumptions would thus be the basic framework around which any regional or area schemes would be structured and could also be a Protocol for the High Seas.

Already we are at a stage where obligations are permanently imposed on ships in certain risk areas, even if there is no risk of collision. The appearance of the 200 mile economic zone alone has literally changed the shape of the world, so ought we not begin now to do something about it, and seek a family of Standards and Recommended Practices (SARPS), like the International Civil Aviation Organization (ICAO) did long ago? Without such standards, which, I believe, call for some sort of Convention of Sea Traffic, I suggest that even the moral imperialism of IMCO may eventually fall apart under the conflict of unilateral schemes demanded by an exasperated and disillusioned shore society. We do not want that kind of chaos, nor would it make any sense economically.

As a start, regional agreements as to concerted radio organization and procedures for defined areas could be set up, so that we can try to ensure that the essentially limited world commodity of radio frequencies and their compatible allocations to a growing multitude of uses by fixed, mobile and satellite services, are not lost to us by default. Already, by its relative inaction over two decades, the marine world has lost out at successive World Administrative Radio Conferences. At the most recent conference in 1979, the maritime interests expressed concern that the air world of ICAO had stolen a couple of years' march by projecting a fully agreed blueprint for their own advance, which of course met no opposition. My message to the marine world is: get organized!

COMMUNICATIONS – THE CATALYST

Central in the whole theme lies the widespread use of radio communications and radio navigation, but these are conducted under the Conventions of the International Telecommunications Union and the Safety of Life at Sea Conferences. Historically and emotionally both these place total emphasis on the *distress* and *safety of life* aspects which, in my view, is unduly inhibitive.

Standardized practice designed to assist proceedings, organized on a continuing basis, can provide highly relevant commercial intelligence by access to the centralized information. So far the needs of this commercial information have been met on what is largely *ad hoc* organization and informal agreements among a host of disconnected commercial activities. On the other hand, for navigation and safety purposes, completely separate services are carried on by ports and governments, navigational or coastguard authorities and the like. The needs in these cases are mostly of a regulatory or safety-monitoring nature. Yet so often these intelligence-oriented services operate in splendid isolation from each other.

Most attempts to thoroughly rationalize this have usually led to each of the interests insisting on having its information edited or obtained by its own man. One result is a considerable overmanning of these services taken in their totality around the coasts and ports, while at the same time depriving each individually of financing the advantages of modern processing and handling techniques and of the instant availability of total information at one focal point. The whole constellation of ideas which we sometimes call routeing measures or traffic management should be adopted and moulded into a set of standard practices.

PROPOSED CODE OF PRACTICE

The need for a Code of Traffic Practice can therefore be seen as the first essential step. In this way the maritime nations could all use a generally acceptable doctrine when implementing new traffic systems. There is considerable consensus already striving towards the widest standardization, through the medium of IMCO and similar consultative organizations. But it has to be accepted that to reach agreement and finalization of a basic code of conduct across such a wide international front would be an extremely lengthy and protracted process. Such a final document is thus likely to take many years before acceptance and general application.

The purpose of the Code proposed is therefore to serve as a basic guideline or doctrine by those administrations seeking to promote and plan their area traffic affairs on a mutually acceptable and generally conforming front, in the immediate future. The object therefore is to make available internationally a set of modular recommendations as a suitable basis for ensuring universality of proceedings, wherever such regulation of navigation by ships is introduced by administrations or authorities, whether nationally or internationally.

The root of the problem is that there is so far no basic agreed, universal philosophy or ethic applying to traffic organization generally. This is what is lacking, and is what will be demanded by the worsening situation. The notion is so relatively new that the few precedents already established have not yet found universal acceptance. The tendency to perpetuate non-standard procedures thus continues rampant. But the Law of the Sea Conferences look as though they provide some similar ingredients to such a convention, and may be expected to be used in this way by coastal states seeking present justification to extend their regulatory powers. Neither can there be any dominant reason why the advent of increased areas of regulation cannot be turned to commercial advantage by making more sensible use of the compulsory data or intelligence demanded by them. There must be a case for cooperating on an area or regional basis, but without the drag of politics.

Once this type of agreement and basic approach is in being, all manner of peripheral information and data systems come into clear focus and offer a range of new economic benefits. These can have a dramatic effect on the route and terminal economics of trade, shipping and port operations in a way not presently available. But the creation of such a Code of Practices is the first essential. Here again the same requirement is often met by totally different methods at different places. The effect to the mariner is one of an increasingly random patchwork of services as he goes from one country to another. The situation can be expected to worsen rather than improve.

The need for closer accord already exists in the operation of modern through-transportation disciplines. The terminal interface requirements extend an increasing influence over the whole approach phase – fuel savings, avoiding delays, economical allocation of facilities such as tugs, pilots, berths etc. The interests of the underwriters and insurers or the cargo, hull and environment, are also closely linked to the well-being of the operational factor. These people also stand to share in the possible economic benefits of the system approach to movement, where this is imposed for sociopolitical reasons.

Basic Levels of Structure and Procedure

There should be a family of fair, undisputed assumptions of doctine which could generally be regarded as agreeable to any administration, and hence applicable totally or in part to any schemes or systems that may be required in any area. These assumptions thus become the basics of the area structure and procedure, with a built-in uniformity and acceptability from the first consideration of any system or organization. This is not a dissimilar approach to that used in the evolution of the ICAO practices of civil air traffic.

The basic assumptions could be stated generally in the following intentions.

- To assist the area traffic flow in the best interest of the safety of navigation, of the environment, and of efficient operations.
- To embrace the general principles of ships' routeing as already established by

IMCO, and additionally to involve local communications in such a way as to actively assist all traffic to comply with the established arrangements.

- To establish the agreed mandatory procedures for the conduct of ships and their communications, in any areas where schemes or traffic facilities operate. Such procedures need to be designed to benefit communal traffic flow in the area, rather than endeavouring to satisfy a stream of individual ships, each in turn.

- To bring together so far as practicable the total communications facilities available in the area, for the assistance of traffic in the agreed way.

- To achieve a closer link between the PTT Coast Stations (International Telecommunications Union Convention) and Marine Traffic Service Stations (Safety of Life at Sea Convention) than that existing at present.

- To require conformity with these procedures by all ships in the areas. The voluntary attitude can no longer be acceptable and the legislation concerned must reflect this.

- To optimize the use, position, and nature of area navigation aids for assisting traffic in lane or zone conformity. The establishment or 'structure' of area navigation aids could be classified as follows: (1) major traffic area, maximum feasible aids; (2) lesser traffic area, at least minimum feasible aids; (3) other special conditions.

- To maximize the use of shipborne radio aids, specifically to assist conformity with the area traffic requirements and to specify equipments to be carried accordingly.

- To develop and improve the IMCO standard navigational vocabulary as basic procedure-mode for conducting vessel traffic services or area schemes. The ICAO precedent is very clear in this.

- To require basic area communications watch.
  Three levels are suggested: (1) for heavy traffic areas; (2) for moderate traffic areas; (3) for other areas.

- To disseminate the flow of vessel movement information to the best community and commercial advantage through an Area Bureau facility (possibly on a subscriber basis) to assist, *inter alia:* safety of traffic; route economics; search and rescue; pollution control; terminal economics; port management; brokers and markets.

- Where National Reporting Systems are operated (whether IMCO-agreed or not), these should be integrated with the wider scope of shipping intelligence applications.

- To document and promulgate essential information on the overall regulatory navigation and radio requirements for the whole area (EEZ), in a standard form of presentation, or route facility chart, for easy use and access on the bridges of ships. The practice, of the airman, to collect every possible item of information connected with a single purpose – organization – and present it on a single sheet of paper might help the mariner who has been brought up with the idea that his information comes in the form of thick bound volumes with annual, monthly and sometimes weekly corrections to go with them.

GENERAL LEGISLATION – INTERNATIONAL TARGETS

To give the force of law, there will usually be need for some international protocol, or decree, applying over all areas in which schemes or services are in operation. The general headings are likely to establish, *inter alia,* the following.

- Purpose is to establish mandatory procedures by which vessels are to conduct their proceedings and their communications, in the defined area, for the general safety of navigation and good order of traffic as well as the protection of the coastal and offshore environment.

- The responsible authority may designate and promulgate zones, routes, and fairways which vessels are to use or refrain from using.
- The responsible authority shall regulate the transit of vessels which could become a danger to other vessels or to the environment. They may also define limits for vessel-operating conditions when necessary.
- The responsible authority may regulate or direct the scheduling or timing of any vessel's progress or movement when considered necessary by reason of traffic or the public interest.

Suggested Area Organization

Organization falls under two headings: radio communication requirements, and information flow requirements. Whenever there are radio communication facilities the extent of these clearly varies, depending on the local area circumstances. When any exchange of information is necessary, it is essential that it reaches the correct points in the organization. The requirements of information flow are thus complementary to the communications requirements. This interdependence is already a rapidly increasing feature of modern movement control or suveillance operations.

Radio communication – typical organizations

These are suggested as falling under three categories of service, namely:

Category 1 service. The level of facilities required in an area of major schemes, high traffic density where high environmental protection and continuous surveillance monitoring are required.

Category 2 service. The level of facilities required in an area of moderate traffic density, where a degree of traffic management is required.

Category 3 service. For other particular areas or localities and their specialized operations (eg canals, waterways, certain port approaches, intensive exploitation areas etc).

Information flow requirement

The transport industry as a whole, of which sea transport is now a totally involved element, is becoming increasingly dependent on correctly processed movement information.

As the traffic develops so will the general level of information to be handled, stored and processed. The rapid flow of such information is an essential component of an efficient movement system and the capital-intensive nature of many of today's shipping operations are such that the whole process of setting up a particular movement in advance demands a much more systematic handling of information than hitherto. This requires the safest, surest and most rapid way of bringing together at one point, and into one balanced process, all data concerning 'what is involved' (cargo, safety of environment), 'what is intended to happen' (ship movement planning), and what is actually happening (departures from planned movements).

Similarly, in the approaches to ports – often long and complex, and involving tidal restraints and problems of traffic congestion both under way and in the anchorages – the projection of the inner problems has serious effects on the safety of navigation, usually leading to delay. Where there are many ships with differing cargo risks the concept of ship population and its related domains comes into focus. Hence the notion of population control by the device of the Safety Factor Index. How many ships should be accepted in a given confined area or waterway? Should particular 'trades' be given particular rules and even particular treatment? If so, on what basis is this acceptable to all other users?

Therefore, a whole body of ordinary operational-type information which is exchanged without any established procedures, other than those of the local sectional interests of the owner or local navigation authority, and the newer concept of properly centralized (and hence more secure), information-handling presents a great potential for dramatic commercial and economic advantage.

THE WAY FORWARD

In the history of nations, not England alone, the cult of the so-called practical man has before now led to a distrust by the Establishment of the intellectual study and research needed for survival or success. We must not be stopped by this. We are at the threshold of a whole new era in sea affairs. Most of the old ingredients have changed, and not only have the ships themselves altered and the trades that they carry, but so has their passage technology. But it seems a pity we still have to go on accepting as realities the contradictions of administrations ostensibly crying out for some control over sea affairs, and an international industry intolerant of any interference to its traditional ways.

The procedures and organization of sea traffic are still in the wilderness. Perhaps the reason for such omissions may be a widely held belief that the problem, because it has not previously been defined in cost-effective terms, is not with us.

And yet it is probable that an independent study of the present lack of system would confirm, in clear economic terms, that if movement is organized through properly presented information and related procedures, even the advantages of introducing dedicated equipment into ships would come into clear light. Was it not through such paths that the navigator and radio officer vanished from the flight decks of aircraft in a decade? And might it not be by the same route that the banking-dominated shipping of tomorrow will choose to tread?

Is there not a commonality of purpose between navigation and the environment? For are not the safety of life and the safety of the environment united in their mutual suspicion and fear of hazardous cargo at sea? This is becoming the chief aggriever of coastal society as far as the politicians are concerned. Time and again we see in each successive saga of sea disaster that catastrophe seems to show itself as the only effective antidote to fixed ideas. Society through its politicians is not likely to tolerate this approach indefinitely, any more than impatient fate will hold back its irrational forces for cosy convenience.

As in the air traffic context, all experience shows that it is the system requirements overall – the organizational framework – which should precede the hardware developments. This should be the basis of all future evolution in the structure of sea traffic; it is essential also that we clear our thoughts very soon, before the full impact of the satellite era bursts on us. If not, the problem will be further compounded. It seems alarmingly true that while talk and counter-talk have been the fashion for nearly two decades, failure to grasp the real problem has led nowhere – and it is almost too late. Can it be that the technology of the sea has run away from the mythology of the mariner and his owner? I hope not, for now beyond all others is the time to turn a fleeting opportunity into lasting actuality.

DISCUSSION

Navigation and safety

The author has made great mention of safety, and we can derive much benefit from such statements. The author has stated that we should develop this control smoothly, and has spoken of an information service and a code of practice. What would be his idea of an ideal?

Author's response. The ideal would be to try to get agreement on the simple matters, such as agreeing to report-in at reporting points using the communications that are already fitted in ships, passing the information to those that need it along the coasts of the countries concerned. That would be a start. There is quite a lot of opposition to this kind of procedure. There was much resistance to getting ships to report-in to the Channel Navigation Infomation Service – which came about over the past two or three years.

It is perfectly feasible to use the equipment and the facilities that are already in ships rather better than they are used at present. In many cases, this could be made compulsory. For example, a ship should not arrive anywhere – perhaps carrying a very obnoxious type of cargo or sailing to a particularly sensitive area of the world – without giving notification that it is coming. It is no longer acceptable for the master of a ship to have the right to say that he is coming by this route, and this route only – as the old wording has it on charter-parties, 'I am the master under God' – that is no longer right and it is how incidents such as the *Amoco Cadiz* accident occur. Therefore, a good start would be compulsory reporting-in at specified waypoints.

Much more than that, we can begin to set up a framework for a system using the methodology and the technique that the International Civil Aviation Organization (ICAO) used when they set up their air traffic system. I am not saying that the control of sea traffic would be in any way identical to the control of air traffic, but that the air world learnt very quickly how to use its information. Many problems that confront us now are those of handling information – passing it on to the right people at the right time, and so forth. But to begin to do that on anything like an international basis does require some kind of a code, or protocol, or convention. I do not limit this to communications alone, but also extend it to things like navigation aids; for example, are there sufficient aids in an area for ships to conform to traffic measures? But we shall never achieve this until there is a basic book of doctrine which can be acceptable through the Inter-governmental Maritime Consultative Organisation (IMCO).

Some progress has been made along such lines. The International Chamber of Shipping (ICS), in conjunction with the governments of Singapore, Indonesia and Malaysia, set up their own routeing scheme in the Malacca Straits where there was a problem of soundings and lack of draught for deep draught VLCCs bound to the East with oil for Japan. In that case the ICS got together with the countries concerned and produced a voluntary scheme which found favour in IMCO. This scheme was a good advance, but the whole question should be considered at a much higher level with all those concerned with the movements of ships meeting together and thrashing out what is acceptable to them. Although some prohibitions or restrictions are highly offensive to a shipowner in one place, in other places he might well like to see those same restrictions imposed on other people for his own safety. These and similar difficulties must be overcome.

We have reached a point where we either simply accept that we cannot help it if the coasts get polluted, that accidents happen and ships run ashore and collide etc, or we agree that we must achieve a set of rules. That set of rules does not yet exist.

Institutional framework

The author has made several references to the need for a new framework in which to pursue these questions. In the context of safety and navigation, has enough emphasis been placed on the role of IMCO? The problem has rightly been referred to as international. Under IMCO there are already procedures for establishing traffic separation and traffic routeing schemes, and areas to be avoided. IMCO is a technical organization which, by and large in this imperfect world, does operate as a technical organization, and is not subject to the group system that causes complications in UNCTAD. Perhaps we have already our framework for proceeding forward in IMCO in an effective technical international organization, and we are simply talking about differences of emphasis rather than the need for any radical restructuring of the international mechanism.

Author's response. Although IMCO can introduce traffic separation schemes, and areas to be avoided, and so on, they do not go much beyond that. For example when the Omani government came to IMCO and proposed a traffic separation scheme off Ras al Hadd, it was passed, and placed on the chart; but this was done without sufficient thinking as to how people are to use it, whether it is likely to need reporting, whether it is to be monitored, and if so how it is to be monitored, etc. When I have talked in IMCO on this theme, the IMCO response was that such considerations were still premature.

Rules, regulations and freedom of the seas

Clearly, we do not want other people's solutions imposed upon us. Recently, US politicians sought to make compulsory the fitting of computer-based collision avoidance systems on a large number of vessels without proper training of those who were to use them. This would have made things worse rather than better for everyone except the electronics industry. We have often heard about the objections that people have to constraints on the freedom of the seas etc, but talking to those in ports and shipping companies, no one has yet objected to any constraints being imposed on those people who are abusing the system for their own personal advantage – the few ships that do not report in when they are coming, the ships that report that they are in a different place from where they actually are, those who abuse the system and thereby cause other people to lose time, to be inconvenienced, or endangered. Everyone is willing to impose constraints, except perhaps those really abusing the system, and there are perhaps not many such people. Thus, if the problem was approached in the right direction, here would not be too much objection to control.

Yet we must remember that there are problems for those on the bridge of a ship. Is more control in some way likely to prevent accidents like the *Amoco Cadiz?* There seems to be no proof of any direct connection between them. More detailed consideration of the problems of the man on the bridge, and a detailed look at how control might affect accidents would mean that something could be done more quickly than it has been. We seem to have ignored technology. We do not know what we want soon enough to be able to reserve the correct radio channels. A Japanese professor visiting Liverpool Polytechnic said: 'We look to the English to take the lead in maritime affairs', but added, 'Why then are you not doing so?'

Author's response. I do know what goes on the bridges of ships, and have done for quite a long time: not naval ships, merchant ships. I believe that people will have to begin to do things. Never mind control, we must just put some order into our affairs. One cannot say that there is any such order in a situation which used to allow ships to come and go exactly as they pleased. One cannot say there is order in affairs which allows a ship that could become a hazard, and for which on both sides of the English Channel there are all sorts of assistance services waiting and available, not to say she is coming so that those services can be properly informed. This is perfectly reasonable. I am open to the fact that this is debatable, but we always debate on extremes.

The Second and Third Presentation of Papers (4-8) and Discussion Sessions were chaired by Mr J. McN. Sidey, DSO.

II. Background papers

1. LINER SHIPPING WITH THE USA

For many years now, the UK's maritime relations with the USA have not been entirely harmonious. This is an unfortunate but nevertheless inescapable fact. There are a number of reasons for this lack of harmony, but the most important one is that the UK's basic philosophy on a number of shipping policy questions is fundamentally different from that of the USA. In the West we have been engaged for over a century in international liner shipping based on commercial standards and practices, involving close consultation with customers and shippers. These commercial relationships have been left free from government involvement by most Western governments. In the USA on the other hand, international liner shipping, whether under the flags of the USA or those of its trading partners or cross-traders, has been subjected since 1916 to the restrictions of Shipping Act of that year and to the regulatory power invested by the Act in the Federal Maritime Commission (FMC). This regulation was the *quid pro quo* for immunity from the US domestic antitrust laws. In the beginning regulation under the Shipping Act was restrained and not offensive in commercial terms but in more recent years a number of Supreme Court decisions and subsequent increasing intervention by the Antitrust Division of the Department of Justice, have severely curtailed the antitrust immunity granted to shipping by Congress in 1916.

US antitrust legislation developed primarily in the years 1890-1914 as domestic laws to protect consumers from abuse of national industrial monopolies. However, as big business increasingly transcended national frontiers, some jurisdictional expansion was inevitable. In principle, national laws recognize both protection of the national interest, territorial boundaries, and the nationality of the victim, as valid bases of jurisdiction; and whether any resultant overlap can be prevented from escalating to jurisdictional conflict depends on how a country is prepared to accommodate its economic philosophy to the territorial sovereignty of other nations (ie its concept of the rule of comity). After the second-world war the 'intended effect' doctrine developed in the US courts, which extended US antitrust laws across its own borders where commercial activities outside the USA had a 'substantial and material effect' on the foreign commerce of the USA. The legal cases in question illustrated that little regard was accorded by the USA to the operation of foreign law within foreign countries' own sovereign territory.

The American obsession with antitrust laws represents a historical American faith in the virtues of a market-ordered domestic economy. But it is significant that an increasing number of US legal thinkers are now joining commercial and economic circles in questioning the wisdom of the courts' interpretation of antitrust laws as they apply within the USA, let alone as they are exported to other nations.

The attempts by the USA to extend its jurisdiction beyond its frontiers have led to inevitable conflicts, not confined to the international business of shipping. But in shipping, this situation was particularly harmful as it developed on the heels of containerization of the US trades, which required massive reinvestment in modern technology by Western shipping companies. The position now is that two basically incompatible shipping regimes are in sharp focus, and this not only tends to stifle the development of efficient liner conference services but also to stifle substantial investments (now and in the future) and has caused an extraordinary diplomatic situation.

The most recent case of serious jurisdictional conflict, which highlighted the commercial uncertainties for shipowners, was the Grand Jury case in the District of Columbia involving a number of Transatlantic shipowners, including two UK companies, which resulted in what the non-US governments considered unjustified fines exceeding $6 million and has now led to a possibility of crippling triple damage suits. In the UK this has been a significant factor in the government's 'Protection of Trading Interests' Bill.

In shipping problems with the USA it is necessary to make a distinction between liner and bulk shipping. The UK has no dispute with the US administration on the commercial aspect of bulk traffic, because we are all in agreement that a free competitive market in bulk shipping should be preserved in the face of increasing pressures in UNCTAD to introduce bilateralism and arbitrary cargo-sharing into those trades.

It is thus only in liner shipping that the UK's and most of the rest of the world's policies are in conflict with those of the USA. With the exception of the USA, rationalized liner conferences have international endorsement as being the most effective economic instrument for providing regular and suitable service for the carriage of non-bulk cargoes in international trade.

The main opposition in the USA to liner conferences comes from the antitrust division of the Department of Justice, which believes they are anti-competitive cartels operating against the amorphous 'public interest'. This stems from a doctrinaire approach based on ignorance of the realities of international liner shipping. An uneasy balance between this philosophy and the realists in the USA resulted in the largely ineffective compromise of the 'open' (non-rationalized) liner conference system being permitted in the US trades. In these 'open' conferences any line can become a member and effective rationalization is impossible. Added to this burden is the unpredictable and uncertain unilateral regulation by the FMC, which is more often than not itself harassed by the Justice Department. The irony of the situation is that it is the non-commercial state-cotrolled fleets – Soviet in particular – operating outside the established conferences that have been able to take advantage of the present chaotic situation in the US trades.

It was not until the late 1970s that US Congressional and administration circles started to realize – having been egged on for years by shipping and commerce – that legislative reforms were urgently needed in the face of increasing conflicts, inconsistencies and rigidities of US shipping legislation. It seems hardly conceivable that the full economic benefit of containerization, in the form of intermodalism, has not reached consumers in the mutual foreign trades of the USA with Europe – the pioneers of this new technology. But that is exactly what the position is: the Shipping Act, 1916, could not have foreseen the age of intermodalism and it is therefore not covered in the Act, and in the void thus created the FMC, the Interstate Commerce Commission and Justice Department are in constant conflict, thus effectively denying any certainty of antitrust immunity for such operations in the US liner trades, and its users the full benefits of this new technology.

The open conference system is a unique phenomenon of the US trades: one of its most damaging effects is that conference members are not allowed to rationalize or pool their resources. Such measures are particularly necessary in the face of extensive rises in the cost of bunker fuel. It is ironic that under the antitrust laws it is a felony (not protected by the Shipping Act) for shipowners to meet to discuss across-the-board rationalization measures to conserve fuel in the mutual foreign trades of the USA and its trading partners. Similarly, the Shipping Act, 1916, does not provide for the possibility of Shippers' Councils, and thus there is no organized pattern of consultation between US exporters and the conferences trading with the USA.

As mentioned above, in the latter half of the 1970s the US Congress started to realize that considerable innovations had to be introduced to bring the 1916 Shipping Act up to date. In 1978 Congressmen Murphy and McCloskey introduced the first legislation to this effect, the Closed Conferences Bill. It was a first effort which received considerable support and criticism at the same time. Unfortunately, this did not lead to new legislation reaching the statute book during the life of the 95th Congress.

However, the seeds of change had been sown and in the middle of 1979 new legislation surfaced in both the House of Representatives and the Senate, the most important of which was the Omnibus Bill, the successor to the Closed Conferences Bill, in the House. Practically simultaneously President Carter, who a year earlier had appointed an Administration Inter-Agency Task Force to report on US federal maritime policies, reviewed the conclusions and recommendations of this Task Force and elaborated on what he considered necessary steps to solve the many problems confronting the maritime industry of his country.

The Presidential message was largely a disappointing policy document as it had to reflect the inability of the Inter-Agency Task Force to reconcile conflicting internal views as to what solutions should be recommended to make US shipping policy effective and bring it more in concert with universally accepted international standards governing the world's liner shipping trades. One of the positive points of President Carter's policy message was his confirmation of the the administration's commitment to oppose government-induced cargo reservation of commercial cargoes. The President's conclusion in this respect was the more important as there are rather powerful forces within Congress which, because of the basic weakness of the US ocean shipping industry, seek to regain its strength by imposing governmental bilateral trade and transportation policies. Both the House Omnibus Bill and various Senate bills, introduced in 1979, contain bilateral provisions.

Despite the unacceptable bilateral features, these bills now further amended and before Congress again, signify an important step forward in that they seek increased immunity from the antitrust laws, and would provide for some form of closed conferences, the formation of shippers' councils in the USA and last, but not least, a reduced regulatory role for the FMC – except in the case of the new Senate Bill, which seeks incredibly to enhance the unilateral regulatory role of the FMC.

It is too early to say what will ultimately come out of this revised draft legislation; in the present unsettled world political situation it is difficult to predict whether Congress will give a sufficient measure of priority to it, bearing in mind the additional factor of its recent preoccupation with internal scandals affecting a number of its prominent members.

In summary, the lack of harmony between the shipping policies of the USA and other Western nations can be condensed in five major issues.

Continuing lack of a cohesive US international shipping policy

The interests of the foreign commerce of the USA are best served by a coherent, consistent and continuing US maritime policy. It is the lack of legislative and regulatory certainty prevailing in US trades that has proved a major disincentive for shipowners to continue to invest and improve their shipping services, which are of considerable importance to the USA and its trading partners. Legislation now before Congress intends in part to create greater cohesion and certainty and deserves therefore general (but not open-ended) backing of Western shipowners and their governments.

Lack of one overriding administration department

The main difficulty for shipowners, and for that matter governments, when dealing with US shipping matters, is that there is not one administration department or agency charged with responsibility for US shipping policy. This effectively means that consultation can only take place involving a number of administration departments. As an illustration, in the October-November 1979 talks in Washington between the CSG governments and the United States, the latter government was represented by no less than seven administration entities, including the White House. The President has tried to find a solution to this fragmentation by designating the Maritime Administration within the Commerce Department as the administration's chief spokesman in maritime affairs, without however restricting the right of individual departments and agencies to voice their own opinions. We believe, therefore, that the President's action does not go far enough and that it would be advisable that one department with cabinet representation is the vehicle which carries overall responsibility in the field of international shipping.

Jursidictional conflicts and the commercial uncertainties

Western governments have made it clear on a number of occasions that the foreign commerce of the USA can best be served by the mutual accommodation of the laws and practices of the USA with those of its trading partners. Shipping is an international activity affecting the interests of all concerned equally and it is vital if conflicts are to be avoided that each country should recognize the policies and practices of its trading partners.

Effects of regulation by the Federal Maritime Commission

Western shipowners, and for that matter their governments, have emphasized to the US administration on numerous occasions that the regulatory authority of the FMC under the Shipping Act of 1916 leads to interminable investigations of what elsewhere are considered normal commercial practices and standards. A large degree of uncertainty exists also, because the Commission is under constant pressure from the Department of Justice to refuse commercial agreements etc which do not, in the view of the Justice Department, conform to its concepts of free competition. Also here the main problem is the US insistence on unilateral regulation of international liner conference operations regardless of the sovereign interests of its trading partners in the international activity of shipping. Because of shipping's international character it is not up to one country to take unilateral action – instead the rule of comity should apply in the case of any conflicts of policy and interest in a business where there is constant overlapping of jursidiction.

Rejection by the President of the UNCTAD Code of Conduct

The President in his July 1979 policy letter stated that the sanctioning of cargo sharing under the UNCTAD Code of Conduct for Liner Conferences is 'neither wise nor necessary'. There appears to be considerable misunderstanding within the US administration about the EEC Compromise on the UN Liner Code. It would be a step forward if the US administration would be prepared to discuss the implications of the

EEC Compromise with a view to establishing rapport with the major trading partners of the USA, most of whom have voiced support for 'the Brussels package'.

Need for policy accommodation

Shipowners engaged in the US trades believe that there are pressing reasons why the USA and its allies should arrive urgently at an accommodation of their divergent shipping policies. In the light of recent disturbing developments on the international scene, in the economic and energy fields and not least in the aspect of Western security, such an accommodation is becoming increasingly urgent.

Recession and the continuously rising cost of fuel oil are unsettling circumstances for shipowners in the trades with the USA as they must be able to rationalize their services and, wherever necessary, to pool their resources. Considering that fuel costs now represent in excess of 50% of fixed operating costs, the question is whether our fleets can afford the luxury of non-rationalized services.

Finally, it is deeply disappointing and a matter of grave concern, even more sharply focused by the attacks of UNCTAD on the free competition shipping of the developed nations, that the USA continues to clash with its allies in one vital area of ocean transportation.

APPENDIX I

UK Department of Trade Press Notice No 523, 4 December 1979

Protection of Trading Interests Bill

Mr John Nott, Secretary of State for Trade, today published two Diplomatic Notes, exchanged between the British Government and the United States Administration, on the Protection of Trading Interests Bill.

Mr Nott was asked in a written Parliamentary question by Mr Charles Fletcher-Cooke MP (Darwen), 'whether he has now received any formal representations from the United States Administration in respect of the Protection of Trading Interests Bill'.

Mr Nott replied: 'Yes. A Diplomatic Note was received on November 9. A reply was sent on November 27 and I have placed a copy of both Notes [US Ambassador's Note No 56; British Ambassador's Reply No 225] in the Library of each House'.

APPENDIX II

US Ambassador's Note No 56

The Ambassador of the United States of America presents his compliments to Her Majesty's principal Secretary of State for Foreign and Commonwealth Affairs and wishes to make the following comments on the Protection of Trading Interests Bill now before Parliament.

I. General Comments.
The introduction of the Protection of Trading Interests Bill gives us concern on several different levels.

As a general matter, we are concerned that it will encourage a confrontational rather than cooperative approach to resolving issues in which both our countries are interested. It comes at a time when several agencies of the United States Government are actively working with Congress and other governmental agencies to ensure that Her Majesty's Government's views on matters affecting international trade are fully taken into account. We will be continuing with these efforts. We trust that Her Majesty's Government, in the same spirit, will give consideration to our views on the Protection of Trading Interests Bill.

We are concerned in general that the Bill forecloses or restricts opportunities for United States views to be taken into account. This is particularly true of Clause 6, which entitles persons doing business in the United Kingdom to enlist the aid of United Kingdom courts in undoing the judgments of American courts, even in some circumstances where American interests predominate over United Kingdom interests. There does not appear to be any flexibility in this procedure for giving due weight to United States concerns. We trust that with respect to other provisions of the Bill, which give discretionary powers to the Secretary of State, channels of communication will remain open so that the Secretary can consider United States views in deciding whether to exercise those powers.

With these general concerns in mind, we turn to our specific comments on the Bill's provisions.

II. Production of Documents.
Clause 2 of the Bill enables the Secretary of State to prohibit compliance with foreign requests or demands for production of certain categories of documents. As it is drafted, it could be applied to prohibit production of some documents located outside the United Kingdom or under the control of persons who are not United Kingdom nationals, even though the United States interest in the documents is greater than the United Kingdom interest in preventing their production.

Clause 2 applies to 'a person or persons in the United Kingdom and to any commercial document which is not within the territorial jurisdiction' of the state seeking the document. It could thus be applied against a United States national found in the United Kingdom (a natural person residing there or a corporation doing business there) even though the requested information is in a third country. The problems with this position are mitigated where the conditions of Subsection (2) are met, but Subsection (3) would authorize restrictions where there is no apparent United Kingdom interest in the requested documents, simply because they are requested at an investigatory or pre-trial stage. Subsection (3) (A) can be read to apply to production of documents needed for a criminal investigation if formal proceedings have not yet been instituted. Similarly, Subsection (3) (B) applies where the documents are sought for pre-trial discovery purposes.

Subsection (3) is not limited by any reference to United Kingdom nationals, United Kingdom territory, or United Kingdom sovereign interests, though Clause 3, Subsection (2) does exclude criminal penalties for acts of non-United Kingdom nationals done outside the United Kingdom. However, we can envision many situations under which there would be no particular United Kingdom interest in the production of documents, though they happen to be either located within United Kingdom territory or under the control of the United Kingdom national. Under these circumstances we do not see why it would be appropriate to impose criminal penalties for producing documents needed in the United States.

III. Enforceability of Judgments.
We understand why the United Kingdom might not wish to facilitate the enforcement

of the non-compensatory portion of United States multiple damage awards. But we read Clause 5 as having a broader effect: it would preclude an action to enforce 'any sum payable under such a judgment'. Thus, even the compensatory portion of the award would not be enforced. There is nothing in Clause 5 that limits its applicability to circumstances in which Her Majesty's Government believes the United States court did not have jurisdiction or circumstances in which United Kingdom sovereign interests are infringed. Thus, Clause 5 could have the anomalous result of precluding enforcement where jurisdiction unquestionably was proper and United States and United Kingdom policies were not in conflict. We trust that the orders of the Secretary of State under Subsection (4) would not be applied in this fashion.

The approach of Clause 5 is inconsistent with the present draft United States–United Kingdom Convention on recognition and enforcement of judgments in civil matters, on which negotiation has been taking place since 1971, and which would contemplate enforcement of the compensatory portion of the award. We would be grateful for an indication of the present status of Her Majesty's Government's consideration of that draft.

IV. Recovery of Non-compensatory Portion of Multiple Damage Award.
We are seriously concerned by Clause 6, both in overall concept and in specific details. As far as we are aware, this provision has no precedent anywhere in the world. In our view, it raises serious questions under the very principles of international law and comity to which Her Majesty's Government is committed.

United States antitrust law reflects a public policy so important to the United States that violations carry criminal penalties. The private treble damage action is a crucial aspect of United States antitrust enforcement. It was adopted as a complement to governmental enforcement tools, in recognition of the limited resources available to governmental agencies to investigate and take action against all violations of the law. It acts as a deterrent to illegal activity in the same manner as governmental enforcement, and provides an incentive to the victims to act as 'private attorneys-general'.

Interference with this mechanism would be as objectionable to us as interference with the imposition of criminal fines. Instead of simply making treble damage awards unenforceable in the United Kingdom, the Bill turns the shield into a sword to be used against a method of enforcement of an important United States public policy given effect by United States courts entering judgments under United States law which in many cases can be satisfied entirely from assets found in the United States.

The theory underlying Clause 6 is apparently that all multiple damage awards are impermissible under international law unless they fall within the narrow exceptions specified in Subsections (2) and (3) of Clause 6. Though the United States and the United Kingdom have taken differing approaches to the appropriate reach of national jurisdiction, Clause 6 could sometimes be used to thwart the exercise of jurisdiction acceptable under even the most conservative jurisdictional theories, and would do so even in circumstances where the United Kingdom has no interest in the transaction.

The benefits of Clause 6 are available to any 'person carrying on business in the United Kingdom', unless that person is an individual ordinarily resident in the United States or a corporation with a principal place of business in the United States, or unless that person did business through a United States branch and the judgment relates to activities exclusively carried on in the United States through the United States branch. We do not understand the theory under which non-United Kingdom corporations doing business in both the United Kingdom and the United States but having a principal place of business elsewhere should be entitled to have a United Kingdom court undo what a United States court has done. We also believe it is unrealistic to insist that a judgment relate to activities 'exclusively' undertaken within one state's territory. In today's highly integrated and mobile world, conspiracies in restraint of trade can be hatched and implemented wholly or partly outside of the territories involved. Clause 6 as drafted would deny the validity of a judgment directed at multistate conduct even where part of the conduct took place in the United States. This would make it possible to evade United States law simply by going outside the United States for part of a course of conduct begun in and adversely affecting the United States.

An example will make the problem clear. Assume that a French company has modest branch operations in both the United Kingdom and the United States. Assume further that officials of the United States branch conspired with its United States competitors to fix United States prices of their product and that one significant price-fixing meeting among the conspirators took place during a trade association meeting held in Jamica. A United States purchaser uncovers the conspiracy and successfully collects treble damages under the United States antitrust laws.

We would trust that such an antitrust action would be of no concern to Her Majesty's Government, and indeed that even the most conservative international lawyers would not claim that the United States courts had acted improperly in entering the treble-damage judgment. Yet Clause 6 would appear to give the French company a cause of action in United Kingdom courts to recover two-thirds of the judgment obtained by the United States plaintiff, even though the United Kingdom had only the most remote contact with the dispute. This is because the French company would be 'a person carrying on business in the United Kingdom' and the United States proceeding was not 'concerned with activities exclusively carried on' in the United States.

Furthermore, in cases where the activities were indeed undertaken exclusively within United States territory, we do not see the relevance of whether the business was carried on through a United States branch or establishment. Thus this condition in Clause 6, Subsection (3) is clearly a superfluity, even under the most restrictive jurisdictional view.

Unlike Clauses 1, 2 and 4 of the Bill, Clause 6 does not leave any room for the Secretary of State or the court to examine the facts of the case and determine either that there is no significant United Kingdom interest in the transaction or that United States interests outweigh United Kingdom interests. Principles of international law and comity, which are applied by United States courts (and we assume by United Kingdom courts as well) in cases of transnational interest, require consideration of the facts of the case and a balancing of the respective national interests involved. Clause 6 denies the opportunity for this sort of case-by-case examination, and does not even include a procedure under which United States views could be taken into account.

We thus strongly urge that Clause 6 be deleted from the Bill. If some version of the concept is to be retained, the Clause would have to be significantly modified to avoid inevitable inconsistencies with the international legal principles which both our governments endorse. One possible modification would be to use the approach taken in other Clauses of the Bill, which permit but do not require the Secretary of State to certify the need for particular measures in light of all the circumstances.

The Ambassador requests that the foregoing comments be brought to the attention of Parliament during its consideration of the Bill.

Embassy of the United States of America, London, 9 November 1979.

APPENDIX III

British Ambassador's Reply No 225

Her Britannic Majesty's Embassy present their compliments to the Department of State and have the honour, on instructions, to transmit the comments of Her Majesty's Government on Note No 56 from the United States Ambassador in London, dated 9 November.

Her Majesty's Government note the US Government's concern that the Protection of Trading Interests Bill will encourage a confrontational rather than co-operative approach to the resolution of issues in which both the countries are interested. Her Majesty's Government wish to assure the Government of the United States that this is not their intention. In introducing the Bill into the House of Commons on 15 November, The Secretary of State for Trade said the following:-

> 'We have not suddenly become belligerent or confrontational in regard to this most powerful and valued friend. This Bill is a response to a situation of a very particular nature which has been developing over several decades, and which in the past few years has become much more acute. It also emphasises that, in so far as the application or enforcement of any foreign law requires the active assistance or passive acquiescence of the United Kingdom, the overseas country in question must have regard to the trading interests of the United Kingdom'.

It remains Her Majesty's Government's firmly held belief that differences between nations over legal and economic issues should be explored and where possible resolved by inter-governmental discussion and agreement. Her Majesty's Government confirm their intention to continue such an approach, which was explained by the Secretary of State in Parliament in these words:-

> 'We recognise this, and we believe that the right way to sort out the resulting differences of policy and approach is by inter-governmental discussion and negotiation through the established international organisations by which trade policy is co-ordinated multilaterally, as well as in bilateral contacts and negotiations between Governments'.

Her Majesty's Government acknowledge the efforts which have been and are being made, both in the United States and by other governments including Her Majesty's Government, to find better ways of resolving issues affecting international trade in which our countries are interested and to which the powers envisaged in the Protection of Trading Interests Bill may be relevant. However, this approach has, from the UK point of view, so far had only limited success, not least because the very aspects of US law to which Her Majesty's Government have objected and which have given rise to differences between our Governments have so far limited the freedom of action of the US Administration in seeking solutions. While continuing to work for better methods for resolving these issues, Her Majesty's Government have therefore considered it necessary to seek further powers in UK law for the protection of the legitimate interests of the United Kingdom. For their part Her Majesty's Government hope that the circumstances in which the Secretary of State may find it necessary and appropriate to use the discretionary powers conferred in the Bill will of course remain open, as they are now, so that the Secretary of State can consider all relevant matters (including, where appropriate, those raised in the US Note) in deciding whether to exercise these powers.

The US Ambassador's Note states that Clause 2 of the Bill would enable the Secretary of State to prohibit compliance with foreign requests or demands for the production of certain documents in situations where the US Government might consider the US interest in disclosure to be greater than the UK interest in non-disclosure. Clause 2, in essence, embodies the principle that demands for compulsory production in one state of documents or information situated outside that state raise issues for other states which may lead these latter states to take such steps as they consider appropriate, within the limits of their proper jurisdiction, to limit or exclude such compulsory production. But Clause 2 is discretionary, and when deciding whether to exercise his discretion the Secretary of State could be expected to take into account all the aspects of any case including the extent of UK and other interests and considerations of international comity.

Clause 5 clarifies a question of UK law by declaring that the multiple damage judgements of other states, which are regarded by Her Majesty's Government as penal, are non-enforceable by the UK courts, just as are other judgements of a penal character. Furthermore both this provision and the discretionary power in Clause 5 (4) reflect the principle whereby sovereign states do not accept an obligation to enforce the public economic policies of other sovereign states. The UK Ambassador's Note points out that under Clause 5 even the compensatory portion of the award would not be enforced and that the provision is not limited in its application to circumstances in which Her Majesty's Government believe that the foreign court does not have jurisdiction. Bearing in mind the objectionable features which appear to Her Majesty's Government to arise from the impact of private treble damage actions on international trade, as well as the general principle just mentioned, Her Majesty's Government sees no justification for proposing that there should be a specific provision enabling UK courts to be used to enforce a part of such judgements.

In relation to Clause 6, which would confer a right of recovery through the UK courts of the non-compensatory portion of multiple damage awards, the US Ambassador's Note states that this provision raises serious questions under the very principles of international law and comity to which Her Majesty's Government is committed. Her Majesty's Government's main objections to the private treble damage action, which is, as the Note observes, a crucial aspect of US Anti-Trust enforcement, are that it has been adopted as a complement to government enforcement, that it provides an incentive to private parties to act as 'private attorneys-General', that such a system of enforcement is inappropriate and in many respects objectionable in its application to international trade. Her Majesty's Government believe that two basically undesirable consequences follow from the enforcement of public law in this field by private remedies. First, the usual discretion of a public authority to enforce laws in a way which has regard to the interests of society is replaced by a motive on the part of the plaintiff to pursue defendants for private gain thus excluding international considerations of a public nature. Secondly, where criminal and civil penalties co-exist, those engaged in international trade are exposed to double jeopardy.

Her Majesty's Government consider that there are further aspects of US civil penal procedure under the Anti-Trust Acts which are questionable in their application to non-US nationals engaged in international trade. A defendant does not have to be present in the US for jurisdiction to be exercised by the courts of that country over him. In the defendant's absence the allegations contained in the plaintiff's pleadings are accepted, ie failure to appear in the US court is treated as tantamount to an admission of guilt. Wide and prejudicial discovery procedures are enforced. The potential penalties can be enormous and totally out of proportion to the alleged mischief, particularly where the activities concerned were entirely legal where they occurred.

Finally, and most important, the US courts claim subject matter jurisdiction over activities of non-US persons outside the USA to an extent which is quite unacceptable to the UK and many other nations. Although in recognition of international objections to the wide reach of anti-trust law enforcement in civil cases, the US courts have begun to devise tests which may limit the circumstances in which the remedy may be available, these tests remain within these wider claims to jurisdiction to which Her Majesty's Government object.

For all these reasons, Her Majesty's Government have reluctantly reached the conclusion that a limited countervailing remedy should be provided to persons in the UK who have, while engaged in international trade, been penalised under laws of this kind.

The remedy in Clause 6 does not depend on the exercise of any Ministerial discretion, since the circumstances in which a general civil right should be available must be objectively determined. To confer a discretion for the sole purpose of creating a private right would be wrong in principle.

Her Majesty's Government consider that they have proposed to Parliament a measure which is appropriate, having regard to all the circumstances, and in tune with the UK view of international law.

Nonetheless Her Majesty's Government will look again at Clause 6 during passage of the Bill, to see whether it is possible to take account of any of the US concerns expressed in the Note without prejudicing the overall objective of this provision. It will of course have regard to opinion in Parliament, which will determine the final form of the provisions.

Her Majesty's Government note the request for an indication of the present status of its consideration of the draft US/UK Convention on Recognition and Enforcement of Judgments in Civil Masters. Further advance in this matter presents certain difficulties which are still under consideration and Her Majesty's Government will reply separately to the US Government on this point.

Finally, in response to the US Government's request that the US Ambassador's Note be brought to the attention of Parliament during its consideration of the Bill, the Secretary of State for Trade made reference to the representations during his speech on 15 November. Copies of the US Ambassador's Note No 56 and of this reply will be placed in the Library of the House of Commons if the US Government so agrees.

Her Britannic Majesty's Embassy avail themselves of this opportunity to renew to the Department of State the assurances of their highest consideration.

British Embassy
Washington
27 November 1979

2. DEVELOPMENT OF USSR AND CMEA SHIPPING

K. A. Moore
(Assistant Manager, General Council of British Shipping)

On the conventional view of Soviet attitudes, one must regard their policies in individual economic and other sectors as being laid down to accord with overall Kremlin purposes and ambitions. The exposition of USSR naval most widely known in the West is Admiral Gorshkov's book *The Sea Power of the State*. He sees the Soviet merchant fleet as a constituent part of the USSR's seapower, which is to be viewed as an integral whole to which the large fleets of naval, merchant, fishing, scientific-research and other types of vessel contribute in different ways:

> *The concept of sea power to a certain degree is identified with the concept of the economic power of the state...Just as economic power determines military power, sea power, mediated by the economy of the state and exerting an influence on it, carries within it an economic and military principle.*

A GDR specialist in 1974 summarized Socialist merchant fleets as having four functions:

(1) to carry the states' foreign-trade cargo;
(2) to contribute to the balance of payments;
(3) to earn foreign exchange;
(4) on the military-strategic plane, to provide lifting potential for defence.

He was apparently rebuked for making a public reference to (4), unexceptionable though this may appear.

The anxiety of Western merchant fleet owners relates mainly to facets of Soviet competition in their own sphere, rather than any problems caused by the shipping or maritime policies of the satellites with their relatively small fleets, or of certain states outside the Council for Mutual Economic Aid (CMEA) which in statistical terms own bigger merchant fleets than the USSR, or which cause various worries of a different nature to the world maritime community.

This paper is a general worldwide survey of overall trends, and it is not possible at the time of writing to indicate what long-term harm Soviet shipping may suffer overall from the consequences of US reactions to the Afghanistan occupation and the exiling of Sakharov. There have, however, been striking immediate local effects in the USA itself from President Carter's curbs on sales of grain and technology and the boycott of Soviet ships by East Coast/Gulf ports' dock workers. There has been severe disruption of Soviet tramp operations with owned and chartered-in ships which had been intended to lift their grain purchases: their East Coast and Gulf cargo-liner services, whose main sustenance has been both-ways traffic between the USA and European states other than the USSR itself (a valued source of hard-currency freight earnings), have been cancelled entirely. Their many trans-Pacific liner services have been substantially maintained but have lost a lot of custom from US and Far East shippers, even though the US Pacific Coast dockers have not so far boycotted Soviet vessels.

Wider-ranging reorganization of tramp and liner operations, necessitated by these developments, is being carried out: its overall pattern and consequences may be clearer at the end of April 1980 than at the time of writing.

The Soviet fleet generally

What follows is based to the greatest possible extent on Soviet and CMEA statistics, which are most complete for the years 1965-78. In Table 1, line (d) reflects slow growth of the Soviet merchant fleet ('Morflot') and line (b) its cargo-carryings, from pre-1914 through a revolution and two world wars, before serious expansion was sought

Table 1. Basic data of development of the sea transport of the USSR Ministry of Merchant Fleet (excluding Central Asian SS Co).

		1913	1940	1965	1970	1975	1976	1977	1978
(a)	Cargo turnover, 10^9 tons/ nautical miles	11.0	13.4	209.9	354.3	397.5	411.5	417.3	446.9
(b)	Cargo carried, 10^6 tons	15.1	32.9	119.0	161.9	202.0	214.5	220.3	229.4
(c)	Average distance cargo carried, miles	726	409	1763	2188	1968	1919	1894	1948
(d)	End-year cargo carrying fleet, 10^6 dwt			8.7	12.6	14.9	16.0	17.1	18.4
(e)	10^3 tons/mile per year per dwt capacity			24.1	28.1	26.7	25.7	24.4	24.3
(f)	Tons orginated per year per dwt capacity			13.7	12.8	13.4	13.4	12.9	12.5

after Suez I in 1956 and Cuba in 1962. The biggest single-year fleet increase was in 1965, 171 ships of 1.3 million dwt. The end-1978 figure was about 18.4 million dwt. Cargo activity almost doubled from 1965 to 1978 in tons originated (to 229 million in line (b)) and more than doubled in ton/miles (to 447 milliard in 1978 in line (a)). Morflot has always been a carrier over relatively short distances: 1948 miles average haul in 1978 in (c) shows only slow recovery to a 1970 level modest in world terms. This is partly, but not wholly, explained because coastal activity is large in tons originated (35-40% of total) but small in tons/mile terms (7-8%) owing to concentration on short intra-basin routes. Tons originated per dwt capacity, for Morflot as a whole, were high at 12.5 in 1978 (line f), more than double world average, but average haul per dwt at 24 000 tons/mile (e) was barely three-quarters of world average.

The fleet has always been heavily concentrated on carrying bulks (Table 2). Liner cargoes formed only a small part of the 11% residue represented in 1978 by 'other dry cargoes' at 26 million tons: the total Morflot liner-cargo performance was about 14.0 million tons, made up from part of 'other dry cargoes' and some elements of general cargo under the remaining dry-cargo subdivisions of Table 2.

Table 3 shows for both tankers and dry-cargo ships that productivity in use of tonnage has in most ways gone down since 1970. Table 4 indicates a slightly better position on productivity of workers employed ashore and afloat: there is in line 1 a switch from ton/miles to ton/kilometres, but the arithmetic matches the earlier figures in ton/*nautical* miles.

Coastal activity uses a lot of relatively small cargo vessels, especially ice-class units, and the USSR's bulk export/import trade is covered by ships which by

Table 2. Carriage of cargoes by sea transport of Ministry of Merchant Fleet in all types of navigation (million tons).

	1940	1970	1975	1976	1977	1978
All cargoes including:	32.9	161.9	200.0	214.5	220.3	229.4
Liquid cargoes	19.6	75.1	91.4	100.9	104.4	108.6
Timber and wood in rafts	0.6	0.4	0.4	0.4	0.4	0.3
Dry cargoes including:	12.7	86.4	108.2	113.2	115.5	120.5
Coal	2.7	9.3	9.2	9.8	10.6	10.0
Timber and wood in ships	1.3	10.6	11.4	11.6	12.6	12.3
Ores	1.5	13.6	17.9	17.4	18.9	18.3
Building materials	0.8	15.3	17.9	17.6	18.7	19.3
Metals and scrap	0.2	6.7	10.0	11.6	10.6	11.7
Grain	1.6	6.5	9.1	9.5	5.9	9.9
Salt	0.3	0.6	0.7	0.8	0.9	0.9
Fish and fish products	0.1	0.3	0.3	0.3	0.2	0.2
Machinery and plant	0.2	2.5	3.8	3.9	4.6	4.5
Chemicals and mineral fertilizers	0.2	5.5	6.3	7.2	7.7	7.6
Other dry cargoes	3.8	15.5	21.6	23.5	24.8	25.8

Table 3. Morflot productivity in use of tonnage.

	1940	1965	1970	1975	1976	1977	1978
Tankers							
Operational speed, miles per day	211	327	333	323	323	325	323
Utilization of cargo capacity, %	49.3	54.6	59.4	59.3	60.8	57.0	59.7
Productivity per day of 1 ton cargo capacity, tons/mile	70.7	133.7	149.8	130.7	129.3	124.5	121.6
Dry cargo ships							
Operational speed, miles per day	175	285	315	314	312	311	306
Utilization of cargo capacity, %	50.4	61.5	65.3	58.5	54.6	55.0	55.6
Productivity per day of 1 ton cargo capacity, tons/mile	25.2	81.1	91.1	82.0	76.8	78.6	79.6

Table 4. Number of workers occupied in carrying cargo, and productivity of labour in sea transport of the Ministry of Merchant Fleet.

	1940	1965	1970	1975	1976	1977	1978
Milliard tons/kilometre performed	25.8	390	658	738	764	775	830
Year's average number of workers employed in carrying cargo, including shore personnel (10^3)	20.9	88.9	113	130	134	137	138
Productivity of one worker (10^3 tons/kilometre)	1 235	4 391	5 822	5 701	5 700	5 666	6 015

contemporary world standards are small and unadventurous, both dry-bulk and tanker: a primary reason is the shallow seas and port draughts available in almost all the USSR's coastal regions, which lie mainly in enclosed seas. Morflot's relatively small ships nonetheless have carried over the years a consistently large proportion of USSR seaborne trade, as shown in Table 5 for the carriage record since 1965 in the different categories.

Table 5. Soviet seaborne trade since 1965.

	1965	1970	1975	1976	1977	1978
(a) Total carriage	119.0	161.9	202.0	214.5	220.3	229.4
(b) Coastal (100% coverage)	62.5	71.6	80.0	80.0	78.7	81.0
(c) Cross trading	7.5	15.0	30.0	30.4	30.2	31.1
(d) Soviet seaborne foreign trade, exports and imports						
(i) All flags	91.8	121.3	155.2	185.1	187.1	194.4
(ii) Morflot	49.0	75.3	92.0	104.1	111.4	117.3
(iii) (ii) as % of (i)	53%	62%	59%	56%	60%	60%

Line (d) (iii) of Table 5 shows that Soviet practices of cif sale/fob purchase, and bilateral intergovernmental cargo-sharing agreements to facilitate pressures of cargo into Soviet bottoms are not new: 60% coverage or so has been the general pattern in the past decade. There is indeed evidence going back to the 1920s of Moscow efforts to restrict second and third flags in USSR trade relations with other states. The column for 1978 shows that Morflot covered the totality of USSR coastal carriage and 60% of national export/import trade, carrying also 31 million tons in cross trades as a bonus. Provisional figures for 1979 are mainly of interest because Soviet officials have said that their fleet carried 140 million tons of USSR exports/imports: this could mean a rise to 70% or more unless the all-flag total traffic for the year moved improbably high beyond the 194 million tons for 1978. It is premature to attempt in Table 5 to add a comprehensive column of 1979 estimates.

Morflot lifting of 60%, 70% or more of particular types of cargo in USSR exports from other countries makes inevitable the compression of individual second flags, and of third flags generally, into a residual share of 40%, often far less. This anomalous situation is by no means ignored by Western governments, but it has not made the impact on the international scene of Morflot's cross-trading on the liner side.

Moderate increase of bulk fleet .

Morflot's acquisition of tonnage to date, and known plans for expansion in the Eleventh Five Year Plan period 1981-85, do not suggest that the growth of dry-bulk and tanker tonnage will, in absolute volume or technological terms, be such as to alarm the West. A prototype 370 000 dwt tanker, long declared as being planned for construction at home, appears to be far from fruition, and 150 000 dwt is the current top limit for 'giant' Soviet tankers actually running, with one vessel built yearly at Kerch since 1975. The USSR may also perhaps be left in peace to exploit its own coastal trade, which is particularly expensive in use of resources around the ice-bound Arctic coastline, notably for running a large ice-breaker fleet, however interesting in technical terms may be the design and achievements of Morflot's three atomic ice-breakers, on which more will be said below. The mainly short-distance intra-basin nature of the coastal trade is emphasized by the fact that to lift in theory for

10 000 miles between European Russia and Vladivostok the 80 million tons total of coastal cargo carried in 1978 would have accounted for 800 milliard ton/miles, or almost double Morflot's total performance in all types of trade of 447 milliard. No, Soviet coastal-cargo carriage is primarily a matter of short intra-basin hauls of bulk cargoes.

Liner operations: national and cross-trades

We are left with the cargo-liner side of Morflot activity. What is the situation regarding liner operations in Soviet export/import traffic and cross-trade? Table 6 gives some 1976/78 details. Soviet liner trade carried by Morflot in Table 6 (b) is each year below one-tenth of Morflot's total carriage of cargo in national trade, which was shown in Table 5 (d) (ii) – 117.3 million tons in 1978. Second and third flags probably carried, because of USSR trading pressures, as little as 10% of the total liner cargoes in USSR national trade, perhaps 1 million tons in each of the three years.

Table 6. Morflot carriage of liner cargo in foreign trade (10^6 tons).

		1976	1977	1978
(a)	Total	14.5	13.5	14.0
(b)	USSR exports/imports	9.5	8.5	8.0
(c)	Cross trade	5.0	5.0	6.0

Apart from a notional 'bonus' of 4-5 million tons annually beyond 40% on 50% coverage by Morflot of this national trade, Soviet vessels acquire an essentially net benefit of 6 million tons/year in (c). This is done mainly because Soviet liner companies remain outside the freight conferences covering most routes and quote to shippers rates of 20% to 40%, sometimes more, below the conference tariff. This 'outsider underquoting' is commonplace and nothing new on the world shipping scene generally: it is also a complex problem and to start an explanation in detail would soon exhaust the rest of this paper. But one can briefly say that Morflot possesses a unique power, as the owner of the world's largest amount of spare cargo-liner capacity under single control, to disrupt as an outsider the economic operation of a wide range of conferences simultaneously. A substantial outsider only needs to attract 5% of a conference trade, with sailings no more frequently than once a month, to send the shippers of the remaining 95% hotfoot to the conference concerned to clamour for the same reduced rates of freight.

The Soviet price for accepting conference membership (where they seek it, and they do not always do so) has usually been too high, in terms of the sailings and cargo-lifting rights they have claimed, to be acceptable as a request from a newcomer at a time when the shares of existing members are under pressure, particularly those of established Western lines which are often being impelled separately to give up a proportion of their rights to new national lines of the developing countries.

Morflot liner cross-trading activity has been increasing year by year and may at present occupy 2.5 million dwt ships' capacity. Even for 1978, which has shown a total of 6 million tons of cross-trade cargo, this means that 2½ million dwt capacity was only fully used for about 2½ single-leg voyages a year, not on the surface an indication of especially efficient use of available resources, but leaving plenty of room to increase liftings further by greater efficiency.

Of what does this 2.5 million dwt cross-trading capacity consist? Just over 2 million is probably short-sea and middle-distance stock of assorted conventional general-cargo ships, converted cellular units and small purpose-built ro-ro and cellular vessels, plus similar tonnage used for ocean liner trading, although really only adequate for use there when operated on the standard Soviet basis of undercutting conferences' freight rates by 20-40% or more. A special interest lies in the remaining tonnage. At end of 1978, Morflot had in service 31 purpose-built ocean-going ro-ro and cellular ships of around 19 000 TEU and 450 000 dwt. With the exception of a USSR export service to Cuba, these vessels are almost wholly employed in cross-trading over various routes, mainly serving US export/import trades in the Atlantic and Pacific. It seems reasonable to assume that the score will rise by end of 1980 to 39 or 40 such ships, 26 000 TEU and 600 000 dwt. Tentative Soviet indications of aims to double 'present' tonnage in 1981-85 suggest that the end-1985 figures in this particular category could be about 60 ships, 46 000 TEU, 1 000 000 dwt.

The present Morflot stock of these new, specialized and highly productive ships is, as mentioned, occupied primarily in cross-trade, and this is probably true to only a slightly smaller degree for the remaining 2.0 million dwt noted above of conventional liner capacity.

Soviet economic development to end-1985 seems barely likely to be such as to provide suitable high-class national manufactured goods in export trade (even less so in import traffic) to raise significantly the present very low proportion of effort of all these ships devoted to USSR national-trade carriage. Will the tonnage continue to rely predominantly on cross-trading cargoes and freight revenues, increasing as it well may from 2.5 million dwt operating now to 3.5 million dwt or more by 1985? Would other nations willingly allow Morflot to increase such third-flag cargo acquisition? This last question is particularly relevant because movement is accelerating in the United Nations towards adoption of a liner conference code based on cargo division 40–40–20 (that is 40% to first or exporting flag, 40% to second or importing flag, 20% to all third flags combined). Outside the UN plane of negotiation, there are growing signs of many states going even further to restrict third-flag participation, and the same result will be likely from Soviet and satellite reservations when ratifying the Code itself. These reservations say that the Code provisions will not apply to the activities of non-conference lines or to joint shipping lines established on the basis of inter-governmental agreements to serve bilateral trade between the countries concerned. Both exclusions would cover a wide range of satellite, and notably Soviet, liner operations: the USSR alone has bilateral shipping agreements with over a dozen developing countries.

All this is setting the pace in the world as a whole as regards the liner-cargo scene, curbing the supply of cargo available in many important liner trades for the whole world third-flag interest (it is worthy of note that the UK-flag cargo-liner industry has at risk a large cross-trade stake in many trades worldwide, but it carries only 38% of UK liner exports/imports while Morflot gets 90% of the corresponding USSR trade).

Should not the USSR be reconsidering its plans for 1981-85 expansion in this area before any firm figures are announced at the end of 1980, for new-ship acquisition, long-term chartering-in and second-hand purchase, as the Eleventh Plan period is about to dawn and any such firm published figures then become as immutable for Morflot as the laws of the Medes and the Persians? Carriage per year of 6 million tons of cross-trade liner cargo now might have to be reduced rather than doubled (or more) in the coming five years, and one might hope for signs from the Kremlin of an intention to retrench rather than further expand its expectations of liner ship-tonnage acquisition, and ability to exploit it via what exists, in Morflot, as the largest world entity under single control devoted to cargo-liner cross trading.

What if no signs appear of a Morflot willingness to be reasonable and accept commercial realities? The next stage can only be in the hands of governments, preferably on a collective basis in the EEC or OECD, to exert their influence. Many individual states already have countervailing powers to meet this kind of situation, but to be effective action must be collective. After a show of initial firmness in the USA to Soviet lines based on a new Controlled Carrier Act, there was a distinct sign of reluctance to press matters by the Departments of Justice and State, but renewed sternness has been one result of the post-Afghanistan reactions in the USA. We must see what happens there and elsewhere.

It is *not* a question of Morflot's overall expansion or policies threatening to disrupt the whole Western World's shipping structure. It is a danger for world liner shipping, probably the most consistently profitable sector. The choices may be threefold:

(1) Admit Morflot to conferences with rights excessively generous by any normal criteria. This would, *inter alia,* perpetuate present Soviet access to an assured, easily earned source of hard currency, where the USSR already has shipping earnings fourth in its league table, the largest invisible after oil, gold and timber.

(2) Leave the Soviets to operate as outsiders over as wide a range of trades as they please, continuing to disrupt freight-rate structures and damage the finances of the many important Western lines to whom the trades are vital, both as national carriers and as third-flag participants.

(3) Persuade governments to induce the Soviets to accept conference membership on terms reasonable in Western, not Soviet terms. This could be on a form of protectionism on the part of Western governments. Western shipowners dislike governmental regulation on principle, but in this special case it seems likely that the problem can only be resolved by state meeting state. A major criterion for Russian admission could be to relate their participation in conferences directly to the amount of cargo which the USSR generates as exports and imports on the trade route concerned. This could in the nature of things exclude the Soviet flag, or allow it only very small shares, over many routes which are cross-trades from the USSR viewpoint.

CONCLUSION

There is as yet no Soviet domination of any sector of world merchant shipping. There is a present serious penetration of one major sector, ie cargo liners, which is worrying and where failure by Western states to act might well lead to the Soviets raising their sights, not only in that specific area but by intensified efforts to penetrate other cross-trade shipping sectors. It can be argued that Western shipowners are unjustifiably worried about existing penetration in one area of their business. *They* do not consider that they are crying wolf unjustifiably and that their case is an isolated one. CMEA states' physical dumping of exports is well known in such manufacturing sectors as shoes and clothing. In the transport sphere, there are real or potential problems, similar to those facing sea-going shipping, regarding road, rail, air and inland waterways, areas which affect the UK's Continental neighbours far more than the UK itself. Some of these are illustrated below in an illustrative record of various Soviet activities and practices.

Features of Soviet activity

Apart from the general tussle between Morflot and free-world shipping, there are several features of Soviet and satellite maritime and intermodal activity that are matters of general interest.

Atomic cargo ships

A recent Tass statement said that work had begun on atomic powered cargo ships, of 25 000 dwt or more, 'for use on the longest cargo routes'. These routes could well not be those in Arctic-region coastal trades, for which the Soviets had earlier indicated that atomic container/ro-ro ships of ice class were being comtemplated. Do the Soviets seriously plan to build for international cross-trading any highly productive container or ro-ro ships of this type, and to overcome incidentally the problems with the world's environmentalist which have dogged the careers of *Savannah, Mutsu* and *Otto Hahn?*

Atomic ice-breakers

The Soviets have the 20 year old *Lenin* and the much more powerful *Arktika* (1974) and *Sibir* (1977). *Arktika* sailed to the North Pole from Murmansk in eight days in August 1977 and *Sibir* escorted an ice-class freighter through high-latitude ice from Murmansk to the Bering Strait in eighteen days in May-June 1978. Year-round navigation in limited sectors of the Western Arctic is now claimed as an achievement, but it remains to be seen how quickly Soviets will secure significant improvements in summer-period regular through navigation around Cape Chelyuskin in 78°N from West to East and *vice versa*. When a fourth atomic ice-breaker comes on the scene, it could well be a replacement for the *Lenin,* not in addition to it. Although the Soviets deny reports about trouble over the years with the *Lenin's* reactors and its reputed sale for scrapping, it will be an old ship, battered by an extremely hard form of service-life, by the time a fourth nuclear unit is ready, in 1981-82 at the earliest.

Soviet ships in UK ports

For a sample quarter, October-December 1977, a check by the UK government showed that 244 Soviet vessels of various kinds made 364 calls at 53 UK ports, mainly in the Thames, Humber, Forth and Mersey. The weekly average over 12 months to June 1978 was about 30 calls per week. These were not all merchant ships bringing in or taking out cargo, but doubtless included trawlers, tugs and other assorted vessels calling to take on water, land sick crew members, take shelter or for any other reason. There was some apparent surprise expressed in official circles that the number was so large. It is not clear if people *should* have been surprised or if anyone asked, 'What can, or should, be done about it?'. No doubt the coastlines of many of the UK's Western neighburs experience the same thing. It is doubtful if, in the average week, there are more than three UK ships in all the ports of the USSR's massive coastline. This is certainly an interesting state of affairs.

Soviet seamen's pay

Theoretically, the average USSR urban cash wage is about R175 per month, plus social security benefits of R60 – say R235 per month in all, or about £40 per week. Seafarers' pay is supposed to be somewhat above this average, but a Morflot ex-captain living in Sweden claimed in 1978 that the able seaman's wage was only about R110 per month in cash, say £25 per week inclusive of social payments.

   In the recent book, *Workers Against the Gulag*, it is stated that earning of the average wage by an individual is not guaranteed, and that money can be lost because of failures in the labour unit or because other individuals are inefficient. It is naturally difficult to make close comparisons with the wages and living standards of Western workers. Nominally cheap Soviet rents for a basic flat have to be set against paying R8 000 for a Lada car, almost four years' average urban cash wage. One doubts if the merchant seaman and his family are all that much better off than the Soviet urban norm.

Passenger ships

With a dozen modern ocean-going passenger ships, two of which come from Cunard, and a large number of smaller units for round-Europe voyages and the like, the Soviets have probably the third largest tonnage for cruising in the world, mainly aimed at the hard-currency wallets of Western customers. Five of the biggest ships have side-loading gear for passengers' cars, a facility barely used in the nature of cruise operations or for the occasional line-voyage like Europe–Australia which the ships carry out. How many troops could be carried in space stripped down from accommodating 700 cabin passengers? What else could be side-loaded/discharged into and from holds capable of holding 250 cars?

Waterways and other modes of transport

To a perhaps surprising degree, Europe is networked by waterways, the key remaining link being between the Main and Danube, due to open about 1985. CMEA mixed-navigation craft will then be technically able to travel for instance from Budapest to Dublin or Grangemouth to Belgrade. Western operators are afraid that, failing action by the EEC or at some other intergovernmental level in Europe, there may be the one-sided result of CMEA ships operating in the West, but little Western shipping running east of Vienna.

One type of Soviet ship to be watched is a new Finnish-built barge carrier, the *Julius Fuchik*. This runs a monthly service from the mouth of the Danube to Karachi and Bombay, presently taking barges loaded with cargo from/to the lower Danube basin for the most part. Its potential hinterland, however, includes the rest of the Danube and parts of Italy and south Germany, and a second ship now in service to the Straits and Vietnam.

Morflot has recently taken delivery of two ocean-going gas-turbine ro-ros, and further developments in this direction will need to be watched: these ships will be mainly cross-traders making intermodal connections in ports of the Western World.

Very similar are the so-called multi-flex frighters, two of which have been built for Morflot in Denmark. Very rugged decks, vertical stanchions and loading ramps are common to many ships in the ro-ro category.

Trans-Siberian Railway

The Trans-Siberian Railway (TSR) is physically a dry-land link from the Soviet viewpoint. However, via short-sea connections at its eastern end and short-sea/rail networks in Western Europe, the TSR is already carrying over 10% of the high-quality containerized manufactures which are the lifeblood of the Western and Japanese ocean-going lines which link the two ends of the trade Europe–Far East both ways. The ultimate capacity of the TSR to handle such transit traffic could be four or five times the present level – a threat to take 50% of the cargo over a vital Western shipping route, unless Western governments do something to curb this growth.

Joint ventures with developing countries

Soviet aid undertakings related to shipping are concentrated on training of sea/shore staff and improvement of ports. The Soviets do little to promote the development of Third World merchant fleets, at least in the sense of making them capable of sharing in the direct exchange of cargoes between their own states and the USSR. The Soviet Union has 50–50 shipping agreements with at least a dozen Third World countries, but in practical terms the partners cannot lift any or all their 50% and leave it to the cooperation of Morflot to fill the gap. The one main exception is India, where an agreement is implemented in practice by 50-50 division, not always to the satisfaction of the Indians.

In practical terms, Morflot's self-interest seems to lie in protecting a large volume of activity in trading with and in the Western World, rather than a smaller volume of involvement in developing nations' commerce: Soviet direct two-way trade by all modes of transport by ruble values in 1978 was 28% with the West and 12% with the Third World (the other 60% being with CMEA). More Western trade moved by land, and Soviet shipping effort in Third World trade might have been expected to be higher than the proportion 12:28. However, this is not necessarily true. One recent exercise by *Lloyd's Shipping Economist* showed that in 1978, out of 237 million dwt of Morflot ship movements to and from Baltic and Black Sea ports in worldwide traffic *other than* with CMEA, 79% was from/to developed world ports. The weighting was especially marked for container ro-ro and break-bulk general-cargo movements.

Shipping policy and diplomacy

Soviet delegates in fora such as IMCO and the Conference on the Law of the Sea have a good reputation for liberal views, common sense and impartiality except when specific national interests require to defended (eg regarding jurisdiction of the coastal state over territorial waters or establishment of baselines of their division). G. A. Maslov, their principal shipping diplomat and troubleshooter, has been a fair and unbiassed chairman of the IMCO Legal Committee.

Regarding the UN Liner Code, there has been consistent Soviet support for the developing countries' stance, but in practical terms it is unlikely that a continuation of this will in itself be allowed to interfere with the defence and propagation of Morflot interests. On flags of convenience and bulk-trade problems generally in the UN, the USSR maintains a low profile, giving overt but often ambivalent support for the developing nations, but emphasizing a well-worn theme about the need to have an international instrument for the regulation of shipping.

Satellite fleets

Other CMEA states follow the Soviet lead more or less reluctantly in diplomatic exchanges and decisions regarding shipping. Polish and GDR liner companies are the only two in the satellites with significant fleets, which have a much longer and wider record than Morflot of cooperation with freight conferences, largely as cross-traders, and are hit almost as severely as Western lines by Morflot's outsider activities in some trades.

Morflot predominance inside CMEA, in tonnage as well as in policy direction, is clear from the fact that at January 1978, the USSR tonnage of all cargo-carrying types was 18.1 million dwt, with 10.4 million for all other CMEA states. The 27.5 million overall total was made up as shown in Table 7, and the division of flags was as shown in Table 8.

Table 7. Division of CMEA tonnage, January 1978 (10^6 dwt).

Tankers	8.8
Dry-bulk	5.3
Other dry cargo	11.8
Various	1.6
Total	27.5

Table 8. Division of CMEA tonnage of by flag, January 1978 (10^6 dwt).

Bulgaria	1.3
Cuba	0.8
Czechoslovakia	0.2
GDR	1.9
Hungary	0.1
Poland	4.2
Romania	1.9
USSR	17.1
Total	27.5

Hard currency shipping earnings

A 1978 Central Intelligence Agency publication calculated that Morflot in 1977 earned a net sum of US $859 million and the TSR another $133 million: the overall total of $992 million represented the USSR's largest single source of invisible earnings, coming fourth after sales of oil, gold and timber. Earlier figures had been 1970 $523 million, 1975 $726 million, and 1976 $855 million.

3. Participation of the Developing World in Maritime Transport

Adib Al-Jadir
(Director, Shipping Division, United Nations Conference on Trade and Development)

T he United Nations Conference on Trade and Development (UNCTAD) is a permanent organ of the United Nations. Its general aim is to promote international trade and economic development, especially the trade and development of developing countries. As an efficient maritime transport system is essential for the development of international trade, the economic, operational and commercial aspects of maritime transport, among other matters, are of direct concern to UNCTAD.

The objectives of UNCTAD's work on maritime transport are twofold: first, to increase the efficiency of maritime transport in international trade with particular attention to the trade of developing countries, and second, to increase the participation of the developing countries in the international shipping industry.

Protection of shipper interests

Shipping services have a critical effect on the flow of trade, because the costs of shipment may determine whether an overseas buyer purchases from one supplier country or another, or whether he uses substitute materials such as synthetics which may not require overseas shipment at all.

Quite apart from the effects of shipping costs on the competitive position of their products overseas, developing countries have a special interest in reducing freight levels to the minimum consistent with efficient service, because the sums which are expended on transport tend to reduce the net returns which the country's producers receive for their export produce and reduce the quantity of goods which a country can import for a given sum.

UNCTAD's work on this aspect has resulted in production of guidelines for developing countries on the question of what can be done to improve shipping services especially in the liner sector. These guidelines were based on the experiences of various developing countries in dealing with their maritime transport, and also on the experiences of some developed countries outside Europe which have similar shipping problems. It has been recommended that developing countries should endeavour to obtain more economical services in the liner trades by:

- establishing *shippers' councils* to strengthen their bargaining position in dealing with the liner conferences;
- setting-up *shipping investigation units* to investigate the efficiency of existing services and the possibilities of more economical alternatives;

- *bulking consignments* wherever feasible so as to switch complete commodity movements out of liner shipping and into the more economical charter and contract services.

The concept of consultations between liner operators and shippers has now been given formal recognition in the United Nations Code of Conduct for Liner Conferences, and there is an accelerating tendency for developing countries to establish shippers' councils to hold consultations in accordance with the provisions of the Code. The establishment of shipping investigation units is an essential complement to the establishment of shippers' councils, since a council needs a unit to ascertain the facts and figures on which to base meaningful consultations, and to ensure that it is not making unnecessary use of liner services for cargo movements which more properly belong to the bulk trades. The three measures recommended by UNCTAD should thus be seen, not as separate measures, but as closely interrelated.

In November 1976, the UNCTAD secretariat issued a report on progress achieved to date in regard to the protection of shipper interests throughout the world. This report analysed the reasons why some shippers have succeeded and others have failed, in obtaining more economical shipping services. The report concluded that the most successful shippers were those who had a *representative organization* backed by an efficient *investigation unit* which has discovered possibilities of adopting *alternative shipping methods* outside the conference. The existence of an alternative is the critical factor which determines whether or not shippers will have any real bargaining power in dealing with a liner conference. Whether or not shippers go so far as to actually adopt the alternatives, they will improve their bargaining power in dealing with the conference if they put themselves into the position where they are *capable* of adopting alternatives. The ability to adopt alternative methods, which would involve signing a shipping contract or series of charter-parties with shipping operators, necessitates having an organization which really does represent the shippers whose cargo is involved, and which has authority to negotiate on their behalves and if necessary to enter into an agreement. Most, though not all groups of shippers who have been able to switch from liner to charter or contract methods of shipping have been *commodity groups* which control shipments of substantial tonnages of a single product.

At the request of the eighth session of the Committee on Shipping, the UNCTAD secretariat has produced guidelines for developing countries on the formation and strengthening of commodity groups. These guidelines, together with another report on the relationship between exporters and importers in dealing with the liner conferences, will be considered by the Committee on Shipping in its ninth session in September 1980.

Expanding developing countries' fleets

The present world fleet stands at about 674 million dwt of which only 9.4% is owned in developing countries. The very limited participation of the developing countries in world shipping has been and continues to be the subject of considerable attention in various United Nations bodies and meetings; in particular, for instance, Resolution 3202 (S-VI) of 1 May 1974 of the sixth Special Session of the General Assembly, which states that: 'all efforts should be made to promote an increasing and equitable participation of developing countries in the world shipping tonnage'. More recently this has been the subject of debate at UNCTAD V.

The basic pattern of ownership of the world fleet has remained virtually constant during the current decade, with only minor variations occurring in the past two years.

About 85% of the world fleet is owned by the developed market-economy countries, either directly under their own flags or under the flags of open-registry countries. The share of developing countries in the world fleet is small, and has increased only slightly during the decade, while the share of socialist countries, which is also small, has actually suffered a marginal decline.

From mid-1976 to mid-1979 the developing countries increased their share of the world's dwt tonnage from 6.7% to 9.4% of the world total, but 75% of the increase is attributable to increases in the fleets of 13 countries which have made more rapid progress than the majority of developing countries in expanding their merchant marines. Thus there is a clear need for measures to increase the merchant marines of developing countries as a group.

In considering fleet development a distinction must be drawn between development in the bulk sector and in the liner sector of shipping. Although the bulk sector accounts for roughly 80% of the world tonnage loaded, past efforts of developing countries in building up their merchant fleets have been concentrated in the liner sector.

In the liner sector, as is well known, international recognition has been obtained of the rights of developing countries to participate in the carriage of cargo generated by their own trade. This recognition has been given formal expression in the provisions of the United Nations Code of Conduct for Liner Conferences. Following declarations which were made by a number of countries at UNCTAD V in June 1979 in Manila, it now appears certain that the Code will come into force within the near future, so from now on the task is not one of developing new principles but one of implementing principles which have been accepted. However, the same cannot be said of the bulk trades.

In 1977, the eighth session of the UNCTAD Committee on Shipping noted the slow progress achieved by the merchant fleets of developing countries in the bulk sectors. In fact their share of the world bulk fleets only amounts to about 7%. For UNCTAD V, the next body to consider shipping, the secretariat prepared a set of proposals to increase the participation of the merchant fleets of developing countries, with special reference to the bulk sectors.

In undertaking this work the secretariat gave special attention to the possibilities of increasing participation in the bulk trades *without* having to incur the risks of trading on the open worldwide market, that is to say, by carrying cargoes which are moving to or from developing countries on a regular basis in such a manner as to provide constant employment for one or more tankers or bulk carriers. At the same time the secretariat pointed out that further opportunities would be opened up for developing countries if there were a phasing-out of flag of convenience operations. The expansion of the open-registry fleets, accounting for roughly a third of the world dwt tonnage at present, has undoubtedly had an adverse effect on the expansion of the merchant fleets of developing countries – as concluded by the *Ad Hoc* Inter-governmental Working Group which met to consider this issue in Geneva in February 1978.

The result of UNCTAD V, which met in Manila 2 May-1 June 1979, was that the Conference adopted by majority vote Resolution 120 (V) which recognizes the right of countries to participation in the carriage of cargoes generated by their own foreign trade, especially in the bulk sectors, and which recommends the application of a number of principles to cover different situations, taking into account pragmatic considerations. At the same time, the resolution called for the reconvening of the *Ad Hoc* Intergovernmental Working Group to consider the desirability of phasing-out open-registry operations. Resolution 120 (V) is set out in Appendix I.

The *Ad Hoc* Intergovernmental Working Group reconvened in Geneva from 14-22 January 1980 to consider the desirability of phasing-out open registries – basing its deliberations on reports prepared by the secretariat on 'The repercussions of phasing-out open registry operations', and on 'Legal mechanisms for regulating the operations of open-registry fleets during the phasing-out period'. The Group reiterated the conclusions which it had reached at its first session – namely, that the expansion of open-registry fleets is adversely affecting the development of other fleets – and there was a unanimous consensus that some action needed to be taken, although the Group did not succeed in reaching agreement on the type of action. The end result was that the Group decided to refer the matter to the Committee on Shipping at its ninth session. The Group forwarded two different proposals to deal with open-registry operations – one submitted by 'the Group of 77' (representing developing countries) and the other submitted by a majority of the members of 'Group B' (representing developed market-economy countries). The first of these proposals calls for phasing-out of open-registry operations over a reasonable period of time, whereas the second represents an attempt to cope with the adverse effects of open registration without actually taking a decision on phasing-out.

Thus the forthcoming ninth session of the UNCTAD Committee on Shipping, which is scheduled for 1-12 September 1980, will be an important meeting. The Committee will not only be called on to make a decision which will affect the future of open-registry operations, but it will review the whole question of the development of merchant fleets of developing countries. In the liner sector, the Committee will review progress achieved towards the entry into force of the United Nations Code of Conduct for Liner Conferences. In the bulk sector, it will review the consequences of the implementation of Resolution 120 (V). In preparation for this session, the UNCTAD secretariat has prepared a report on 'Merchant fleet development – guidelines for developing countries' (UNCTAD document TD/B/C.4/186), which will form the basis for much of the discussion. In addition, the Committee will consider the issues detailed above in relation to the protection of shipper interests, as well as a number of other items in the field of shipping, ports, legislation, multimodal transport and technical assistance.

Looking to the future

When looking to the next 10-15 years, it is easier to predict what the trends will be than to predict the precise extent of those trends, or the precise timescales involved.

The general trend will be towards a redistribution of the task of supplying the world demand for shipping: it appears certain that the developed market-economy countries will not maintain their dominant position as suppliers of 85% of world shipping. At a more specific level, two future trends are discernible. First, insofar as cargoes can be tied to the countries creating the demand, there will be a considerable increase in the practice of reserving cargoes for the trading nations concerned. Second, as regards cargoes that cannot be readily reserved to the trading nations, the developed market-economy countries will play a diminishing role as suppliers of worldwide shipping services: it appears inevitable that open-registry operations will be phased-out sooner or later and the present role of the developed market-economy countries will be taken over by those countries which can operate economically under their own flags.

APPENDIX I.

UNCTAD document TD/RES/120(V), 27 June 1979

UNCTAD Resolution 120(V) Participation of developing countries in world shipping and the development of their merchant marines[1]

The United Nations Conference on Trade and Development,

Recalling its resolution 70 (III) of 19 May 1972, which recognized that developing countries should have an increasing and substantial participation in the carriage of maritime cargoes,

Recalling also General Assembly resolution 3202 (S-VI) of 1 May 1974, which called for efforts to be made to promote an increasing and equitable participation of developing countries in the world shipping tonnage,

Recalling further resolution 28 (VIII) of 22 April 1977 of the Committee on Shipping, which considered that past efforts on the part of developing countries to develop their merchant fleets had not been successful to the extent desirable, and which noted with concern the present position of the fleets of developing countries among the world merchant fleets, in particular among the tanker and bulk carrier fleets,

Noting that no appreciable progress has been made in the area of shipping under the International Development Strategy for the Second United Nations Development Decade and the Programme of Action on the Establishment of a New International Economic Order,

Considering that the insignificant share of developing countries in the carriage of bulk cargoes and refrigerated cargoes is a matter for serious concern,

Recognizing the right of all countries to an equitable participation in the carriage of cargoes generated by their own foreign trade, especially in the bulk sectors,

Convinced that there is a particular need to overcome the obstacles to increasing participation of developing countries in international shipping,

Taking note of the desire of many countries to phase out open-registry operations,

Taking note also of the Report of the *Ad Hoc* Intergovernmental Working Group on the Economic Consequences of the Existence or Lack of a Genuine Link between Vessel and Flag of Registry which met in Geneva in February 1978,[2] and of the resolution adopted by it,[3]

1. *Calls upon* governments to take steps to ensure for developing countries equitable participation in the transport of all cargoes, and more specially bulk cargoes, generated by their own foreign trade by national vessels of the respective trading countries or by vessels otherwise operated by them;

2. *Recommends* the application of the following principles, taking into account pragmatic considerations:

(a) That the transport of regular bulk and refrigerated cargo between a pair of exporting and importing countries should have equitable participation by the national lines of the respective trading countries, or by vessels otherwise operated by them;

(b)   That other bulk and refrigerated cargoes should be the subject of bilateral agreements between the trading partner countries providing for the equitable participation in the trades by the national lines of these trading partner countries;

(c)   That until developing countries achieve an equitable share of world tonnage, contracts between developing and developed countries for the sale or purchase of bulk cargoes, or for the exploitation of natural resources which give rise to bulk cargoes, should stipulate that a substantial and increasing portion of cargoes shall be carried by the national vessels of developing countries or by vessels operated by them;

3.   *Urges* developing countries which import bulk cargoes especially in less-than-ship-load quantities to take measures among themselves for joint bulk shipping operations in co-operation with the exporting developing countries;

4.   *Requests* the UNCTAD secretariat to identify the movements of bulk cargoes between developing countries which might form the basis of joint fleet development by developing exporting and developing importing countries, and also the less-than-ship-load bulk imports of developing countries which might form a basis for joint bulk shipping operations;

5.   *Requests* the Secretary-General of UNCTAD to call a meeting of representatives of interested governments with a view to taking measures which would ensure that, as far as feasible, all bulk cargoes shipped between developing countries should be carried on vessels of the national lines of the respective trading countries or by vessels otherwise operated by them;

6.   *Requests* the UNCTAD secretariat:

(a)   to undertake in-depth studies of the possibilities of expanding bulk fleets of developing countries on specific bulk trade routes, and to examine the manner in which the cargo is currently tied to trading partner countries or to transnational corporations;

(b)   to investigate, in co-operation with the appropriate bodies, the controls which are exercised by transnational corporations over bulk movements of commodities such as iron ore, coal, grain, phosphate, and bauxite/alumina;

7.   *Further requests* the UNCTAD secretariat:

(a)   to undertake in-depth studies on trade and maritime transport of refrigerated cargoes, both liner and non-liner, and to recommend measures to promote the increasing participation of developing countries in the carriage of such cargoes;

(b)   prepare guidelines to assist developing countries in the introduction of containerization and multimodal transport and the modernization and improvement of their infrastructure, including ports, so that those countries can derive the maximum from new technologies;

(c)   Carry out, in co-operation with the International Civil Aviation Organization appropriate studies, on air-cargo movements in the context of multimodal transport so as to increase the air transport fleets of developing countries and to facilitate the export of goods by air as desirable;

8.   *Calls* upon the Committee on Shipping to review at its regular sessions the whole question of the participation of developing countries in world shipping and the

development of their merchant fleets, and the problems with which developing countries are confronted;

9.   *Calls* upon the UNCTAD secretariat, in consultation with other related agencies, to:

(a)   Undertake further studies in respect of the repercussions of phasing out open registries, its economic and social impact on the economies of developing countries, its effect on world shipping, and how the phasing out of open registries would ensure simultaneous development of the merchant fleets of developing countries, with a view to taking a decision on the desirability of phasing out;

(b)   simultaneously study the feasibility of establishing a legal mechanism for relating the operations of open-registry fleets during the corresponding period, stressing the need to adopt such legislative measures as might enable them to ensure that substandard vessels do not operate to their disadvantage;

10.   *Requests*   the Secretary-General of UNCTAD to reconvene the *Ad Hoc* Intergovernmental Working Group for the purpose of considering these studies on phasing out of open-registry operations;

11.   *Requests* the *Ad Hoc* Intergovernmental Working Group to report its conclusions and recommendations to the Trade and Development Board or the Committee on Shipping whichever session takes place earlier, for decisions, as might be appropriate.

171st meeting
3 June 1979

REFERENCES AND FOOTNOTES

1   The Conference adopted this resolution by a roll-call vote of 81 to 23, with 9 abstentions. The result of the voting was as follows:

In favour: Afghanistan; Algeria; Argentina; Bahrain; Bangladesh; Barbados; Bhutan; Brazil; Burma; China; Colombia; Comoros; Congo; Cuba; Democratic Kampuchea; Democratic Yemen; Djibouti; Dominican Republic; Ecuador; Egypt; Ethiopia; Fiji; Gabon; Ghana; Guatemala; Guinea; Guinea-Bissau; India; Indonesia; Iran; Iraq; Ivory Coast; Jamaica; Kenya; Lesotho; Liberia; Libyan Arab Jamahiriya; Madagascar; Malawi; Malaysia; Mali; Malta; Mauritius; Mexico; Morocco; Mozambique; Nepal; Niger; Nigeria; Oman; Pakistan; Peru; Philippines; Qatar; Republic of Korea; Romania; Rwanda; Sao Tome and Principe; Saudi Arabia; Senegal; Singapore; Somalia; Sri Lanka; Sudan; Swaziland; Syrian Arab Republic; Thailand; Togo; Trinidad and Tobago; Tunisia; Turkey; Uganda; United Arab Emirates; United Republic of Tanzania; Uruguay; Venezuela; Viet Nam; Yemen; Yugoslavia; Zaire; Zambia.

Against: Australia; Austria; Belgium; Canada; Denmark; Finland; France; Germany, Federal Republic of; Greece; Ireland; Israel; Italy; Japan; Luxembourg; Netherlands; New Zealand; Norway; Portugal; Spain; Sweden; Switzerland; United Kingdom of Great Britain and Northern Ireland; United States of America.

Abstentions: Bulgaria; Byelorussian Soviet Socialist Republic; Czechoslovakia; German Democratic Republic; Hungary; Mongolia; Poland; Ukrainian Soviet Socialist Republic; Union of Soviet Socialist Republics.

2   TD/B/C.4/177-TD/B/C.4/AC.1/3.

3   *Ibid*, annex.

4. The Inter-governmental Maritime Consultative Organization

T. A. Mensah (Director, Legal Affairs and External Relations Division, IMCO)

The Inter-Governmental Maritime Consultative Organization (IMCO) is a Specialized Agency of the United Nations System. IMCO was established by a Convention adopted in 1948 by the United Nations Maritime Conference as an instrument for intergovernmental cooperation in the field of governmental regulation and practices relating to technical matters of all kinds affecting shipping engaged in international trade.

Objectives of the Organization

The major objectives of the Organization are:

(i)   to provide machinery for cooperation among governments in the field of governmental regulation and practices relating to technical matters of all kinds affecting shipping engaged in international trade; to encourage and facilitate the general adoption of the highest practicable standards in matters concerning maritime safety, efficiency of navigation and prevention and control of marine pollution from ships; and to deal with administrative and legal matters related to the purposes of the Organization;

(ii) to provide for the consideration by the Organization of any matters concerning shipping and the effect of shipping on the marine environment that may be referred to it by an organ or specialized agency of the United Nations; and

(iii) to provide for the exchange of information among governments on matters under consideration by the Organization.

Functions of the Organization

For the achievement of its objectives, the Organization:

(i)   considers and makes recommendations upon matters within its competence that may be remitted to it by Members, the United Nations or any specialized agency of the United Nations or by any other appropriate intergovernmental organization;

(ii) provides for the drafting of conventions, agreements or other suitable instruments by convening such conferences as may be necessary and recommends the resulting instruments to Governments and to intergovernmental organizations for acceptance, implementation or enforcement as may be appropriate;

(iii) performs functions assigned to it by or under international instruments relating to maritime matters and the effect of shipping on the marine environment;

(iv) promotes measures for the effective implementation and enforcement of international standards and regulations adopted by the Organization or contained in international treaty instruments;

(v) facilitates, as necessary, technical cooperation within the scope of the Organization, including the provision of services and other appropriate assistance to governments, particularly those of developing countries.

Fields of activity

The fields of activity of the Organization, current and envisaged, include the following:

A. In the field of maritime safety

(1) Measures to improve maritime safety and efficiency of navigation in general including:
   (a) the implementation, technical interpretation and improvement of conventions, codes, recommendations and guidelines;
   (b) procedure for the control of ships including deficiency reports;
   (c) casualty statistics and investigations into serious casualties; and
   (d) harmonization of survey and certification requirements and guidelines for survey and inspection.

(2) Training, watchkeeping and operational procedures for maritime personnel including seafarers, fishermen, maritime pilots and those responsible for maritime safety in mobile offshore drilling units.

(3) The manning of sea-going ships.

(4) Measures to improve navigation safety including ship's routeing, requirements and standards for navigational aids and ship movement reporting systems.

(5) The development of a global maritime distress and safety system and other maritime radiocommunication matters including navigational warning services, shipborne radio equipment and operational procedures.

(6) Survival in case of maritime casualties and distress including life-saving appliances and the provision of maritime search and rescue services and their harmonization with aeronautical search and rescue.

(7) The safe carriage of timber, grain and other cargoes by sea including containers and vehicles and dangerous goods carried including containers and vehicles and dangerous goods carried therein or in packaged form, portable tanks, unit loads, shipborne barges or intermediate bulk containers (IBCs).

(8) Emergency procedures and safety measures for ships carrying dangerous goods, medical first aid in case of accidents involving dangerous goods and the safe use of pesticides in ships.

(9) The safe handling and storage of dangerous goods in port areas.

(10) Intact stability, subdivision, damage stability and load lines for all types of ships.

(11) Tonnage measurement of ships.

(12) Safety considerations for machinery and electrical installations.

(13) Manoeuvrability of ships.

(14) Noise level aboard ships.

(15) Matters pertaining to fire safety in all types of ships.

(16) Safety aspects of the design, construction and equipment of all types of ships, such as finishing vessels, oil tankers, chemical tankers, gas carriers, dynamically

supported craft, mobile off-shore drilling units, special purpose ships, off-shore supply vessels, nuclear merchant ships, roll-on/roll-off ships, barge carriers, dry cargo ships carrying dangerous chemicals in cargo tanks and barges carrying dangerous chemicals in cargo tanks and barges carrying dangerous chemicals in bulk.

(17) Cooperation with the United Nations and other international bodies on:
   (a) the carriage of dangerous goods by all modes;
   (b) freight container safety in transport by all modes;
   (c) maritime training, the manning of sea-going ships, watchkeeping and operational procedures;
   (d) navigation safety and radio matters;
   (e) the safety of fishing vessels.
   (f) noise of nuclear merchant ships; and
   (g) the safety of nuclear merchant ships; and
   (h) the safety of offshore drilling units.

(18) Organization of seminars, symposia and workshops on the above matters.

B.   In the field of prevention and control of maritime pollution

(1) Procedures for the effective enforcement of the International Convention for the Prevention of Pollution of the Sea by Oil, 1954 (OILPOL) and the International Convention for the Prevention of Pollution from Ships, 1973 (MARPOL) as modified by the Protocol of 1978.
(2) Clean Ballast Tank (CBT) and Crude Oil Washing System (COW) Specifications and Operating Manuals.
(3) Oily-water separators and monitoring equipment.
(4) Interpretation of the provisions of the 1973 MARPOL Convention as modified by the 1978 Protocol.
(5) Surveys and Certification under the 1973 MARPOL Convention as modified by the 1978 Protocol.
(6) Reception facilities.
(7) Procedures and arrangements for the discharge of noxious liquid substances.
(8) Reporting systems on incidents involving pollution.
(9) Comprehensive Manual on Oil Pollution.
(10) Protection of particularly sensitive sea areas.
(11) Regional cooperation in combating marine pollution.
(12) Dumping of waste at sea.

C.   In the field of facilitation of maritime traffic

(1) Standardization of documentation on the carriage of dangerous goods by all modes of transport.
(2) Automatic data processing (ADP) of shipping documents and documents used for clearance of ships.
(3) Establishment of guidelines for the use of ADP with Standardized IMCO Model Forms.
(4) Collection and dissemination of information on shipping documentation required by and available in different countries.
(5) Documentary requirements for ships carrying nuclear (radioactive) and other noxious cargoes during 'innocent passage'.

D. In the legal field

(1) Consideration of a draft convention on liability and compensation in connection with the carriage of noxious and hazardous substances by sea.
(2) Consideration of legal questions arising from the *Amoco Cadiz* disaster.
(3) Consideration of the legal status of novel types of craft, such as air-cushion vehicles operating in the marine environment.

E. In the field of technical cooperation

The Organization provides assistance to developing countries in all areas of its activities including, in particular:

(1) Maritime training.
(2) Maritime safety administration and maritime legislation.
(3) Technical port operations and management.
(4) Prevention and control of marine pollution.
(5) Shipbuilding research and design.

F. General

Consideration of measures and procedures for the speedy entry into force of international instruments and the effective and wide implementation of international regulations and standards for promoting maritime safety; prevention of pollution and efficiency in shipping and related maritime activities.

5. THE INTERNATIONAL LABOUR ORGANISATION

E. Argiroffo (Chief of the Maritime Branch, International Labour Office)

Since it was first estabished in 1919 as a result of the Treaty of Versailles to serve the cause of peace through social justice, the International Labour Organisation (ILO) has devoted special attention to social and labour questions in the maritime industry. Although an intergovernmental organization, which in 1946 became the first specialized agency of the United Nations, the ILO is tripartite in structure, employers' and workers' representatives taking part along with government delegates at conferences and other meetings, with the right to vote independently. However, maritime labour questions are in general considered in the first instance by a bipartite body, the Joint Maritime Commission, composed of representatives of shipowners and seafarers, which advises the Governing Body of the International Labour Office on action to be taken in the maritime field and adopts proposals leading, among others, to the adoption by the International Labour Conference of maritime labour Conventions and Recommendations.

Thus, through the years 32 Conventions and 25 Recommendations in the maritime field have been adopted by the International Labour Conference and these, when taken together, comprise what has come to be known as the 'International Seafarers' Code', a comprehensive set of international minimum standards governing practically all aspects of seafarers' employment conditions. These standards have acted as a model for national maritime legislation and have had an important effect on the terms of collective agreements throughout the world. A list of these instruments is attached in Appendix I. In addition to formal standards the ILO, through the Joint Maritime Commission, regional maritime conferences and other meetings, has adopted various Resolutions leading to government action in favour of seafarers, as well as guidelines and codes of practice.

Since the second world war other specialized agencies of the United Nations have been established, and the ILO has cooperated with these organizations on matters of common interest. Special mention may be made in this regard of the joint committee of the ILO and the World Health Organization, of which one of the major achievements was the adoption in 1965 of the first edition of the *International Medical Guide for Ships;* this comprises in one volume a medical guide giving advice on first-aid and further treatment of those sick and injured at sea, recommended contents of the ships' medicine chest and the medical section of the *International Code of Signals*. The Guide is at present in course of revision.

Since the establishment in more recent years of the Inter-Governmental Maritime Consultative Organisation (IMCO) and the United Nations Conference on Trade and Development (UNCTAD), the maritime industry is receiving growing attention on a worldwide scale, and this largely because of its importance, from both the economic and safety points of view, among the many problems such as pollution of the seas, the dialogue between industrialized nations and those in course of

development and the vexed question of open-registry vessels or 'flags of convenience', with which the world is faced at present. The ILO is cooperating with both
these bodies. A Joint IMCO/ILO Committee on Training, which first met in 1964, has
adopted and revised from time to time an international maritime training guide, and
the Committee undertook preparatory work leading to the adoption by IMCO in
1978 of the International Convention on Standards of Training, Certification and
Watchkeeping for Seafarers.

The picture, then, has changed radically since the ILO first paid attention some
60 years ago to what were then the major social problems in the maritime industry. It
may be said that from being among some of the most underprivileged of workers of
the day, seafarers at present in general enjoy conditions of work and life which, apart
from the difficulties involved in long absences from home and consequent limitations
on normal social life, are not inferior to those of shore-based workers. Nevertheless,
this situation is not universal. There are many ships sailing the seas today which, often
by registration in foreign countries, are able to avoid control measures, and which do
not meet internationally recognized standards as regards safety and employment
conditions on board. The problem in itself is not new; in 1958 the International
Labour Conference had adopted the Seafarers' Engagement (Foreign Vessels)
Recommendation and the Social Conditions and Safety (Seafarers) Recommendation, and the question was kept under review subsequently. In 1970 the
International Labour Conference, at its 55th (Maritime) Session drew attention to the
fact that the number of vessels registered under flags of states with which the
shipowners concerned have no national connection had continued to increase, and
called for a study to be made on the extent to which governments had implemented
the provisions of the two Recommendations mentioned above. The study in question
was submitted to the Joint Maritime Commission in 1972 and, on the recommendation of the Commission, the question of 'substandard vessels, particularly those
registered under flags of convenience' was placed on the agenda of a Preparatory
Technical Maritime Conference in 1976 and of the 62nd (Maritime) Session of the full
Conference in 1976.

The latter Conference adopted what are perhaps two of the most important
instruments of recent years – the Merchant Shipping (Minimum Standards) Convention, No 147, and the Merchant Shipping (Improvement of Standards) Recommendation, No 155. The former instrument, which as a Convention is binding on
governments which ratify it, lists subjects on which laws or regulations shall be laid
down, and provides that effective jurisdiction shall be exercised over ships registered
in the ratifying country, that proper procedures exist for dealing with complaints, and
that seafarers employed in these ships shall be adequately qualified for their duties. A
list of other international labour Conventions adopted previously is appended to the
instrument as an Annex, and ratifying countries are required to ensure that provisions
of national laws and regulations are substantially equivalent to those of the Conventions listed, insofar as they are not otherwise bound to give effect to them. A most
important article of the Convention empowers the authorities of a ratifying country,
in case of a complaint or evidence that a ship calling at a port in the country does not
conform to the standards of the instrument, to report thereon to the government of
registration of the ship and to the Director-General of the ILO, and to take measures
as necessary to rectify any hazardous conditions on board. The Merchant Shipping
(Improvement of Standards) Recommendation, which is not subject to ratification
and thus not binding, also lists in an Appendix various ILO instruments whose
provisions governments should ensure are applied through laws and regulations or

collective agreements. It is expected that the Convention in question will shortly have received the required number of ratifications to enter into force.

It may thus be said, in regard to the question of open-registry vessels, that while UNCTAD seeks to reach agreement between all countries concerned with a view to phasing-out such registry over a period of years, the policy of the ILO is not to deal with the question of registration under foreign flags but to try to ensure that minimum labour standards are applied on board ship whatever the flag of registration.

A further question of topical interest which the ILO is studying at present, and which will be discussed by the Joint Maritime Commission at its meeting in October 1980, is that of foreign seafarers. The employment by traditional maritime countries, whether under national or foreign flags, of seafarers from developing countries where average national wage rates are very appreciably lower than those of Western countries, has given rise to considerable controversy, particularly on the part of the international trade union organizations concerned. Large numbers of seafarers from in particular Asia and the Pacific region are employed on board ships of traditional maritime countries. While this situation is of advantage to the former countries who thus benefit not only from the appreciable amount of foreign exchange which the seafarers earn but also from the provision of employment for their nationals, it creates problems for those engaged in the shipping industry of Western countries who tend to lose their jobs to cheaper labour. The International Transport Workers Federation is already acting on this question, as on that of flags of convenience, and it is expected that the Joint Maritime Commission will give guidance at its coming meeting as to steps which the ILO may be able to take to reach agreement and possible solutions to conflicting interests on the question of what have come to be known as 'crews of convenience'.

While the ILO has thus largely fulfilled the expectations placed in it in the early years through a wide improvement in standards of general conditions of work of seafarers, it must now look forward in a changing world to new and more complex social problems in the maritime field. As social questions are inseparable from, and greatly influenced by, the economic situation and technical developments, cooperation between the ILO and such organizations as IMCO and UNCTAD will have to be continued and developed in future years. In this it will benefit, as in the past, from the advice of the industry itself through its tripartite structure.

APPENDIX I

List of ILO instruments relating to seafarers

Conventions

7   Minimum Age (Sea), 1920
8   Unemployment Indemnity (Shipwreck), 1920
9   Placing of Seamen, 1920
15 Minimum Age (Trimmers and Stokers), 1921
16 Medical Examination of Young Persons (Sea), 1921
22 Seamen's Articles of Agreement, 1926
23 Repatriation of Seamen, 1926
53 Officers' Competency Certificates, 1936

54 Holidays with Pay (Sea), 1936
55 Shipowners' Liability (Sick and Injured Seamen), 1936
56 Sickness Insurance (Sea), 1936
57 Hours of Work and Manning (Sea), 1936
58 Minimum Age (Sea) (Revised), 1936
68 Food and Catering (Ships' Crews), 1946
69 Certification of Ships' Cooks, 1946
70 Social Security (Seafarers) 1946
71 Seafarers' Pensions, 1946
72 Paid Vacations (Seafarers), 1946
73 Medical Examinations (Seafarers), 1946
74 Certification of Able Seamen, 1946
75 Accommodation of Crews, 1946
76 Wages, Hours of Work and Manning (Sea), 1946
91 Paid Vacations (Seafarers) (Revised), 1949
92 Accommodation of Crews (Revised), 1949
93 Wages, Hours of Work and Manning (Sea) (Revised), 1949
108 Seafarers' Identity Documents, 1958
109 Wages, Hours of Work and Manning (Sea) (Revised), 1958
133 Crew Accommodation on Board Ship (Supplementary Provisions), 1970
134 Prevention of Occupational Accidents to Seafarers, 1970
145 Continuity of Employment of Seafarers, 1976
146 Annual Leave with Pay for Seafarers, 1976
147 Minimum Standards in Merchant Ships, 1976

Recommendations

9 National Seamen's Codes, 1920
10 Unemployment Insurance (Seamen), 1920
26 Migration (Protection of Females at Sea), 1926
27 Repatriation (Ship Masters and Apprentices), 1926
28 Labour Inspection (Seamen), 1926
48 Seamen's Welfare in Ports, 1936
49 Hours of Work and Manning (Sea), 1936
75 Seafarers' Social Security (Agreements), 1946
77 Vocational Training (Seafarers), 1946
78 Bedding, Mess Utensils and Miscellaneous Provisions (Ships' Crews), 1946
105 Ships' Medicine Chests, 1958
106 Medical Advice at Sea, 1958
107 Seafarers' Engagement (Foreign Vessels), 1958
108 Social Conditions and Safety (Seafarers), 1958
109 Wages, Hours of Work and Manning (Sea), 1958
137 Vocational Training of Seafarers, 1970
138 Seafarers' Welfare at Sea and in Port, 1970
139 Employment Problems Arising from Technical Developments on Board Ship, 1970
140 Air Conditioning of Crew Accommodation and certain other Spaces on Board Ship, 1970

141 Control of Harmful Noise in Crew Accommodation and Working Spaces on Board Ship, 1970
142 Prevention of Occupational Accidents to Seafarers, 1970
153 The Protection of Young Seafarers, 1976
154 Continuity of Employment of Seafarers, 1976
155 Improvement of Standards in Merchant Ships, 1976

6. SHIPPING AND THE EUROPEAN ECONOMIC COMMUNITY

R. Le Goy (Director-General, Transport Directorate-General of the Commision of the European Communities)

T he purpose of this background paper is to describe and comment on recent action in the European Economic Community (EEC) in the field of shipping. Since the summer of 1977 the Council of Ministers of the European Communities has adopted nine items of legislation on shipping. Before 1977, it had adopted none. Indeed, in the earlier years of the Community several member states took the view that the effect of Article 84(2) of the Treaty of Rome was that the Treaty did not apply to shipping at all. However, the Court of Justice of the European Communities declared in April 1974 that the 'general rules' of the Treaty do indeed apply to shipping. This means, in the Commission's view, that what the Treaty says about such matters as the free movement of labour, freedom of establishment, state aids and competition between undertakings applies to shipping just as much as to other sectors of the economy. This judgment of the Court implies that shipping automatically becomes in some senses a Community matter.

At about the same time, other developments occurred which had the effect of encouraging the member states and the Commission to pay increased attention to shipping in the Community context. The accession of the UK, Denmark and Ireland to the Common Market in 1973 significantly increased the importance of shipping to the Community: the UK and Denmark were themselves maritime powers, and the seaborne as opposed to the landborne carriage of Community trade became much more important.

It was in the early- and mid-1970s, too, that the member states became increasingly conscious of being faced with a number of intractable problems of international shipping policy where action at national level alone did not seem likely to have enough impact, and where member states were therefore ready to examine whether action at Community level might be more effective. The concrete actions which have been taken by the Council of Ministers in the past three years fall into this general framework; they are actions in which advantage is taken of the Community dimension to produce a result which might be thought to go beyond the scope of action at national level. The Commission, for its part, and subject of course to ensuring respect of the requirements of the Treaty, is anxious to identify areas where action at Community level in shipping can make a real contribution to promoting the shipping and trading interests of the member states and the Community, and to developing sensible shipping policies worldwide. Thus in a communication to the Council in June 1976, the Commission indicated how the Community countries' interests might be looked to in dealings with third states. It is not interested in Community-level action for its own sake and at all costs.

The measures adopted so far reflect and take account of the importance of shipping and trade to the Community, and the need for Community shipping on the one hand to remain competitive in the world markets in which it operates, and on the other to retain as much freedom of access to those markets as possible. The Commission believes that member state fleets, and Community trade generally, stand to gain from the preservation wherever possible of commercial modes of organization for world shipping activity, but that the Community needs at the same time to equip itself to defend its essential interests against countries whose maritime policy is different and harms or threatens to harm our trade and shipping.

Consultation procedure

The first measure adopted by the Council of Transport Ministers in the shipping field was a decision reflecting the feeling that a Community dimension could usefully be inserted into the dealings of the member states with third countries in the shipping area. Council Decision 77/587/EEC of 13 September 1977 setting up a consultation procedure on relations between member states and third countries in shipping matters and on action relating to such matters in international organizations[1] provides for a member state or the Commission to request discussion, among all the member states and the Commission, of shipping questions coming up in wider international organizations (OECD, UNCTAD, IMCO etc) as well as of the shipping relationship between any member state and a third country. This consultation procedure has since been employed for both these purposes. The information exchange and the consultation for which it provides are covered by professional secrecy, but it can be said that the procedure has been and continues to be a very useful mechanism for identifying common interests among the member states and deciding on any appropriate action, eg the coordination at need of their position within another international organization dealing with shipping, such as the OECD.

Liner conference shipping organization

Probably the most significant achievement of the Community in shipping so far is represented by the Regulation which the Council adopted in May 1979 on the subject of the United Nations Convention on a Code of Conduct for Liner Conferences.[2] The text of the Liner Code had been adopted at an UNCTAD conference in 1974. The Code contains a series of rules for the organization and behaviour of liner conferences, covering such matters as conditions for conference membership, principles for cargo-sharing between shipping lines members of conferences (including the so-called 40–40–20 principle), the setting of freight rates, consultations between shipowners and shippers, and the settling of disputes between conference members or between conferences and shippers.

At the outset the Code of Conduct was a divisive influence as between the member states, basically because some felt that their fleets would gain by the application of the 40–40–20 principle, while others were equally anxious to avoid such cargo reservation. The Council of Ministers understood, however, the centrality of this subject to world shipping policy, and was always anxious to reach a common position on it. After long and difficult negotiations the Council agreed in May 1979 on a compromise solution, sometimes known as the 'Brussels package'.

The Council Regulation provides for the member states to ratify the Code Convention; their adherence will achieve the total to bring the Convention into force, and the Code will then be applicable in liner conference trades between the Community and other contracting parties not belong to the OECD. The Community regards this as a significant contribution by it to the North–South dialogue. At the same time the member states will, when they ratify the Code, make reservations disapplying (except to developing country shipping companies) important parts of it, and in particular its cargo-sharing elements, in liner conference trades between member states (and, on a reciprocal basis, between the member states and other OECD countries), and also as between member state (and, on a reciprocal basis, other OECD) conference members in trades between the Community and other non-OECD contracting parties to the Code Convention. The Regulation thus seeks also to respect the OECD tradition, which in the Commission's view is in the Community's interests, of basing the shipping relationship between OECD member states on purely commercial considerations.

The Community's approach to the Liner Code of Conduct has aroused wide interest. A number of other OECD countries seem likely to adopt an equivalent solution, and the Council Regulation can generally be seen as a central contribution to world shipping policy making. The member states are currently preparing the national legislation which will allow them to ratify the Code; and the Community now needs to get the best out of its decision. This will involve, for example, resisting collectively any attempts by non-OECD contracting parties to obtain more than their cargo entitlement under the Code or to extend its principles into areas in which they would not in our view be appropriate; deciding what attitude the member states should take to damaging reservations made by other countries on ratifying; and encouraging other OECD countries likely to become contracting parties to adopt an equivalent solution to that of the Community.

Problems of non-commercial competition

Another problem which has occupied a good deal of the attention of the Community in the shipping field – and indeed still does so – is that of the difficulties caused to member state merchant fleets by the activities of shipping under other flags which is perceived to be indulging in practices of a non-commercial kind. Some member states have also been concerned by shipping operating under the open registers; but the main focus of concern in the past three or four years has been the pressure exercised by the merchant fleet of the USSR, operating as a cross-trader outside the liner conferences in the important liner trades between the Community and developing countries. The non-commercial features have taken the form of the undercutting of freight rates to levels which cannot be matched in the long term by shipowners operating within the commercial constraints set by the organization of the western economies but which can be offered idefinitely on the Soviet side because of the nature of Soviet economic organization (command economy, shadow pricing etc).

The Council of Ministers has adopted two measures in this area. A Council Decision of 19 September 1978 concerning the activities of certain third countries in the field of cargo shipping[3] requires each member state to institute a system allowing it to monitor the activities of the fleets of third countries whose practices are harmful to the shipping interests of the member states. The Decision also envisages future Council Decisions in favour of the joint application by member states, in relation to a 'problem fleet', of appropriate countermeasures forming part of their national legislation. Most member states already possess legislation which would, for example, permit them to place quantitative limits on the carryings of Soviet shipping to and from their ports. The effects of the isolated use, by a single member state, of such powers might be evaded; joint use by all the member states together would certainly be much more effective.

The Council of Ministers has not yet judged the time ripe for a Decision in favour of the joint use of countermeasure powers, although the member states and the Commission have together studied the national laws in detail so as to establish how they might best be used jointly. The Council has, however, embarked on a monitoring exercise directed at two important liner trades where the Soviet presence is believed to be relatively marked. Council Decision of 19 December 1978 on the collection of information concerning the activities of carriers participating in cargo liner traffic in certain areas of operation[4] provides for the member states to collect information on all carriers involved in the liner trades between the Community on the one hand, and East Africa and Central America on the other. Information is called for on liner services operated, on cargo carried, and on freight rates charged. The monitoring period is 1 January 1979 to 31 December 1980; the member states forward the results to the Commission every six months. The Commission is currently examining the early results and will be reporting on them to the Council.

The point should be made that the Community is by no means opposed to cross-traders in shipping, or to liner operators who choose to operate outside the conferences, provided that they operate commercially and thus compete fairly. It does, however, reserve the right to keep non-commercial practices within bounds; and it has the power to do so.

Shipping safety and the prevention of pollution from ships

The *Amoco Cadiz* pollution disaster on the Breton coast in March 1978 caused the Community to decide that it must play a significant part in promoting shipping safety and preventing pollution, mainly oil pollution, from ships. In playing this part it is, naturally, anxious to complement the work of IMCO and not to duplicate it or conflict with it. And in fact it is clear that the Community can fulfil a most important complementary role in the field of the enforcement of the international Conventions on shipping safety and pollution prevention which are drawn up by IMCO. When agreement is reached on a Convention in the IMCO framework it has first to be brought into force as a piece of international law by being ratified by a certain number of states (eg 25) responsible for a certain proportion of world shipping tonnage (say 50%). Then, once in force, the provisions of the Convention must be effectively applied by the contracting parties. The Community can make a major contribution on both these fronts. In the context of the initial entry into force of the Conventions, the Council of Ministers has adopted two Recommendations[5] which, together, encourage the member states to ratify by specific dates five major IMCO and International Labour Organisation shipping safety and pollution prevention Conventions. The member states can, of course, make a significant contribution here because they represent almost 20% of world tonnage and, when Greece joins the Common Market on 1 January 1981, will represent almost 30%.

As for the actual enforcement of the standards set by the international Conventions, once these have entered into force, the Community has again a major role to play in the Commission's view. First, the member states need, as flag states, to ensure that the ships under their own flags meet the standards. The Commission has taken the view that no specific action at Community level is needed to ensure this. At the same time, however, the member states have a particularly important role as port states; the Conventions empower contracting parties whose ports are visited by shipping under other flags to ensure that this shipping meets the standards set in the Conventions. Because of its importance as a trading power the Community receives, of course, in its ports the shipping of all nations. It is thus in a strong position to make a significant contribution to shipping safety through port state enforcement.

With this in mind the Commission has already proposed to the Council that the member states should regard as binding the provisions of two IMCO Resolutions on port state enforcement.[6] This Decision has, for juridical reasons, not yet been adopted by the Council of Ministers. However, the Commission is now preparing a further proposal in the same field. It has in mind to propose a Council Directive under which the member states would institute, as port states, procedures designed to identify every ship entering their ports which does not meet the standards set by the international Conventions, and to require it to put the deficiencies right.

In this same field of shipping safety and pollution prevention the Council of Ministers has also adopted two Directives. One of these[7] sets requirements for oil, gas and chemical tankers of 1 600 grt and over entering or leaving Community ports. They are required, *inter alia*, to give specified information to the competent authority before entering, complete a 'tanker check list', and make use of radar and pilots in accordance with local practice. Pilots must inform the appropriate authorities of any deficiences which may affect the safe navigation of tankers which they are piloting, and a member state becoming aware of a pollution hazard posed to another member state must inform it as soon as possible. Minor amendments were made to this Directive in a supplementary Directive of 6 December 1979.[8]

The second Directive relates to deep-sea pilotage (as opposed to local and harbour pilotage).[9] It requires member states with coasts bordering the North Sea or the Channel to ensure the availability of a sufficient number of properly qualified and certificated deep-sea pilots, and to encourage those of their ships which require a deep-sea pilot in these waters only to use a properly certificated one. In addition, the Community has recently supported an initiative in IMCO designed to encourage the shipping of *all* countries only to use properly qualified and certificated pilots in the Channel, North Sea and Skagerrak.

Assessment of Community activity

The above account shows that, after a late start, the Community has in recent years developed significant activity in the shipping field, with the adoption by the Council of Ministers of a series of measures in the fields of consultation mechanisms, liner shipping organization, non-commercial competition, and shipping safety and pollution prevention. Generally, these measures have made use of the capacity of the Community as a unit to take action not available, or not available in as effective a way, to the member states individually; action in fields where the member states were faced with problems set outside the Community, whether by flag discrimination by developing countries, non-commercial competition from state-trading countries, or substandard shipping visiting member state ports.

A glance at the future

The authors of this paper certainly pretend to no clear view of Community shipping in the 1980s. But a few remarks may nevertheless be made.

The Commission will continue to explore with the member states the scope for useful actions for the Community to take in shipping, and to apply the general rules of the Treaty to shipping in a sensible way. The Commission does not aspire to advocate a global, overall shipping policy, but some basic points are clear. The Community is the biggest trading power in the world, and most of its trade moves by sea. So it has a vital interest in efficient shipping services provided at a reasonable price. Shipping under the flags of its fleets owned by the member states, should be able to play an important part in meeting this need for efficient and reasonably priced sea transport; our shipping should also remain as free as possible to carry, as a cross-trader, the trade of other countries. It is difficult to say whether the Community should aspire to control any particular percentage of world shipping. With Greek accession to the Community, the member states will, as mentioned, have almost 30% of world tonnage under their flags. A reasonable aim might be through free and commercially normal conditions to see that this proportion does not fall significantly in coming years. To achieve this, we need, as suggested above, to seek for policies which, on the one hand, ensure that our fleets remain competitive, and, on the other, retain access to their markets instead of being excluded from them by protectionist policies of others. As to specific areas of possible future action, the Commission's intention of making a formal proposal in the field of port state enforcement of safety provisions has already been mentioned. In addition, the following indications can be given.

1. Application of the competition rules of the Treaty to shipping

Shipping and air transport are the only areas of the economy for which a Regulation providing for detailed application of the Articles of the Treaty dealing with competition between undertakings has not yet been adopted. The Commission is currently preparing a proposal for a Regulation applying the competition rules of the Treaty to shipping. It aims at proposing a measure which, while correctly applying this part of the Treaty to shipping, will not prevent the efficient and profitable operation of liner conferences and might make a significant contribution to finding a *modus vivendi* with US law and practices on liner conferences.

2. Bilateral relationships of member states with third countries in the field of liner shipping

The Commission is considering whether, in relation to those liner trades with non-OECD countries to which the UN Code of Conduct will not apply because the trading partner in question has not ratified the Code, there would be advantage in developing at Community level guidelines for any agreements made between a member state and such a country, or between the shipowners concerned. The Commission suspects that such guidelines, firmly applied by each member state, would allow more advantageous agreements in terms of opportunity to be obtained.

3. Bulk shipping

All OECD countries are strongly in favour of the preservation of the existing commercial market in dry- and wet-bulk shipping, without flag preference. This is necessary in order to keep transport costs down and transport services efficient. The Commission will play its part in maintaining this stance against current pressures aimed at giving the countries which generate bulk cargoes the specific right to carry a certain proportion of them.

4. Open registers

The Commission shares the view of the majority of member states, that current pressures in favour of the gradual dismantling of the open registries should be resisted. At the same time any abuses as to standards affecting safety associated with the operations of these registers should be dealt with.

5. State aids to shipowners

Articles 92-93 of the Treaty, dealing with state aids to enterprises, apply to shipping, but their implications have not yet been followed up in detail. The Commission is now examining, via a study by consultants, the current factual situation as regards government aid to shipping, not only in the member states but also in other important shipping countries. In the light of the results of this study the Commission might then make formal proposals for the treatment of shipping aids in the Community. In doing so it would, of course, take account of the need to maintain the competitive position of member state fleets against those of other countries which give aid to their shipping.

6. Cooperation between the Community and developing countries

The new Lomé Convention between the Community and nearly 60 African, Caribbean and Pacific (ACP) countries contains a joint Declaration on shipping. This recognizes the importance of efficient and reliable shipping services to the development and promotion of trade between the ACP states and the Community; emphasizes the importance here of the Community's position as regards the UNCTAD Code of Conduct for Liner Conferences; and makes clear the Community's willingness to contribute to the development of the shipping sector in those ACP States which so request. The Commission is now exploring possibilities here; one useful action might well be to support the training of shipping safety inspectors in ACP countries, as a contribution to ensuring the highest possible standards of safety for their merchant fleets.

References

1   *Official Journal,* No L 239/23, 17 September 1977.
2   Council Regulation (EEC) No 954/79 of 15 May 1979 concerning the ratification by member states of, or their accession to, the United Nations Convention on a Code of Conduct for Liner Conferences; *Official Journal,* No L121/1, 17 May 1979.
3   Decision 78/774/EEC; *Official Journal,* No L 258/35, 21 September 1978.
4   Decision 79/4/EEC, *Official Journal,* No L5/31, 9 January 1979.
5   Council Recommendation 78/584/EEC, 26 June 1978, on the ratification of Conventions on safety in shipping *(Official Journal*, No L194/17, 19 July 1978; Council Recommendation 79/114/EEC, 21 December 1978, on the ratification of the 1978 International Convention on standards of training, certification and watchkeeping for seafarers *(Official Journal,* No L 33/31, 8 February 1979).
6   Proposal for a Council Decision rendering mandatory the procedures for ship inspection forming the subject of resolutions of the Inter-Governmental Maritime Consultative Organisation *(Official Journal,* No C 284/3, November 1978).
7   Council Directive 79/116/EEC, 21 December 1978, concerning minimum requirements for certain tankers entering or leaving Community ports *(Official Journal,* No L.33/33, February 1979).
8   Council Directive 79/1034/EEC of 6 December 1979 amending Directive 79/116/EEC concerning minimum requirements for certain tankers entering or leaving Community ports *(Official Journal,* No L315/16, 11 December 1979).
9   Council Directive 79/115/EEC of 21 December 1978 concerning pilotage of vessels by deep-sea pilots in the North Sea and English Channel *(Official Journal*, No L 33/32, February 1979).

III. Study Groups

STUDY GROUP 1: POLITICAL ASPECTS

Rapporteur: Professor A. D. Couper (Head of Maritime Studies, UWIST)

The Group examined five main questions:

- Attitudes to UNCTAD policies and the developing countries.
- The activities of Soviet shipping.
- The shipping regulations of the USA.
- The role of the EEC in shipping.
- The problems of British shipping.

UNCTAD policies

In relation to UNCTAD, the discussion started by considering whether any lessons could be learned from the negotiating strategy adopted by the UK with respect to the United Nations Code of Conduct for Liner Shipping. It was thought that this might provide a guide as to how we should approach the current UNCTAD proposals on allocation of bulk cargoes between national fleets and the phasing-out of flags of convenience (FOC).

It was clear from the outset that the UK was opposed to the UN Code of Conduct. The shipping industry made it plain to the government of the day that the Liner Code was unacceptable to them. They adopted this attitude primarily because the principle of cargo reservation was alien to the UK and to other Western shipping countries. It would have been very difficult for the UK to suddenly accept such a philosophy. The UK also objected to many specific articles in the Code which it considered as confusing, contradictory, and legally problematic. In this they were in agreement with the USA and the Scandinavian countries.

Whatever the merits of the British attitude the effect was, very early in the Code negotiations, to place the UK outside many of the policy-making discussions. Britain as a result appeared to have lost influence within the EEC where Germany was a supporter of the Code.

In retrospect it was felt that the UK should have taken a greater initiative earlier within the EEC. By not so doing, and by straight opposition to the Code, the UK may also have lost some credibility in shipping circles.

This led the Study Group to a consideration of the UK response to the current UNCTAD proposals on bulk cargoes and the phasing-out of the FOC. It was pointed out that most UNCTAD resolutions evolved in a series of documents as proposals from the Secretariat. Each document receives some support and it undergoes frequently a relatively fast transition. For example, a progression in the order – 'Right to participate'; 'Right to share'; 'Enabled to share'; 'Obtain an equitable share' – that is, a move from an acceptable principle to a strictly mathematical division.

It was considered by the Group that many developing countries, in particular, do not always appreciate all the implications of these resolutions, and that those developed countries most involved in shipping have not the time nor the mechanism available to explain the likely problems which may as a consequence arise in world shipping. They are generally unable to enter into a dialogue with the developing countries before lines are drawn at the international level. The result of this is that Group B opposition appears at UNCTAD without the benefit of detailed discussion with the Group of 77 beforehand. Some developing countries are often suspicious of Group B and they have to turn to the Secretariat for an explanation of Group B motives. Group B attitudes are often seen by the Group of 77 in the context of self interest and a lack of understanding of the Third World problems of poverty, difficulties in promoting manufacturing industries, lack of markets, and tariff barriers etc.

The Study Group considered that there was a new approach. It was necessary to acknowledge the problems of the developing countries more resolutely, and to be seen to be prepared to study their shipping and trade difficulties objectively. This approach may be put in the context of the Brandt Report. We should avoid overreacting to initial proposals but rather should approach the developing countries in a positive way.

In considering the future, it was agreed that not all developing countries are likely to enter the liner or the bulk trades. Those that do may not proceed to a 40% or 50% share of their trade generation. It was felt that the developed countries should be prepared to explore to a greater extent the opportunities of joint ventures.

It was also felt that the developed countries should demonstrate clearly that their concern is genuine for the damage which may be done to international trade through ill considered measures. For example, it was necessary to prove that the 'open market' did exist, and did operate to the benefit of the world community in the carriage of bulk cargoes; also that a move to flag reservation would result in a rise in freight rates, and that the allocation of cargoes on the basis of cargo generation may have disadvantages for those developing countries which had entered shipping but were not major generators of bulk cargoes. It was noted, for instance, that the main gains from the allocation of cargoes on this basis would be to the oil-producing countries. The effect of this would be a further transfer of greater incomes to the rich oil producers, and a possible rise in freight rates. These matters had to be explored with the developing countries in a more objective way.

It was clear that there was a need for better channels of communication between developed and developing countries. Governments could do more in this respect, and certainly the EEC and the OECD should grasp the initiative. There could possibly be more ministerial visits to developing countries, and a better mechanism created to discuss the facts of shipping in the context of aid than was available at UNCTAD meetings.

It was considered important to provide assistance to developing countries in shipping and ports. One area of assistance is that of educational and training courses. These would enable developing country administrators and commercial entrepreneurs to more realistically evaluate entry into shipping, and to compete on fair economic grounds to the benefit of the international community.

It was pointed out that merely reiterating that the free market was best, and that there were no barriers to entry into shipping, was not sufficient. In many developing country economies the free market was an unfamiliar concept, and these statements coming from the developed countries often reinforced suspicions as to motives.

In effect, it was felt there was a need to acknowledge the political realities of the world, to seek compromises and not to dismiss proposals out of hand; rather, it was necessary to take the initiative in examining these. It was recommended that discussions along these lines should be initiated at the EEC and that the Community should speak with one voice. The UK should take the lead in this and formulate a clear policy in shipping *vis-à-vis* the proposals emanating from UNCTAD. They should find the best means to get their views across to the Group of 77, and, in particular, to seek for joint ventures in the provision of British management expertise and officers and crews, in those cases where there is general agreement that further shipping investments would prove of real value to the economy of a developing country.

In relation to the phasing-out of FOC, it was emphasized that the bulk cargo sharing proposal and the FOC phasing-out proposal were closely related. If phasing-out were to proceed without the adoption of cargo allocation to national flags it was very likely that the flag of convenience ships would be repatriated to the owner states. There was already evidence that ships move back to their owner states rather than to developing countries when they leave flags of convenience.

The Study Group considered the main point made by UNCTAD, ie that FOC were preventing the developing countries from establishing bulk fleets, as FOC was a device whereby the high-wage countries were able to own ships and operate them with crews drawn from the developing countries, and in so doing they were eroding the comparative advantages which the underdeveloped countries had in their supply of low-cost labour willing to go to sea. It was argued in the Study Group that this was, in fact, a rational use of resources combining capital and labour on an international basis.

Members of the Group were also sceptical of the claim that phasing-out FOC would necessarily raise the standards of ship safety. There were poor standards of shipping in several developing countries, and the highest rates of casualties in recent years, as a percentage of shipping directly owned, were attributable to Greek vessels.

There was clearly a need to improve standards and make owners, including those owning FOC vessels, more responsible. It was felt that the scenario painted by UNCTAD of a transfer of ships from FOC to those of developing countries was not necessarily the only one. There were many other possibilities, some not advantageous to developing countries or developed countries, and it was up to the shipping community to examine these clearly and to communicate the range of possibilities to the UNCTAD Secretariat and the Group of 77.

USSR and CMESA shipping

On the question of Soviet competition, it was pointed out that the USSR had a much bigger liner fleet than it required to meet national trade needs, as indeed had the UK. The question posed was whether Soviet competition was any more serious than say Brazilian competition. The answer is this lay in the strategic implications of Soviet vessels which were affecting UK shipping in the East African trades by offering low rates, and were eroding German and other Western flag shipping in various areas.

There were some complex problems in this respect. Shippers were free to choose vessels offering the lowest rates; the governments of France and Germany, in particular, valued their trade with the Eastern bloc and had no wish to antagonize the USSR over questions of shipping. It was thus difficult for the EEC to talk with one voice in relation to the non-commercial practices of Soviet shipping.

There was, in any event, a problem as to how to deal legally with this type of strategic threat. It would be possible to subsidize Western shipping in some vital routes where the USSR was presenting non-commercial competition, but this was unlikely to be successful in the long run. It was also possible, in theory, to prohibit shippers from using Soviet shipping, but this was not considered to be a practical method.

The best solution which the Group could foresee was achieving EEC action on a more coherent basis and influencing the Soviet government on the matter of operations as outsiders, and also abtain their adherence to the Code of Conduct on Liner Shipping. It was considered sensible to negotiate with the Soviet shipping organizations and show willingness in inviting them to join Conferences. It was felt that some eastern shipowners had no wish to see Russians in the Conference, but in the main shipowners were considered pragmatic and prepared to acknowledge the political realities involved.

The question of the Trans-Siberian landbridge *vis-à-vis* shipping was raised, and the Soviet aim of capturing increasing quantities (up to 50%) of high-value cargo between Europe and the Far East was discussed. The Group could see no way of preventing the use of the Trans-Siberian railway by Western shippers, but they pointed to the problem of an increasing build-up of this and the consequences of a sudden change of policy by the USSR in carrying Western cargoes to the Far East, thus leaving shippers without adequate transport in the short term. Once again there was a need for EEC-level discussions on this problem, although no ready solution could be foreseen.

US shipping regulations

The policies of the USA were clearly of concern to British shipping, and in particular the US Anti-Trust Legislation. The Group was not optimistic about achieving a fundamental shift in US policy regarding Conferences. They acknowledged there was a very strong attachment in the USA to anti-trust philosophy, and it would be at least another generation before this was likely to change fundamentally.

The greatest concern was expressed at the continued application of US Laws extra-territorially as part of the American effects doctrine – what took place externally has an effect and therefore the USA has a right to act. It was strongly felt that the USA needed to modify the territorial reach of its anti-trust laws and to come to some more sensible accommodation with its trading partners. It was perhaps worth exploring offers of qualified regulation in the US trade, and certainly there was a need to shift this discussion to OECD level and find some basis of agreement between the OECD countries and the USA on this issue.

Role of the EEC in shipping

It was quite clear that the EEC had become more involved in shipping over the past few years in relation to the Code of Conduct and other matters, and was showing at last increasing interest in the questions of Soviet shipping, US legislation and ship safety etc. Other issues which were arising with respect to the Treaty of Rome in shipping involved social standards, wages, taxation and fiscal policies, access to coastal trades, mobility of seamen between EEC flag ships, subsidies, substandard ships, and so on. The question was posed as to how far EEC should be encouraged to proceed in the shipping field.

The choice appeared to be that the EEC would act on an *ad hoc* basis in relation to problems as they arose. Alternatively, they could build up a maritime administration in the EEC and deal with problems on a more controlled and long-term basis. There was clearly a dilemma in these choices. The EEC was likely to be criticized for not acting coherently enough, or in time, or with sufficient knowledge, due to a lack of maritime expertise and staff. On the other hand if the EEC recruited a large maritime administration it would be open to accusations of increasing bureaucracy and the danger of over-legislation from Brussels.

It was felt there was a real danger of the EEC applying regulations in the same way as the USA; there was no enthusiasm for seeing within the EEC the development of the equivalent of the Federal Maritime Commission. On the other hand it was agreed that since the EEC was obviously getting more involved in maritime matters it should obtain the best possible advice on these issues from the member countries, and that the maritime organization of the EEC needed to be strengthened.

Problems of British shipping

The final discussion focussed on British shipping. Some of the main characteristics were the declining numbers of ships, the low rates of return (less than 4%) in many sectors, the world overtonnaging, and the various issues already referred to.

It was noted that some fundamental changes were coming about in the attitude of several companies. In the attempt to solve financial problems, shipping companies were diversifying into transport, hotels, breweries etc, and were also being incorporated by other organizations. In many cases these had managements different from those founded on original family shipping traditions, and they regarded shipping less as a way of life than as a commercial undertaking which must be capable of reasonable profits for its investors. They would consequently make an appraisal of the best possible investments, and if shipping was not attractive would expand elsewhere. The solution of diversification by shipping companies of their activities may therefore have inherent dangers in terms of the survival of the shipping sector of a company if the low rates of return continue. The UK may also be losing some of its wage advantages in shipping competition.

However, some entrepreneurs clearly continued to find shipping worthwhile. The C.Y. Tung bid for Furness shipping was a case in point. The idea of government restrictions on this type of activity was not favoured by the Group. If an owner wished to sell his ships he should be free to do so – one could not argue for the free market on the one hand and restrict it on the other. But this road did lead in a very difficult direction.

The question now was, what could be done to preserve British shipping from any further decline? Costs, it was felt, had already been trimmed a good way. It was, however, pointed out that British ships using British ports as their main base were still at a disadvantage in terms of turn-round times. Improvements in port industrial relations would be of considerabe help to British shipping. It was considered also that the stricter enforcement of safety standards on ships would even-up some of the competition internationally, since British shipping had for many years applied high standards to equipment and levels of training and certification.

The Group considered the role of government in assisting British shipping. It was acknowledged that very good relations were maintained between the shipping fraternity and government regardless of which party was in power, and political support for shipping was always forthcoming. The point was made, however, that if the industry was to receive the backing of government ministers and civil servants on the many issues requiring political support, the industry must be willing to supply sufficient and accurate statistics and information.

In conclusion it was felt that the British fleet would continue to be competitive, but it did require government support politically – and we should move some of this to EEC and OECD levels. It was also reiterated that one of the best courses of action was to explore joint ventures with new maritime nations. Points which were posed but could not be considered by the Group due to lack of time included: How can the British fleet operate in a non-free market? And what size of merchant fleet is essential for strategic purposes?

Discussion

Flags of convenience

It was suggested that if flags of convenience were phased out, ships under Liberian flags, say, would transfer to the flag of their beneficial owners. Is it seriously suggested that American owners of these ships, say, would transfer to the American flag? Further, in the course of the Group's discussion about flags of convenience, was the British flag included in that context, bearing in mind that 27% of the UK fleet in ship terms and 44% of the fleet in tonnage terms are owned abroad, not including the probable Tung acquisition of Furness Withy?

Rapporteur's response. It was seriously considered that American owners would transfer their flags from the Liberian back to the American flag. The USA has permitted its nationals to register under flags of convenience provided they can retain control of that tonnage. It seems very unlikely that the Americans would be happy if this tonnage disappeared from their control. The Americans are very large shipowners, and to have their tonnage disappear to the flags of other countries where political reliability is not too great would probably not be acceptable for strategic reasons. Rather, the USA might be prepared to subsidize its shipping to get it back under its own flag if it could not operate in this way, and US seamen would be employed.

On the other hand, one can see these vessels being transferred to Greece, perhaps, or to the UK or elsewhere, which are not such high-wage-cost countries. There are all sorts of possibilities. The UNCTAD Secretariat has raised one possibility that the flags could be transferred to the developing countries but this does not necessarily follow. They might be transferred to the developing countries only if these countries were given an allocation of cargo rights which would be shipped under their own flag and could not be shipped elsewhere. Then such a possibility might occur. But there is a range of possibilities. Our point was that the one scenario raised by the developing countries may not be the right one, and they could be heading towards something of a disaster with regard to this.

We did not consider specifically the second point, on the British flag, although we did consider the movements of capital internationally in shipping. There has always been a clear movement of capital, and perhaps this combination of capital, labour and skills in the world as a whole in order to promote international trade is a good thing. There was no great opposition to these movements of capital or to the transfers of ships in this way – whether it was Swedish ships to the British flag or some British ships to other flags.

Soviet merchant shipping policy

Granted that the Soviet Merchant Navy is completely state-owned and state-controlled, did Study Group 1 find the Soviet approach to the problems of its business different in kind from that of any other merchant navy?

Rapporteur's response. We were fortunate that we did have at least one or two people with this type of experience, and their view was that the Soviets seem to be businesslike and becoming more so.

Group member's response. The Soviet negotiators adopt two different stances. One derives from whether the service which they are operating is one which they consider predominantly in terms of political ends, for example, the service to East Africa. That trade has always been dominated primarily by political rather than commercial aims. On the other hand, the services that they have operated to some Eastern areas, such as India, have been dominated more by commercial needs, and there the USSR has perhaps adopted the attitude of seeking foreign exchange earnings rather than the more political ends which might be considered.

But, when one does discuss a business proposition with the Soviets, eg their joining a conference, one finds them extremely practical and extremely businesslike in their attitude. Experience has been (eg in discussions with men such as Mr Cassenko and Mr Overin) that when asked to put pressure on their shipping organizations such as the Black Sea Shipping Company to enter a commercial arrangement, they refused under the plea that if they did and the venture failed commercially – in other words, if they were out of pocket at the end – they woud then be called upon by the Black Sea Shipping Company to make up the difference by way of some kind of internal subsidy. Whether this is true or not, it certainly led to the belief that the approach in the initial stages to such a venture was a practical one.

This leaves aside the inherent question as to whether they are working from the same costing basis as, for example, the British. It is most evident that they are not. They do not have anything like the same costs for fuel, crew, perhaps replacement costs, and certain other matters. The issues are entirely different, and one can thus always assess their approach to the problem through the realization that they are in fact operating at a basically lower level in terms of costings, and therefore they have that edge in terms of negotiations.

Relevance of political and social scientific considerations

It may have surprised some of us here to find that we could spend five hours usefully discussing politics – which everyone knows is a nonsense – and discussing political problems that are of real commercial significance to the industry as the industry itself described it, not as the political scientists present imagined it. The CBI Education Committee has submitted a report to the UK government, in which it states that the CBI is particularly anxious that universities concentrate more on teaching useful subjects, like engineering. Presumably the unspoken thought was that less time should be spent on rubbish like politics and sociology. It was apparent from the Study Group's discussions that some problems encountered by the British shipping industry stem from a certain unfamiliarity with how to analyse political and sociological problems. Very interesting observations were made on, for example, the variations in productivity between docks as shown in turn-round time and the incidence of labour troubles. This seems pre-eminently a subject for a concerted study by social scientists of various disciplines. About half a dozen subjects were mentioned during our discussions, by the Chairman and others, as being something to which the universities might devote some resources. The fact of the matter is that it might be possible within the UK for one of these large areas that were mentioned to be studied. But if, for example, people want a study of public administration because it is relevant to business interests, they should be aware of the fact that there are not enough public administration graduates in the UK to do all the research tasks which from time to time business and industry think need to be done for commercial and economic reasons. Next time industry feels like making a submission to the government on the subject of higher education, it should consider that at some point in the future it will be needing social scientists, or at least it will be coming up against problems on which it thinks social science expertise might be commercially valuable to it, and should give some thought now to the future supply of such people. Of course this is a self-interested argument, but a lot of the shipping people are here today because they feel that shipping is a very important industry and its case should not go by default. Academics too think that theirs is a very important industry, and are concerned that their case also should not go by default.

Chairman's comments

An articulate plea has been made on behalf of the social sciences. For some time I have felt fairly strongly that the proper study of mankind should focus on 'Man'. The social sciences have got off to rather a bad start and it is unfortunate that in practical terms we have not made more use of the expertise and the disciplines that they have developed. Almost every aspect of all subjects under discussion at this conference touches upon training, attitudes, behaviour, industrial strife, roles, jobs, recruitment, training. It is impossible to divorce the human factor, which we know to be the primary one; and the science of the human factor, as I understand it, is what the social sciences are all about. I believe that it is worth considering seriously a study of where applied social science can help in the problems being discussed.

STUDY GOUP 2: ENERGY, ECONOMICS AND TECHNOLOGY

John Holt (Senior Lecturer in Maritime Economics, Liverpool Polytechnic)

Given peace and reasonable rates of economic growth and trade development the Study Group could not foresee any major immediate problems with regard to the supply of fuel oil for propelling ships.

The possibility of sea transport becoming displaced by alternative modes of transport during the next 15 to 20 years has to be dismissed. The specific features of a ship as a cargo carrier, such as the low tonnage of the ship in relation to the weight of cargo which can be carried, the large cargo capacity and the low consumption of energy relative to other forms of transport, result in sea transport being the cheapest in international trade. Despite the progress in other modes of transport, especially air, pipeline and landbridge, there are no indications that the dominant position of shipping will be changed radically. Therefore, for large bulk commodity movements the surface displacement ship will continue to be the answer, provided reduced speed is accepted, given the overall transport efficiency the ship provides.

The world fleet at present is comparatively young and most sectors of the industry are still subject to overtonnage and low profitability. Therefore, it is envisaged that there will not be any dramatic change to other forms of motive power and that there will still be a large diesel-engined world fleet in the 1990s running on oil.

However, it is recognized that the supply of oil is finite, and its price, relative to the general inflation rate, will rise in real terms. Further problems may arise with regard to its quality and availability for shipping, therefore there must be a significant response to this situation in the present.

Alternative power sources and fuels need careful consideration and it is important to identify time horizons for the development and operation of these alternatives.

Wind-driven vessels

The Group's view was that despite recent design improvements sailing ships are unlikely to offer a viable solution before at least the start of the next century. Wind variability and thus the unpredictability of voyage times, difficulties of ship manoeuvring in ports, rivers and canals, the possibly larger required crew sizes and crew training costs, provide just some of the technical difficulties, but the Group did support further investigations in this area, particularly into alternatives to sails such as ducted wind turbines.

Coal

Coal-fired ships do not provide a fundamentally new technology and so offer most promise for rapid development.

At present, the price of coal relative to oil in many parts of the world appears low even after allowing for the lower energy efficiency of coal, and proven coal reserves –

though, like oil, finite – are extensive and favourably distributed in politically stable areas. Apart from the coal trade, other trades, particularly grain, could benefit by the introduction of coal-fired ships as coal produced locally or imported is available at one end of the voyage or along the route. More than two-thirds of the world's grain trade is generated from the USA, Canada and Australia, and therefore the most attractive primary routes for coal-fired ships, it is argued, are Australia–Japan, South Africa–Europe, South Africa–Japan, US east coast–Europe, and Canada–Japan.

In other dry bulk and general cargo trades shipowners will delay investing in coal-fired tonnage until special facilities have been developed. Feasible locations for coal bunkering stations may be South Africa, the English Channel, Panama, the Red Sea or Suez, and Gibraltar. Therefore, the logistics problems associated with the reintroduction of coal require investigation, especially with regard to the bunkering requirements and port requirements to facilitate bunkering.

The main questions on coal relate to the form in which it is to be used. The Group agreed that the use of pulverized coal has to be rejected because of the shipboard space requirements of pulverizing machinery and the risk of explosion. Although there are no insuperable problems in adopting a combined oil-firing and coal-burning system in the same boilers, this alternative would not maximize the economic benefits from utilizing coal. Similarly, the problem of engine damage renders coal–oil mixtures unattractive, and in any case this does not provide a real alternative to oil. Therefore, the easiest option appears to be that of burning solid coal directly, since the boiler and turbine requirements are known and pneumatic methods of coal-handling could easily be developed. In this respect the group recognized the development of the fluidized bed boiler to be particularly encouraging.

It was suggested that coal would primarily serve to reduce the operating costs of larger vessels with perhaps little immediate advantage for vessels up to Panamax size. The ships would have less risk of fire and explosion than their oil-burning counterparts, with a reduced risk of pollution. Research efforts should thus consider alternative systems of automatic control, coal-handling and pollution control.

The Group acknowledged that it was not practical to convert existing oil-fired boilers to coal-firing unless an owner was prepared to accept a considerable loss in speed. Shipowners should thoroughly investigate ways of installing coal-fired boilers and bunker capacity sufficient to maintain full speed with the minimum reduction in cargo-carrying capacity for existing vessels, together with the implications for stability. For example, bunkers may be positioned in areas not normally used for anything but tanks or voids.

Overall, the Group felt that subject to detailed economic assessments the technical design of a coal-burning ship is feasible and that the UK should play a leading role in the evolution of coal-burning vessels; otherwise both shipbuilders and owners may have systems imposed on them by others.

Nuclear propulsion

There is the view that because coal is also in finite supply, its price too could start to rise significantly in real terms towards the end of the century and therefore we should ignore it as an alternative and proceed to nuclear power – which in any case provides the inevitable solution. The group, on balance, took the view that a resurgence of interest in nuclear power many occur in the 1990s but the environmental lobby and problems of safety of operation and waste disposal, together with the need to develop the necessary support infrastructure, do not render it a viable alternative in the next decade and a half.

Therefore, the coal ship will play a significant interim role with nuclear ships only emerging in the much longer term and even then, if reactors do not become smaller, only for the largest vessels. Some of the Group did suggest that there was some likelihood that other countries with no access to supplies of fossil fuels may move down the nuclear path more quickly.

Conservation measures

In parallel with the development of alternative power sources and fuels the Group gave consideration to a range of energy conservation measures in both ship design and operation. The consensus view was that relatively small energy savings in a number of areas could produce a creditable overall energy saving.

In particular, on the design side, the following appear desirable:

- the closer study of unconventional hull designs;
- a metallurgical approach to ship-resistance reduction and streamlining improvements to ships' superstructures to reduce wind resistance;
- reductions in lightshipweight and the fitting of fins to improve aft-end flow;
- development of stern arrangements and propeller sizes to maximize propeller efficiency.

Perhaps the clearest message the Group had in this area was that in many cases optimum ship speed will fall possibly producing significant savings. In this regard, double-engining for speed flexibility should be further considered, particularly on trades with directional or seasonal trade variations. A further point was raised that side and bow thrusters together with active rudders could save energy by reducing tug dependence.

Elsewhere savings were considered possible with regard to energy recovery, energy-reducing systems such as the use of variable speed pumps, and in insulation, particularly in the maintenance of insulation.

The question of reserving oil for use by shipping in the 1990s was raised. However, on balance, it was thought that the market would ration oil usage adequately, and even if a crisis arose shipping may not be given high priority since there are at least some alternatives to oil for shipping.

In the area of automation and reduced manning costs it was argued that the development of automation would continue but its reliability, maintenance and future training of officers all require attention.

Ship size and types

The final part of the Group's deliberations related to possible areas in which further economies of ship size may be obtained in the 1990s. Such economies would also produce energy savings. In tankers, maximum ship size is unlikely to be greater than today simply due to environmental considerations and port restrictions. Pipelines may continue to make inroads in this sector but the political risks are likely to increase.

The technical progress in shipping, so dynamic in the previous 10-15 years, has begun to stabilize and in the near future will be characterized by a wider application rather than further developments. In particular, the market share of the fully cellular containership is expected to have expanded by the 1990s, particularly on routes between developed and developing countries. Typically, the cargo liner of the 1990s may be a fully cellular vessel probably not exceeding 1 800 TEU in capacity and may be a geared ship where complex route itineraries have to be served.

Although the small conventional general cargo vessel may continue to service smaller ports with poor cargo-handling facilities, its role will probably decline, but the group envisaged a continuing and expanded market for both larger hybrid and multipurpose vessels. The view was that such vessels are not simply a transitional stage to the use of cellular containerships, roll-on roll-off ships or bulk carriers, but they have a future role in their own right although they may have to move from route to route to be profitable. Improvements in ship turn-round time in port will provide an incentive to further investments in ship size and should be encouraged.

Barge systems also provide the opportunity for economies of scale in the marine sector and energy savings with regard to cargo distribution by barge. The commercial success of the barge carrying system, however, has still to be proven especially where it is in direct competition with other unitized cargo carriers; therefore the prospects of a general expansion in this area should be viewed with caution. Nevertheless some opportunities will exist to exploit this technology, especially where semi-bulks dominate a trade in sufficient volume, where extensive waterway systems exist for cargo distribution by barge without additional cargo handling, and where port infrastructure is poor.

A continuing market for dual-purpose ferries which will probably be larger than at present was also envisaged for the 1990s, and serious consideration should be given to the possibilities of expanded coastal trade as an alternative to road and rail.

More generally, the group felt it important to avoid duplication of services and excess capacity, and the attitude of UNCTAD is a problem in this respect.

Research and development

Finally, it is clear that more research and development in a number of areas is desirable. However, the Group could not be precise as to whether the shipbuilders, shipowners or government should provide the main impetus and funding. However, well formulated proposals made jointly by research agencies and shipowners should receive favourable consideration from government, especially where the potential benefits from energy saving can be clearly identified.

Conclusions

(1) The surface displacement ship will continue to be economic for large bulk commodity movements, although typically ship speeds will fall.

(2) There will not be any dramatic change away from oil as the main form of motive power and therefore there will still be a large diesel-engined world fleet in the 1990s.

(3) The coal-burning ship is technically feasible and will play an important interim role with nuclear-powered ships evolving only in the longer term.

(4) The logistics problems associated with the reintroduction of coal require investigation especially with regard to bunkering and port requirements to facilitate bunkering.

(5) Shipowners should thoroughly examine ways of installing coal-fired boilers and bunker capacity sufficient to maintain an acceptable speed with the minimum reduction in cargo-carrying capacity for new and existing vessels.

(6) Wind-driven ships are unlikely to be economically viable within the 1990s, but research, particularly into alternatives to sail, should continue.

(7) A whole range of energy conservation measures in both ship design and operation could provide a creditable overall energy saving.

(8) The development of automation will continue, but its reliability, maintenance and implications for the training of officers all require consideration.
(9) Technical progress in shipping is likely to stabilize during the 1990s with the wider application of current technologies rather than further developments.
(10) The fully cellular containership, typically less that 2000 TEU in capacity, will dominate general cargo trades in both developed and developing countries and thus provide potential economies of scale.
(11) Barge systems also provide the opportunity for further economies of scale to be reaped, although perhaps on a limited number of trades.

Discussion

Fuel alternatives

One advantage of boiler fuel when it came into use was the considerably smaller volume needed for bunkers on-board ship. Presumably if we revert to coal burning, the reverse would apply. To what extent did the Group consider the effects of this on the payload to deadweight ratio, which would presumably mean a larger number of units or larger units?

Rapporteur's response. We discussed it at reasonable length, and came to the conclusion that some sums will have to be done. I mentioned the logistics problems with regard to the worldwide bunkering facilities that would have to become available. The point was that it was technically feasible but that ships would have to be bigger to be economic, and further work would have to be done in the area.

Energy R&D

Did the Study Group consider what is being spent and how it is being spent on research and development in the general field of energy replacement which might have an application to the maritime problem?

Rapporteur's response. We did not. The feeling was that it was quite small.

Group member's response. The point was that a very great deal of work is being carried out on fluidized beds etc, under the National Coal Board with industrial and US involvement, but employing a great deal of British expertise. We shall have to wait and see how that develops for the benefit of shipping. The research is quite far advanced and there is a large amount of money involved. Prototype sets of 80 mW are being built at present which will, we hope, lead to production units in due course, probably of larger sizes. The shipping side is not doing this work but is keeping a watching brief.

Rejoinder. This work would have application to the shipping side, but the knowledge of what is being done and whether the effort is sufficient should be obtained, if it has not already been, by the shipping industry as a whole, and pressure, if necessary, should be exerted to improve and enhance the kind of research being carried out. The shipping industry has a most evident priority in the outcome of such research and therefore ought to be especially energetic in promoting activity in this field.

Chairman's comment. The UK government, through the Requirements Boards, has in fact been spending a certain amount of money on energy research relating to ships. It has even spent a certain amount of money on studies of wind propulsion of ships, on the adaptation of diesels to use lower-grade fuel, on the saving of heat losses etc. This money has been fed through the Ship and Marine Technology Requirements Board whose budget has been drastically cut in 1980, and all wind propulsion studies, for instance, have been stopped. The money has flowed in the past and one hopes it will flow in the future, but it is not flowing very fast at the moment. I am referring here, of course, to government money. There is nothing to stop any shipowner or shipbuilder funding such research. Research organizations exist to spend it for them: they are just waiting to see the colour of the money.

Research needs and the problems of funding

On the question of funding, there is currently an urgent list of research topics in the field of ship safety, all requiring early investigation; this runs to three pages of titles alone. Just seeking the funding for research takes up a large proportion of one's time. On six occasions at least in Study Group 2's deliberations, shipowners and representatives of research bodies stated that more work needs to be carried out in this area, and at no time did we adequately address ourselves as to exactly what mechanisms should be established to pay for it. The shipowners, who will be the main beneficiaries of more economic and safe shipping, ask how they are to be expected to pay for research projects of uncertain outcome – by definition research is an uncertain outcome – when they are struggling themselves. Shipbuilders will not often take the lead in innovation, because not only are they in financial difficulties themselves, but they will often say that they do not intend to innovate because they have no orders to do so. They will only innovate in response to firm orders, and that is often too late. The customer who wants a ship with a specific performance wants it in a few months, a year or two at the most, and that does not give enough time to set up a comprehensive research project. Government research bodies now have a virtually complete ban on recruitment for new projects. Many shipbuilders are in financial difficulties themselves, and a number of important projects have recently been dropped. The universities are suffering very severe financial setbacks and are not able to fund research projects themselves, except those of a fairly trivial nature. But the money must be found: if we do not innovate, plenty of other nations will, notably the Japanese. Japan has a noticeable lead particularly in respect of ship automation research, the application of simulators to shipbuilding, and similar work. The UK could catch up, but something needs to be done quickly.

The solution seems to lie possibly in fora such as this, where all the bodies in the marine world and the marine community meet together and talk to each other. In this way the needs can be identified, and possibly the people to do the research can be brought together, and some way of obtaining the money – from joint funding, perhaps, between shipowners, shipbuilders and government – can be found.

Research and the market

Those last remarks made me somewhat impatient: the UK is supposed to be an entrepreneurial country, but the whole attitude to research is thoroughly non-entrepreneurial. If we are moving towards a post-industrial society where we have to live on our wits and not our services – and research is *par excellence* the type of service that can provide – then those who can supply services should get into the market place. I am not referring to the Social Science Research Council funding type of market place, but centres of expertise such as the Economist Intelligence Unit where a service is supplied, and although the charge maybe high, the results fulfil needs and the research is not undertaken from behind but from in front. In other words, such work can identify the needs of which no one in industry has yet become sufficiently aware because they are too close to it; the professional researcher, however, can look further ahead. There are investment funds available if one goes out and finds them; but this is a job for marketing rather than funding of research. It is this different attitude which has to be absorbed by universities – universities need to be thinking that they are providing, or can provide, services that can be sold in the marketplace, and they will not be sullying their own souls by doing so. The need for such a change of attitude must be absorbed and considered very seriously indeed.

Group Chairman's comments. This is clearly an important problem, but it does happen that when a research organization goes out into the marketplace and sells its services, it is not UK bodies which are the customers. In my own organization we have been working for the Korean Ship Design Organization. Whether this is a good thing or not is a moral problem.

Rapporteur's response. A number of points were made by the Group. One was that the government would be very willing to fund good, well presented, projects with a number of industrial sponsors jointly with research, and possibly academic, institutions. Yet there was a general view of disbelief that it was a statement of intent, that there was no real will there. The short discussion we had at the end should now be widened, and some of those who joined in that discussion might now contribute further.

NRDC policy

Although there have been considerable cuts in government funds for research such as that funded by the Science Research Council and the Requirements Boards, the National Research and Development Council (NRDC) still has reasonable amounts of money to spend, preferably jointly with industry. It is very happy to consider projects coming from equipment manufacturers, from ship operators, or from a whole range of other firms, people, organizations, sometimes jointly with universities and some-times not, where the work seems to make general economic sense. It is not a charitable organization, but provided there is some prospect of getting the money back in the long term – and the long term may be very long term indeed – then the NRDC is very willing and anxious to get more involved in projects. It is not in the business of turning projects down, but of trying to find more things to support. One problem is the difficulty or the willingness of firms to get together and talk about projects. One result of a forum such as this is that it may encourage people to get together in groups and consider these things further.

Research priorities

Are we spending the taxpayers' and our own money in the right areas of research? It was astonishing to notice recently that we are spending more on astronomy than on engineering research. This must surely be wrong today. It has been stated also that the number of bureaucrats in the UK at present including local government as well as central government officers, pro-rated to population, is 1.7 million more than FR Germany and France employ to administer their countries. Britain cannot have research, schools, and roads etc, if there is this enormous overlay of bureaucrats that competitors do not find necessary in other industrialized countries.

Subsidy policies

The universities are in the business of going out and selling their services – they have many services to sell – but people have to be prepared to buy them.

Turning to the findings of Study Groups 1 and 2, there is a divergence between the economics group and the politics group and it concerns profitability. I come as a newcomer to the subject of shipping, but listening to these discussions and the helpful answers and information given, one problem of shipping seems to arise directly from the subsidy policies of various governments. These must contribute a good deal to excess capacity, and thus reduce the profitability of individual companies. Perhaps this bears particularly hard on the British shipping industry which, according to what has been said here, is one of the least subsidized industries. If this is right, it will be important to British shipping in the 1990s that there should be a debate on the effects of subsidy policy on the profitability of shipping. Perhaps there has already been one, and perhaps the results just did not get drawn together, but one thing that the General Council of Shipping might decide to buy – and it would not necessarily be very expensive – would be a study for the worldwide effects of subsidy policies on the profitability of various shipping industries. The findings of such research could be fed into UNCTAD, for example, because such considerations affect not only the profitability of British shipping, but also the costs which have to be borne by shippers throughout the world, and particularly by Third World countries.

Rapporteur's response. The overlap between the two groups was not made particularly clear in the discussions, because we became involved in a discussion of research expenditure. But one point was raised on a number of occasions during Group 2 discussions – namely the question of the need to conserve energy. This relates to such matters as excess capacity, overtonnage, cargo sharing etc – all things that in the political environment could lead to too many ships moving around inefficiently, and will lead to problems with regard to energy supply and use.

Finally, one underlying issue to be considered in the longer term is the energy cost of having an oversupply of too small ships moving around at uneconomic speeds at less than the economic payload.

Defence aspects

We are faced at present with extreme crisis, both economically and in the military sense. One does not want to be alarmist, but one should be a realist. We are told that the fuel supply system we have been used to over the years is to come to an end in the foreseeable future, and before that happens, we are faced with an increasing rate of costs of this fuel. This will have implications both in terms of economics and for the defence of the UK by merchant navy support for the Royal Navy in time of war.

It is suggested that there is a need for dissemination of all information available about the so-called finite limits to fuel supplies – the dissemination of information about what is being done to meet the needs for the future, both for existing fleets from the point of view of conservation, and also from the point of view of the design of the ships to operate on the new fuel systems which will shortly be entering into service. This is an urgent task that should be undertaken. There is a great deal of knowledge, and a great deal of research is being undertaken, but this is not commonly known throughout the shipping industry.

But this of course begs the question of funding. In normal peacetime circumstances one would say that is was up to owners and shipbuilders perhaps, to provide funding. Yet it is suggested that the UK is now facing a grave national threat, both economically and on defence grounds, which calls for support from government, and not simply by directives, through perhaps a body such as the General Council of British Shipping, to coordinate the information available and to plan a path for future development.

STUDY GROUP 3: MANPOWER REQUIREMENTS

Captain L. A. Holder (Head of Maritime Studies, Liverpool Polytechnic)

UK fleet size and type

Manpower requirements depend on the size and type of ships in the UK fleet and the management and crewing services provided for overseas flags. The Study Group preferred to make one 'guess' at the position in the 1990s, rather than considering several alternative and/or limiting scenarios.

General comments on the UK fleet envisage a reduction in the number of ships, brought about by continued pressure from UNCTAD and developing countries. The balance of the fleet envisaged would be:

- a stabilized liner provision, mainly container/ro-ro ships;
- short-sea traders, with perhaps a modest growth in services;
- specialized bulk carriers and product carriers increased in number and size, with operation remaining in the UK as a developed country, because of the complex management and skilled technical requirements.
- simple large dry bulk/combination carriers and crude oil tankers reduced in number. Movement of processing plants to points of primary production and the ability of low-cost countries to operate 'low' technology vessels would encourage this trend away from UK flag operations.

Fishing requirements are very dependent on political decisions in the EEC and were not considered in detail, other than to offer encouragement to the UK colleges and research establishments to take a lead in providing European centres of expertise. New ventures such as seabed exploration, fish farming etc, would not, we believe, have a major impact on manpower requirements and could be met from the main manpower provision.

Crews in UK flag ships are likely to have a single or comparable wage structure regardless of national origins either within the EEC or outside. Some exchange of seafarers between countries is envisaged, if only as a damper on the cyclical nature of shipping demand.

UK management services for overseas flag vessels will depend on the quality of expertise provided, and the availability and cost of manpower. Short-term expansion of management services can moderate the effect of a contracting UK fleet on the manpower requirement by absorbing skilled seafarers and managers. In the long term the scope of provision for overseas flag vessels will be determined by cost-effectiveness of the UK in comparison with other rapidly expanding centres of competence such as Hong Kong and Singapore.

In any case, such services are not likely to require UK ratings, although they may involve officers and, of course will require managers, even though managers comprise a relatively small number of people in the shipping scene. Some managers as individuals may travel abroad to work for overseas companies in their operational headquarters. Some developing countries using UK expertise at present are tending to 'indigenize' their operation progressively as their own people are trained for senior posts. Thus, management services are not likely to lead to significant changes in manpower needs in the longer term.

Criteria for efficient manning on board

Blanket regulations for the industry are not likely to be efficient and manning must be determined by companies for individual ships or classes of ship with reference to the seafarers' organizations and regulatory bodies. Factors to be taken into account in determining efficient manning must include:

- normal operational requirements;
- peak workload requirements;
- safety of the ship and people on board;
- maintenance policies.

The useful life of a ship is likely to be about 20 years. Minimum time for design to completion is about 2½ years. Time to train a qualified officer (Master/Chief Engineer) is about ten years. This leads to a repetitive circle of events which inhibit change (see Figure 1).

Ships are designed taking into account the available range of skills and expertise. The design is a major factor in determining manning levels. The operational experience then 'trims' the manning level and feeds into future ship design. Any ideas on radical changes in manning find the training – with its ten year lead-time – unable to respond other than through major disruption and retraining. Therefore manning needs to be used to initiate change, not to respond to it (see Figure 2). Fortunately not all vessels will change overnight, and in the 1990s a large number of vessels will be of conventional type, as they are already in existence now. So if we start now, people can be trained for the 1990s.

The general characteristics of the operation of vessels will be smaller, more highly skilled crews, more automation, and many boring and repetitive jobs will be 'designed-out' of the ship. The smaller officer team will need to have a greater overlap of their body of knowledge and experience, so as to be a more cohesive team and

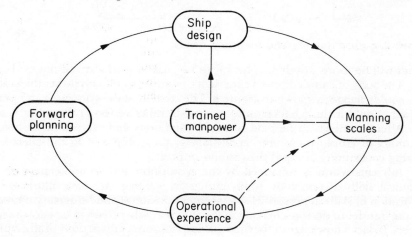

Figure 1. Factors inhibiting change.

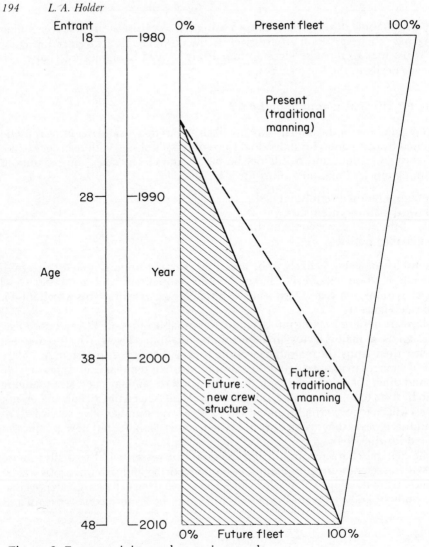

Figure 2. Future training and manning needs.

ratings will be more closely involved with the skilled work carried out on board.

The body of knowledge and experience required by officers (other than catering staff) could change as shown in Figure 3. The content of the syllabuses and practical training should include background on coal-burning vessels and nuclear vessels.

Attention needs to be paid to social conditions and recreation on board, to continuity of employment, and crew stability on a ship and to the effect on the working community of rapid turn-round in port.

Job satisfaction is enhanced by the acquisition and demonstration of skills. Technical skills acquired by some ratings in welding etc, have illustrated this. Acquisition of skills in personnel management, financial and budgetary monitoring and the transfer of decision making to the ship is another trend to be encouraged for officers. In fact, knowledge of the financial implications of the actions of all employees on board would be useful.

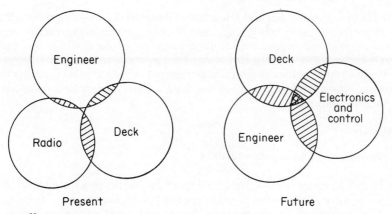

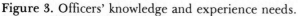

Present   Future

Figure 3. Officers' knowledge and experience needs.

These suggestions need to be taken up now if they are to be implemented by the 1990s; in fact, for senior officers it is too late for *ab initio* training, and retraining will be necessary.

Collective identity and recruitment

Present industry-wide recruitment fails to illustrate to potential employees the range of skills that can be acquired and experience that can be gained at sea. It also fails to illustrate or illuminate possible later career paths into shore management, teaching, ship broking, pilotage, port services etc.

With a falling school population, it will be necessary to broaden the intake to include entrants from all school and college leavers, and possibly post-experience mature entrants, in order to select on aptitude and attitude as well as academic standards.

The industry does not have a good image with schools or the public in general. Methods to improve the image should be explored and might include better access for the public to docks and ships. Sea voyages in vacations for students or undergraduates might provide direct interest and recruitment, even if only on passenger vessels rather than normal cargo carriers.

The conclusions in the above paragraphs broadly support the paper by Mr Peter Sharpe in its references to continuity of employment and company involvement in creating small well motivated shipboard teams.

Education and training structure

The present mix of sea experience and college periods seems suitable in its broad concept, but there is scope for improvement in the syllabuses for professional qualifications. Much greater emphasis on management (both financial and personnel aspects) is needed for the future and not solely on the safety subjects which the Department of Trade (DOT) has statutory duties to supervise. Syllabuses need to be determined by colleges in consultation with companies, and examinations could be transferred to colleges with the DOT monitoring minimum standards in safety subjects.

Present manning structures and work roles on board do not encourage high calibre ratings to stay at sea and few attempt professional examinations. Changes in the skill content of rating work, improved ship design and organization, may attract and retain higher calibre personnel and more may be encouraged to seek qualifications as watch-keeping officers, but this is not seen as a major source of officers.

It would appear that change must be initated by individual companies as there is no national control to bring about *radical changes*. This can only be done at a company or individual ship level.

DISCUSSION

EEC countries' manning standards

The Group's findings could be accused, perhaps, of being a little bland. Seafarers have the impression that efficient manning for the shipowner often seems to revolve around having the minimum number of men on board; it is disappointing to note that the Group decided that no blanket rules should be laid down for minimum manning. Some manning scales allowed by EEC countries are particularly low. If one considers small ships, if these are to work at maximum efficiency – which means 24 hours of every day either steaming or in port – it is surprising that the Group did not consider it necessary to look at such legislation and to make minimum blanket proposals. Several papers at this conference have suggested that the UK should take a lead in developing EEC-type legislation and in exercising some influence through the European Commission. One should examine the legislation of some EEC countries and look at their minimum standards of manning. We have an obligation to decide whether it is safe, and there is no doubt that we should bring pressure to bear through this Forum.

Rapporteur's response. In the discussions in the Group it was said that a number of ships, particularly those ships in and out of port once or twice every day, were running with so few officers and crew that they were not giving the crew or officers proper rest, and therefore were a danger to both themselves and to others.

The point that the Group wished to make and agreed upon, was that if blanket regulations of any kind are applied, then each ship is not made as efficient as it might be. For each ship there should be a minimum number, depending on what trade the ship is involved in, and we should not insist on artificially high numbers simply to cover the few ships that need that number. Decisions need to be made for each individual ship on the basis of its route and the quality and quantity of the officers and crew that are needed for that route. If that is not done, there is the risk of being uncompetitive.

As an illustration, a Belgian pilot was told that a British Rail vessel had a crew of 21, and he remarked that it was not surprising that British Rail had financial problems: a Dutch ship of that size would have a crew of five. Yet he admitted that the Dutch ship had its problems; when it had run into fog he had rung the telegraph to slow and the man on the wheel had said that it was no good ringing that; he was the engineer! The Group wished to indicate that in that case the Dutch ship had too few people on; yet at the same time the British ship had too many. Somewhere in between the two there must be a happy medium where the operator is competitive but safe.

The Study Group considered training for the UK fleet and manpower requirements for the UK fleet. It did not look at undermanning on foreign vessels; that is another question that the Group did not address, and it is one that the Forum should consider.

Education and training

Could the ideas on training be enlarged on? The Group report stated that it takes ten years to train an officer, and that this would be divided between sea experience and college experience. How should this be done?

Rapporteur's response. In terms of education, the two ends of the spectrum we looked at were, on the one hand West Germany and Japan, where at one time people were given three years of college education with no practical experience before they were sent to sea, and on the other the UK system, where because of the amount of leave that people were getting they were coming back for masters' certificates when they were into their 30s and when they found the study for certificates very difficult. The Group considered that the position has now been reached were the mix of periods at sea and periods in college is just about right. People are sent to sea early in their careers – so that they know what industry they are going into and why they are going to college to study; they are then sent to college to be taught what they should do, and they then go back to sea for more experience in the hope of putting into practice what they have learnt. It would be interesting to know if people think we have got the mix wrong; and that others have got it right. Present opinion indicates that this is one of the things that we have done quite well. Within the Study Group there was a wide spectrum of people representing views from different parts of the industry, and they seemed to agree with that consensus.

Rejoinder. Perhaps the ten year training period is a little short for engineers who will man the more complicated ships; training and experience will take longer than ten years for these men to reach the maturity they need. On the other hand, the main engineering training must be early in their 20s: it cannot be later. It is most difficult to absorb the mathematics and the rest later on, after a break of several years.

Methods of training

Did the Group have any thoughts on novel methods of training? The rapporteur referred to the automated ship, the new electronics requirements in the ship. Was any thought given to more training at sea and more ship-based training, for example the placing on-board of computerized training equipment linked with the ship's more elaborate equipment. Further, was consideration given to the training of ships' officers to conduct training and to take packages away to sea, so that much of the more elaborate training might be conducted on board ship. The packages could be prepared and used in colleges, but a transfer to sea might be an alternative.

Rapporteur's response. The Group did not consider things in that degree of detail. The general theme of the Group's discussion was that our efforts should be devoted to what actually occurs on board ship and what skills are required to run the ship, rather than what skill is required to pass an examination taught and set by somebody sitting ashore who is not actually in the ship.

These comments probably coincide with the general views of the Group that anything that can be done to get the training down to the 'nitty gritty' of what is actually needed to be done by people today and in the weeks ahead on a particular ship, must be a valuable contribution to the efficiency of that ship and of the fleet.

Pool system

Individualism is one of the difficulties encountered when recommending that there should be people in teams, that they should be well motivated, and that they should have continuity of employment. One suddenly finds that there are a number of people, all individualists, who do not want to be associated with this type of collective experiment and who will go their own way. We must take this into account in not changing over to a pool system altogether. Human nature will demand some flexibility and movement of pool numbers etc. We shall probably need both types of system.

Management and financial implications

It is very important that the budgetary requirements of a ship are appreciated by those who operate them if they are to have any control over it. Again this is extremely difficult to achieve there is a concerted effort. In 1978 the Nautical Institute held a Conference on Maritime Commercial Practice, the idea being that a number of seafarers had expressed an interest in commercial matters and the desire to have a better insight into it; yet in the event the actual number of seafarers at the conference, out of a hundred delegates, was one. Again, it is perverse: seafarers are told that they need to understand financial factors, and yet they omit these topics on their certificates because it is not examined and they take no interest in it. The Nautical Institute would like to offer any help it can to the development of the management and financial side, either directly or in collaboration with others, although one is aware that there are enormous difficulties.

Rapporteur's response. On one of the ships where I spoke to the master after a new financial system had been devised, he said, 'Aye! I think it's a marvellous system this, and it's really excellent, but I dinna want it on my ship'. The problem was that he had never been taught anything about accountancy, economics, the financial side of chartering, or any related matters, and suddenly, overnight, he was supposed to become interested and enthusiastic and involve the whole crew in this. With regard to training, if you want people to be good at anything in the 1990s, you start training tomorrow, not in 1990. If people are properly prepared for this, then it will be accepted with no problem at all. If people are bludgeoned into doing it suddenly they become awkward and will refuse: it is up to those involved in the educational side to encourage this now to be ready for the 1990s.

Problems of automation

How would highly qualified and highly skilled personnel be reconciled with high automation when at the same time they would be expected to have job satisfaction? With the totally automated ship, there could be nothing for the highly skilled and highly qualified people to do. If minimum manning is intended to enable the ship to operate efficiently with the smallest number of men required to navigate from one part of the world to another, and if ships are to operate with maximum efficiency over 24 hours, the ship sails as soon as the last load of cargo or the last container is on board. Is it anticipated that they will not have any responsibility for the work being done aboard the ship whilst it is in port, loading and so on? In that case, who is responsible for the stability and the safety of the ship?

There are a large number of questions to be answered on the proper manning of ships, and not least perhaps is the skill that they will need to have in occupying their leisure time at sea, and how to achieve compatible crews with such small numbers.

Rapporteur's response. One topic that the Group stated to be in need of consideration was the shipboard community. When it comes to minimum numbers, the Group agreed that what had to be considered in minimum numbers were normal operational requirements at sea and in port; this is not likely to yield the minimum number because consideration must then be given to peak load requirements, which on a number of ships are in the berthing operations when the greatest number of people are likely to be needed. There was a view that if a ship was manned by a small integrated team working well together, the stewards and the firemen would assist in other tasks: in other words, flexibility needs to be improved so that when the men are on-board and are needed at peak load times, they are willing to take part in whatever needs to be done.

The other aspect involved, which never seems to be mentioned by the technical experts who say how well automation can reduce numbers, is that a lot of people are required on-board to carry out maintenance. How are the ships to be maintained? There are very few ships where the personnel on board are simply there to take it from A to B: they are there to take it from A to B and also to make sure that it can go from B to C when it is ready for its voyage. These things need to be considered for each individual case, and we must consider the likely emergencies that may occur such as a failure in the engine room automation where the engine room will have to be manned, perhaps a fire on-board, the need to abandon ship, etc. All these scenarios must be taken into account in establishing minimum efficient manning levels. When it is known how many personnel are needed on-board, one can then consider how they will be employed the rest of the time to keep them interested.

But some ship automation has led – the same as in factories – to the semi-skilled jobs being removed and people being left to wash paint at one end or doing very clever things pushing buttons on computers at the other, with nobody in the middle. That problem has to be settled at the design stage: we shall have to try to design out the boring jobs, otherwise we shall just go on the way we are at present.

Chairman's comments. The impact of automation on the human factors involved is a very complicated issue, and automation applied unfeelingly can create chaos.

Rejoinder. The issue of maintenance was discussed briefly in the Technology Study Group. It needs emphasizing that maintenance is a major issue, and reliability of automated equipment is by no means a foregone conclusion. The Technology Group conceived of mobile teams coming out and carrying out the maintenance, and suchlike schemes. This is a most important issue in consideration of manning, and it is probably the reason why it is not feasible to go down to the irreducible minimum purely on an operational basis.

Technology and automation – Royal Navy experience

The UK Royal Navy's experience of automation may provide some helpful ideas. The first lesson learnt was that the introduction of automated equipment does not necessarily reduce the number of people needed overall. It may reduce the number of people needed in a particular case to do a particular job, but the support required increases while the number of operational people required tends to drop. Next, it was discovered that, although equipment may apparently be very reliable while in use, nevertheless one knows that it might break down: one group of people operates the equipment while another team waits to mend it if it goes wrong. It follows that while the equipment is in use it cannot be maintained, and while it is being maintained it cannot be in use. A 'double group' of people thus began to come about, almost twice as many people as it had been thought initially would be needed. In consequence the Navy is now moving very much towards the concept of what is called the 'operator-maintainer', where the person who uses the equipment, is, if it should go wrong, in broad terms also the person who mends it. Thus a much higher educational qualification is required by the person operating the equipment if he is also to maintain it.

The other interesting aspect is that the rate of technological advance and the rate at which people say, 'We must have one of those because it is there; let us fit it because it will have some advantages', actually outpace the experience of those who have to make use of the equipment. There occurs a 'mismatch' between men and machines. The new equipment sits there on ship. The people who come to use it, although they may have been trained for a length of time ashore, when it comes to the moment of use (and this is particularly applicable to the naval situation which is more dynamic than the merchant shipping situation), cannot actually make proper use of the gear fitted because they do not have the experience that is relevant to the newness of the equipment that they are called upon to operate. The Navy had found more difficulty in the introduction of automated equipment than was foreseen initially, and it is quite a race to keep up.

Rapporteur's comments. This mismatch has been with the shipping industry for a long time as well. Radar at the end of the war was a prime example of that: we had the equipment before we really knew how to use it, and the accident rate went up accordingly.

Fishing industry

It was particularly pleasing to hear the fishing industry mentioned in the Group's report. The manpower situation there is currently disastrous. But the fishing industry worldwide has tremendous opportunities, and the UK's expertise is enormous in all aspects. There is a multitude of implications of the 200-mile limit for the industry: this must be viewed as creating opportunities for disasters. The EEC must solve the situation in the 'European Pond' but the opportunities for the joint ventures overseas, reemployment of UK nationals abroad etc, are very large indeed. Those already abroad are well received in most of these countries – the White Fish Authority, and many skippers, mates, engineers, and so on.

Rapporteur's response. Those comments conform with the views of the Group.

DFDS experiment

In some of the papers we heard of the growth of ferry services. DFDS, for example, has had a shipboard management scheme for some time. Presumably such a scheme creates greater opportunities for the people on-board to get themselves involved in a wider range of interests in the ship, and operating the ship, and different aspects of running a ship. Did the Group examine this type of management, and what were their conclusions about its efficacy and its relevance to our own industry? Obviously it has more relevance to the short-sea services than perhaps the deep-sea, particularly the bulk trades.

Rapporteur's response. The DFDS experiment was talked about at length. The first thing of interest in that experiment is that when a company is about to go into liquidation, it is desperate and must do something. It then starts to act. By that time it is too late to start training people properly; some scheme is introduced in a rush and not very efficiently, and it takes a long time to overcome the problem. DFDS have overcome it now and are in a position where it is running smoothly. They have also capitalized on the experience they gained in those traumatic days at the start by selling their mistakes to other people so that they need not go down the same difficult path.

At present no one at this meeting has told us how to break into this circle and initiate change. The members of the Greenwich Forum should give it consideration. but in the DFDS crisis the company was in desperate financial straits and finished by sacking about 400 people from the shore-side of the industry; it is only desperate financial straits that encourage anybody to do anything and that is perhaps the only way we shall break into that circle. The Group believed that we would be much more efficient if we broke the circle earlier and started to think further ahead.

Onshore change

We have heard nothing of the implications of technological change on-shore. Was there any investigation of this – the new systems, computerized systems, computerized systems of freight booking etc – and is a contraction foreseen on-shore in terms of numbers of people employed in the industry, similar to that likely at sea?

Rapporteur's response. The Group did not look at a reduction in numbers of people ashore. In setting the scenario originally, it was noted that we did not just have to consider the ships, but also the overall transport service which is to be provided. The shore organization is very expensive; the operator will not be viable unless his shipboard operation is correspondingly cheap. Whether or not he sells his service depends on the overall picture, and to be successful he must look at economies in both parts of the operation. But we did not specifically consider the shore side.

Trade union questions

There has been mention of making economies in crewing through individuals doing jobs outside their normal or traditional range: firemen pulling on ropes, operators maintaining as well as operating, and so on. These are precisely the things that have caused the most difficulty in factories with regard to union demarcation. Is this – the union aspect of this approach – a problem at sea or are there different considerations from the union point of view?

Rapporteur's response. One difference between factories and ships is that no one has to live in a factory when he works in it. A problem shared by shipowners and unions is that there is – among the ratings – a very rapid turnover in people. Therefore, experienced and skilled men are easily lost, and everybody is interested in retaining people within the industry. Presumably the unions are interested in improving the skills and experience of their members, because in that way they will raise their productivity and raise their wages as well.

There does not seem to be the same problem – as long as change is introduced with proper consultation and with a fairly long lead-time, and half the crew is not suddenly left on the quayside because there is no longer a need for them. It is different from the shore situation.

Rejoinder. The problem may not appear so difficult, but experience in the Sea-life programme showed that this is a buried problem, and it is also a large one not helped by the fact that there are five unions trying to become three. Ultimately, two will remain, and those two are likely to be in conflict for a long time. The matter must be approached slowly, and is best controlled at company level rather than at national level; otherwise there will be a confrontation of the monoliths similar to those we are seeing in other British industries at present. But let no one pretend there is no problem. There is a very difficult territorial problem as far as work on the ship is concerned.

Rapporteur's summary

When the Group started discussions, I thought that we should not come to any consensus at all, but after everybody had put their point of view, we reached a reasonable consensus, and I hope that is what the Forum intended us to do. That consensus does not seem to have been wildly upset by the discussions that have just taken place.

Study Group 4: Regulation of Shipping Movements

Dr J. F. Kemp (Head of School of Navigation, City of London Polytechnic)

The total system to be considered consists of the ships and their cargoes, the sea area, the coastal geography, manning of ships and shore installations, safety requirements, communications networks, regulatory enforcement etc. All these items formed the subject of discussions during which it was borne in mind that each was part of the overall system.

Manning standards

Regulations affecting the movement of shipping can help in improving safety but must be taken together with the need for crews of sufficient number (particularly in the short sea trades) and competence to comply with procedures. Any EEC national can serve legally in any EEC flag ship, thus easing the problem of finding properly qualified crew for some fleets. Greece joining the Community should at least in theory overcome the shortage of officers to man the Greek fleet.

Equipment standards

In order to comply with traffic regulatory schemes, equipment standards are needed for navigation and communications purposes and these must be enforced. The standardization of radio and radar equipment to a common European specification is progressing. Fully international standardization was seen as the ultimate aim.

Enforcement

The impending introduction of a reporting system for defects in ships' equipment was welcomed, but it was suggested that the enforcement of adequate standards should be the responsibility of a central organization such as the Department of Trade. If it is left, as appears to be the intention, to port officers, it was felt that interpretation would vary from port to port and that small ports would not be able to deal satisfactorily with situations which might arise, due to lack of manpower and expertise.

It was suggested that a European Navigation Service (or similar) should be established to devise and enforce both manning and equipment standards.

Subsystems

Accepting that the total system as defined above comprises the complete movement of ships from berth to berth, it was suggested that three subsystems might then be considered: (i) ports; (ii) open sea; (iii) intermediate zones – port to and from open sea. The regulatory requirements for each subsystem were then discussed.

Requirements for ports

In many ports there is already a large measure of regulation and control of marine traffic. Procedures vary from port to port and some standardization on at least a regional basis, perhaps through a European Navigation Service, would be desirable.

Requirements for open sea

There should be a requirement for ships to report their positions, at least to the owners, not less frequently than once per day.

Requirements for intermediate zones

Mandatory reporting points should be established, to which should be added, if necessary, separation schemes, surveillance facilities etc. Satisfactory communications systems and means of identifying ships would be needed. Identification was seen as essential for effective communications and it was felt that the use of transponders for this purpose should be fully explored and evaluated. The Dover Strait and Ushant are examples of intermediate zones which have already been established.

Research needs

It was suggested that research was required to establish the need for further traffic regulation through the analysis of traffic patterns and densities in appropriate areas. The possibility of introducing regulation at various levels to match real needs should be considered and it is desirable to adopt the simplest of the options compatible with the desired level of safety. Methods of assessing safety levels need to be established; casualty records alone are insufficient. Also, investigation and analysis of radio traffic was needed as a prerequisite to the improvement of communications.

There are a number of problems in this area: problems of frequency allocations, limited ranges, VHF etc were all mentioned, but they appear to be capable of solution although they do need to be thoroughly investigated. It was pointed out that on the US coast, some frequencies are actually shared by the railroads.

Format of systems

Regulatory schemes should conform to a general international format but be adapted for local geographical and other requirements. Final schemes should be examined by an IMCO sub-committee consisting largely of experts with recent practical experience, to avoid unrealistic schemes being adopted which have been devised by local bodies with little maritime tradition.

Survey requirements

Many candidate areas for intermediate zones including several around UK coasts, eg the Minches, had been imperfectly surveyed. In such cases, hydrographic surveys must be carried out before regulatory schemes are introduced.

Implementation

It was suggested that direct control of ship movements from a shore station on lines similar to air traffic control would not generally be practicable because of lack of local information concerning individual ships (such as sea state and the presence of small craft which do not show adequately on the surveillance radar) and because of lack of practical expertise on the part of the shore station operators. It was therefore felt that the term 'Operational Information Zone' might usefully describe the regulatory function in the intermediate zones. It was suggested that public pressure will eventually demand more control of marine traffic and that it is important that such schemes are properly considered in advance of public opinion, so that those adopted take a practical form. Some categories of ship such as cross-Channel ferries might safely operate in Operational Information Zones without any control, although subject to monitoring. Other categories, such as large tankers and those carrying noxious cargoes, could be subject to certain controls, although final decisions concerning specific manoeuvres etc would be taken on the ship's bridge.

The reason for exempting the ferries and some other ships regularly and frequently operating in these zones was that it was considered that the competence of their officers was of a high standard and that they would usually be in a better position to make decisions than anyone ashore. What should be done, of course, is to provide them with all the relevant information that is available so that they can make the best decisions possible. We do need to be careful about what regulations are imposed on competent mariners. Additional regulations do not necessarily mean additional safety.

Costs of regulating traffic

It was felt that investigation was needed to estimate the costs of operating regulatory systems at varying levels of sophistication. This would include costs to shipowners from fitting additional equipment and from delays on passage, and also costs to the coastal states operating shore stations. The possible methods of recovering the costs were also discussed and it was suggested that a similar method might be used as for the collection of light dues. However, operating surveillance schemes – communications, radar networks etc – is expensive.

Many non-European flag ships already carry North Sea pilots when navigating in the English Channel and the southern North Sea. It was suggested that the increased use of pilots would, at relatively small expense, help to ensure the proper conduct of ships passing through regulatory zones, and also perhaps help offset low levels of manning.

It was felt important to reinforce the use of IMCO English in order that efficient communication should be established and maintained from ship to shore and from ship to ship. Communications are vital to all aspects of safe operation and regulation of marine traffic.

It was suggested that an important principle should be that no ships should be prohibited from passing through a regulatory zone since this could interfere excessively with the freedom of trade and applied in any of a large number of straits in various parts of the world.

DISCUSSION

Regulations outside port jurisdiction

The control or otherwise of ships which it had hitherto been considered should be exempt from control, needs to be studied carefully in relation to proposed new regulatory schemes. There are occasions where ferries leave ports and rapidly enter international waters. The following experience was reported recently.

The master was proceeding in a very fast ship from the South Goodwin Light Vessel towards Folkestone, anticipating passing the port of Dover, some two miles distant. As he approached the port, doing something in the region of 20-21 knots, a ferry left the Eastern entrance. His ship had a very advanced radar, with advanced collision avoidance procedure capability. The alert officer on the bridge said that another ship had locked on to a collision course and was closing at a speed of 18 knots. The pilot then asked for a track to be kept on it, and in a very short space of time the officer again said that it was still closing on a collision course and had now increased to 20 knots. The ship in transit then reacted; fortunately she had a variable pitch propeller, and reduced speed from 21 to about 14 in a matter of seconds to avoid that collision, only to be confronted by a second ferry leaving Dover which did precisely the same thing; it locked on to a collision course with increasing closing speeds – again 18-20 knots.

The point is this. The ship outward bound had traffic on her port bow and the right of way, but the ferry was locked on to a collision course. The ship with the right of way had to give way to starboard, and finished up a quarter of a mile from the breakwater of Dover Harbour which is a busy port. One cannot pass it without meeting at least four ferries and two Hovercraft, no matter what the speed and what time of the day. There is a case for control of ships even in international waters to prevent that sort of conduct.

Financing equipment

The problem of paying for surveillance schemes and navigational aids was raised. Did the Study Group consider the position of those countries on the intermediate parts of voyages, eg between the Arabian Gulf and Japan, or where adjacent countries are being asked to supply this type of navigational aid, surveillance etc to ships in transit, and there is no mechanism for the beneficiary countries to pay for this aid. How do we pay for this? How do we pay for this 'common good' item supplied by countries – particularly adjacent to straits?

Casualty records

It was stated that little help or information could be derived from casualty reports or records; that was a rather surprising statement. Lloyd's now has a very good databank which can be accessed. It gives the distribution of casualties in the world by squares covering any part of the world: the type of casualty, the flag and the apparent cause. We are not talking about hundreds, but about thousands of ships per annum. It gives those that are total losses, and those that are merely accidents at sea but not a total loss. An analysis of this shows some surprising patterns of casualties emerging – the real accident black spots in the world, of which there are many in addition to the Straits of Dover.

Rapporteur's response. As far as areas like the Malacca Straits are concerned, the Study Group did not come to any conclusion as to how they could be covered.

As regards casualty records, they are helpful when dealing with reasonably large areas. When looking at relatively small areas, eg Land's End, and perhaps trying to decide whether setting up a traffic regulatory scheme is justified, the annual number of collisions or strandings is normally so small that significant trends from year to year cannot be identified. In bigger areas this is possible; looking at general areas where traffic regulatory systems might be introduced, the casualty analysis is perfectly good. For specific areas which may be limited in size to the range of surveillance radar – which makes them generally quite small – it is quite difficult to get statistically reliable results.

Standards of seamanship

With regard to the question of pilots on ferries, we must be extremely careful before we recommend increasing their use. Hundreds of voyages across the channel are made from Dover and Folkestone every year; since the second world war the only ferry that has sunk and had major loss of life was the ferry off Stranraer, and that was not a collision. The standard of seamanship of the masters and officers of those ferries is extremely high, and to start of from one individual case and say that all should be limited would be wrong. The correct way would be to examine the safety record.

The report of this Study Group compliments the masters of cross-Channel ferries, and specifically states that we were thinking of extending them the privilege of not entering into direct control. Although this may appear to be at odds with this contention, it is a direct compliment to the seamanship and competence of the ferries themselves. Pilots only take them out of and into the ports; they do not pilot them across the Channel. The navigation of Hovercraft is also excellent, and needs defending.

CNIS records

The master of the ship transitting past Dover should have reported the incident with the two ferries to the Channel Navigation Information Service (CNIS), which would have been able to take some retrospective action in that there is a photographic record and a videotape record, and they could have identified the ships and called for an explanation later. Of course, CNIS has no control over ferries if they pop out like corks from Champagne bottles.

Standardized procedures

The Study Group report stated practically everything that needs to be considered, but from the practical point of view, one or two points need emphasizing. On the subject of ports, the report mentioned how the procedures vary. Would the Forum consider whether we should not be working towards a service that supplies staff and procedures, rather like Air Traffic Control which is universal, so that when a master comes into the English Channel, for example he knows what he will be told to do, the language in which he will be invited to do it, and if he then goes to, say, Southampton, he will be talking with people with whom he is familiar in recognized language using familiar procedures, and similarly through the Dover Strait and then into London or Rotterdam, talking to people all the time with the same trained disciplines. It is not suggested that HM Coastguard should take this over, but that some other body should take over this part of HM Coastguard's responsibilities.

Communications problems

On the question of communications, which is really the nub of the problem, no initiative is being taken towards making it mandatory for ships to listen to what the CNIS is doing in the Dover Strait. As a ship leaves a port, there is nothing by law to prevent the VHF set being thrown overboard at that moment, and we shall get nowhere until ships are required to set watch; having done so, then they must be required to use a language which everybody can understand.

A recent incident emphasized this need. A Greek ship called up and said he was leaving Folkestone Bay bound for Calais and that he would be steering 081°, which is not a right angle to the main traffic flow. The relevant section of the regulations was read to him, that he should cross at right angles or as near thereto as practicable. He then asked what a right angle was and he was given a course of 135°. Here a very serious mistake was made, because it was not true to say that he should steer 135° without knowing where he had started from, and no one had checked this. He headed off straight for le Colbert Bank. Fortunately the senior watch officer of the CNIS spotted what had happened and the situation then got into a ballgame into which CNIS is definitely not supposed to be drawn; the captain had to be persuaded to turn round as quickly as possible. Fortunately it was possible to do so and he reversed his course and headed back towards Folkestone – the whole time asking what is the right course and being told right angles. The CNIS then managed to talk him round down the south of le Colbert Bank, during the course of which he admitted that the only chart he had on board was a 20 year old small-scale French chart, without any traffic separation lines shown on it.

There are communication difficulties to this day, and although that ship was Greek, it must be emphasized that the Greeks have recently dropped very low on the list of rogues.

Navigation research

The Forum has been told that we need research into any extra regulation which may be forced on us, possibly as a result of public pressures in the wake of another disaster. We do seem to progress from disaster to disaster, but who would carry out the research which we should be doing now on whether speed limits should be introduced or whether there should be no overtaking? There are a number of these concepts which come from road traffic engineering, and others that relate to air traffic, such as streaming where, for example, 20 miles should be kept between VLCCs. We should be doing such research now, so that when we do get what the statisticians tell us is the inevitable nasty accident, we are not then stampeded as we were after the *Amoco Cadiz* accident.

Systems approach

The Study Group report did a good job of summarizing the very diverse opinions of the Group. It was brought out that we do seem to go from crisis to crisis, and that is how our regulations would appear to proceed also. What we are looking for, if we are looking to regulating shipping in the 1990s, is a systems approach to the whole problem, where we look not at manpower alone, nor at traffic separation schemes alone, nor at equipment alone, but at the whole in a total system, where every element is related to the other. If things are to be done for all to be right for the 1990s and before there is some major disaster involving an extremely hazardous cargo, we should get down to thinking most specifically and definitely about a systems approach to the whole matter.

Research on transponder

One of the current research programmes at Liverpool Polytechnic covers transponders. This research is to be carried out on simulators rather than at sea, because one will be able to see what it would be like if everybody had transponders, all of them working properly; it is important to consider the goal we are aiming at before deciding whether to go along that path. It is hoped that this research will take place over the next couple of years – provided that the research budget has not disappeared in the interim.

Code of practice

These discussions have highlighted the need for some kind of agreed code of practice. But this kind of progress can only be made if there is agreement internationally. Although the process may of necessity have to begin at the national level, for any scheme to be fully effective there must be international agreement. It is encouraging that there may be progress on this within IMCO, although as a secretariat IMCO will only undertake what it is requested to do by the member states.

Collision regulations and enforcement costs

The potentially disastrous confusion of traffic in the intermediate zones, and perhaps equally in some port zones, occurs because we rely so much on the experience of individual ferry masters. Is there a case, perhaps, in some of these intermediate zones for looking again at the collision regulations in such restricted areas, as part of the overall picture?

Much expertise is being acquired in the whole field of administration, organization, equipment and systems for surveillance and control in these various zones, but we must remember the extreme cost of some of these items. Perhaps when we start to provide the information, help and expertise abroad, we ought to promulgate a good deal more about the costs before people jump on the bandwagon and start to apply these ideas in various parts of the world. The capital and operating costs are high, and one should not commit oneself lightly to having to pay them.

Chairman's comments

It is difficult for the pilots – in this sort of forum at any rate – to beat the drum about their own expertise without looking as if they are trying to build empires. If it comes to pass that 'Operational Information Zones', for example, are thought to be practical propositions, the people required to operate them are likely to be the pilots. This does not cast any reflection at all upon those who operate so successfully within present limits; the Channel Navigation Information Service, for example. I only say that if the responsibilities within certain zones become more precise, even if these zone are not brought under direct control, then the authority of acknowledged and credible maritime experts, shipmasters, with of course the local knowledge of the pilots, would seem to be indispensable as the basic qualification for the operation of such zones.

With regard to the question of radio traffic analysis introduced in Study Group 4's Report, at risk of repetition, several points are involved. First, there does not seem to have been any general analysis of the way in which radio communications and other electronic communications are utilized today in merchant shipping operations. Second, the rate of change of technology in that area is extremely rapid. Third, the structure of the jobs and the roles in the merchant services at present is such that the radio shack is inhabited by, as often as not, an employee of one of the manufacturers of the equipment – Marconi, or a similar company. He is acknowledged to be an expert, and very much a man apart from the ship's officer core and the operation of the ship in general. He has a highly specialized skill, and however good in his ship, he does not progress in general to a sphere where his expertise can be deployed as a general part of the operational work and development. Therefore, I believe, there has been no serious analysis of these communications problems, and it is for that reason that I would hope that a university or polytechnic might find it possible to undertake, on behalf of the industry, a radio traffic analysis of this kind as the basis for what one can say is probably the cheapest way of achieving operational improvements – namely, by standardized procedures that are appropriate to what has to be done. It is not costly to introduce proper procedures, except that a social psychologist will probably be needed to help get it accepted.

Study Group 5: Land/sea Interface

Professor J.H. Bird (Professor of Geography, University of Southampton)

At the outset it was agreed that the remit should not be interpreted too narrowly, and the day's discussion divided into three broad headings:

(1) the organization of seaports, particularly from the point of view of safety of operation and control;
(2) general trends of British trade, with particular reference to differential development of British ports;
(3) the general relationship between ports and the location of industry.

Seaport organization

Sensitive areas of the land/sea interface are constantly being extended not only in connection with new oil harbours dealing with cargoes that could cause environmental hazards but also because of the increasing pressures for control and responsibility along the coastline outside of harbours (*vide* Commander Richardson's paper). There are a large number of bodies responsible for functions such as lighting, pilotage, hydrographic survey, and traffic surveillance. For example, in the event of a rescue operation a port authority, coastguard, Ministry of Defence, RNLI, and air/sea rescue might all be involved, yet it is nobody's responsibility to act as a coordinator. Apart from this functional separation, there is a real separation of responsibility along the coastline, such that a survey has revealed that about 100 separate bodies have some form of authority for maritime safety.

As far as ports are concerned, many are answerable to nobody but themselves, and are often responsive more to user groups than to the community, which might increasingly expect them to be protectors of the coastal environment. This has already happened in the cases of Rotterdam and Amsterdam where environmental lobbies have successfully blocked port expansion. Thus while the problems of the physical interface have increased, powers to deal with these problems have not kept in step, often hardly changed since the days of the 19th century enabling acts which set up some of the UK's long-established ports. The study group also considered that the powers and scope, and indeed the experience of some ports were insufficient to match the scale of the problems that might suddenly come upon them. A port might find itself dealing with 75 million tons of crude oil per annum, yet still be administered as though it were a local authority answerable only for a local operation. Each port is moreover the judge of its own facilities and organization, and yet it might be just a small group of people responsible for large areas of a very busy waterway; one port authority is responsible for no less than 600 miles^2 of estuarial and coastal waters. Matters have reached a pass where we expect such old-established bodies to bear responsibilities for which they are not qualified.

20 years ago the move towards rationalization was based on the concept of estuarial grouping – an areal or regional approach. The Study Group now sees a need for a functional approach but the possibility of a new root and branch organizational change appeared to be impractical in view of the mass of legislation which would be

necessary to dismantle the present system. The following three-stage step-by-step approach is therefore recommended.

(I)   Establish a national quality control and coordination system in a code to deal with safety, conservancy, and environmental coastal protection, to bring some order into the present chaos.

(II) Because of the plethora of existing bodies, we should build a requirement function on to the existing structures, such that for example there should be a standard code of control and practice for each harbour and intervening stretch of coastline.

(III) Finally, an attempt should be made to cut away overlap of existing intertwined responsibility. This tier of national involvement is necessary because at present safety is often being handled solely within a commercial context.

The Group realized that port licences were already required for explosives, meat, and passengers, that North Sea oil spillage had been dealt with under a recent plan, and that IMCO is considering hazardous cargoes for which individual by-laws are in operation; but the group nevertheless feels that the UK should give a lead in attempting to integrate these initiatives. This could be effected in cooperation with work being done in Common Maritime Traffic Systems by the European Communities Committee for cooperation in Scientific and Technical Research (Project 301). In this area we finally recommend that the Greenwich Forum should draw these problems to the attention of the UK Royal Commission on the Pollution of the Environment. The moves for any integration of traffic control should be allied to a European port information bank based on a European network of complete information about vessel movement available to a VDU system.

We feel that ports are often not aware of the special nature of oil exploration feeder traffic – the urgency requirements of the service for example – and it would be helpful if southern and west coast ports which may be developed in this field could keep themselves fully up-to-date with current experience of the North Sea operation (eg the recent Channel Offshore '80 conference at Southampton).

British trade trends and impact on ports

The Study Group believes that the swing to European traffic in UK national trade (see K.A. Heathcote's paper, Table 1) will be confirmed and increase possibly in the 1990s as a trend away from what can now be seen as a 19th century aberration – an empire based on long-distance markets and suppliers encouraged and protected under Imperial Preference. Instead UK markets and supplies are reverting where possible to their nearest neighbours – the proximate market. This trend may be accelerated by the need to avoid the high energy costs of long voyages. At present the European Communities have a North Sea focus which has given great stimulus to ports of the Tyne–Solent coastal facade. When the Communities become enlarged to include the southern European countries of the Mediterranean, a circumferential new sea-route round the Iberian Peninsula may give a stimulus to UK west coast ports.

We observed the forecast in Michael Graham's paper that penetration of container ships into world liner trade will increase from 50% to 75% by 1990. However, container vessels may themselves be under threat from the part-bulker or the scheduled bulker, as shipowners respond to the lure of Mr Meek's dream of a simple, slow ship. The cellular container ship may turn out to be too sophisticated for some cargoes, and concepts like the bulk packaged timber ship and the car carrier may be extended to other trades. In *Lloyd's List*, 24 April 1980, there was notice of a

6 900 ton deadweight bulk chemical carrier that could be adapted for bulk whisky! It would make life certainly easier for the port if more loading and unloading could be arranged through side-ports eliminating the costly quayside cranes for lo-lo operations, and perhaps enabling the naval archietect to design a cheaper, simpler, and stronger box cross-section for the hull. In short, we believe that ships may become more versatile, but would stress that a minority of British cargo is deep-sea, and a minority of British cargo is non-bulk.

All the signs are that there are more than enough berths in Britain to cope with the present trade, but we must reiterate the point that came out in the discussion of Mr Heathcote's paper – the requirements and future of British merchant shipping do not match the evolution of the direction of British trade routes.

Relationship between ports and the location of industry

Based on the Rotterdam-Europort model, the Midas (Marine Industrial Development Areas) project was promoted some ten years ago. These schemes were based on the idea that the source of bulk materials required by primary industry was increasingly the port and that therefore inland transport costs would be minimized if that primary industry, together with the secondary and tertiary industry dependent on it, was located in industrial areas immediately adjacent to the port. The idea did not catch on in this country although the French promoted such developments at Dunkirk, Le Havre and Marseilles-Fos. One could recapitulate the remark in K. Heathcote's paper: 'It is the ports which are generated by the economic activity, however much it might be the other way around in an underdeveloped country'. In case Teesside should be cited as an example of a successful Mida, we would point out that this industrialized estuary has been developed by steady increments on a historic industrial base since the middle of the 19th century and is not a greenfield, or bluecoast, Mida planned *ab initio.*

This led the group to believe that completely new ports were also unlikely in view of the necessity to fit in with the existing network of major roads which itself was unlikely to be adapted for the sake of a new port, even if the present over-provision of berths in many existing ports did not make that unlikely anyway. We expect to see berths grow and decay in existing ports, a different emphasis of present stance rather than a major step forward.

One initiative, which might affect port areas such as the Isle of Dogs, is the designation of enterprise zones for small manufacturing industry as outlined in the Chancellor's 1980 budget speech. These zones will be 'minimum regulation tones' freed from much of local authority and planning legislation, but not free of customs zones, for this would be contrary to the Treaty of Rome, although existing freeports like Hamburg have not yet been abolished; the advantage of the siting of these zones in ports would be their short communications to export markets.

The group would be in favour of more experiments using barges along the lines of the Dutch Bacat system on the Aire and Calder Navigation; this ran into trades union difficulties, and the Study Group believes that novel solutions may be frustrated by social and political factors of a tradition-focused workforce. We appreciate that the dockers draw strength from the National Dock Labour scheme, but have to note the popularity of non-scheme ports, and the energy displayed by new trades, such as the North Sea oil supply industry, in avoiding ports that have poor or inflexible labour practices.

In conclusion, the Group was fully aware that the land/sea interface was a much wider question than the subject of seaports, but the discussion seemed to show that because ports exist to mediate between land and sea traffic, many problems that arise in the interface do so with greatest acuteness in seaport areas.

DISCUSSION

Artificial islands

Did the Study Group consider the development of offshore islands for port terminals as a possibility? The Group states that it is unlikely that there will be further new ports, but there is considerable resistance in Europe at present to the siting of noxious and dangerous industries within existing port areas, whether it be at Canvey Island or the Dutch industrial areas. From time to time artificial islands have been put forward as a proposal – that perhaps some joint port development in the North Sea between the Dutch and the British, for LNG terminals and so on, might be a possibility.

Rapporteur's response. The Group did not discuss such ports. My own feeling is that the idea of the 'no port' or the offshore port is generally only considered for liquid cargo. The difficulty is that the port is always having to mediate between land and sea traffic, and if it is offshore, by definition it is not doing a very good job for the land traffic. I take it that the offshore port is mainly concerned with bulk liquids to some other installation by pipeline, or some form of transshipment, but in the present investment state of many ports I do not think it has been considered.

Group member's comments. The rapporteur stated that the topic of offshore island ports was not discussed. This was principally because the members of the Group were all conscious that the general subject of the land–water interface is a very large subject, and the amount of ground that could be covered was fairly limited. Three topics of interest were therefore selected and focused on. But there is a large number of other subjects that could have been discussed.

Royal Commission on Environmental Pollution

The Commission on Environmental Pollution is currently undertaking a study of oil pollution of the sea caused by routine discharges and accidents. The Greenwich Forum was asked to make comments to the Commission, and we should certainly take the matter up after this conference. Because the Commission is still taking evidence, many points raised in this Study Group's report are of great relevance in this respect.

Project 301

Can we be given a fuller explanation of Project 301?

Rapporteur's response. Project 301 stems from the EEC's Committee for Cooperation in Scientific and Technical Research. It is essentially an EEC subcommittee on new means of transport which considers a variety of topics, including electric trams. Marine transport is one of these topics. Until now, this subcommittee has only held one meeting; this meeting considered a draft proposal concerned with working towards some commonality in maritime traffic systems as they exist around EEC waters. This extends slightly from the points that have been made in the discussions in

Groups 4 and 5, particularly that we should have some standardization; but by standardization what we mean here is that there should be some basis of common procedure throughout all these marine traffic systems – some skeleton common procedure upon which the flesh of local requirements can later be added. This project has yet to get underway. In EEC terms progress is quite good: it takes only a year to get a proposal agreed. The procedure is that the subcommittee first looks at those areas around EEC waters where it is felt there is a need for some traffic regulation or management, ie areas where something is going wrong at present. Having identified them then it is considered what usefully could be done to reduce accidents in those areas. The work seems to be concentrating on two points. First, a report on the work to be carried out on reduction of collision has already been drafted. A collision happens basically because no one knows where the ship is – the way to get around this, perhaps, is through better traffic information.

The second subject is that of groundings. We all know that ships go aground because there is insufficient water, but they usually find the insufficient water because they are out of position, so the shore base would look towards providing better position-fixing information.

It will be about a year before the Project actually starts, and there are great hopes that something useful will emerge as guidelines which all EEC member states can develop for their own sea areas.

Chairman of the presentation of Study Group reports and following discussion was Vice-Admiral Sir Ian McGeoch KCB DSO DSC.

BACKGROUND COMMENT

BRITISH SHIPPING: CAUSES FOR CONCERN

G. J. Bonwick (Mercantile Consultants and Investments)

My name appears on the List of Participants at this Forum immediately below Sir Frederick Bolton, which must be the closest that he and I have been on anything. 14 years ago we had a slight disagreement in the *Financial Times*. He did not agree when I wrote that 'The British shipping industry's record in modern times gives cause for serious national concern and certainly does not inspire confidence in the future'. I did not agree when he wrote that British shipping led the world 'not necessarily in size of fleet but in efficiency and competitiveness'. In my opinion, it did not then, it does not now, and never will again.

I refer back briefly to October and November 1966, which was probably the most dramatic peacetime year in the long history of British merchant shipping. Some weeks later, when it became clear that Sir Frederick had terminated the engagement with me, the Investors' and Shareholders' Association took the industry to task in the *Financial Times*. It stated that it had closely studied the industry for many months on behalf of its shipping investors and did not like what it had seen. This was 'an industry with vast potential but little or no achievement; an industry earning *a derisory return on capital employed* [which hardly supports Mr Bolton's claim that it leads the world in efficiency and competitiveness]; and an industry in which nepotism obtains on a colossal scale', etc.

1966 was a dramatic year by any criteria – perhaps traumatic would better describe it: this was the year of the British seamen's strike, the year of Lord Pearson's shipping Court of Inquiry, and the year the establishment of a Committee of Inquiry into Shipping was announced from Downing Street. This was on 16 June 1966, less than a month after I had strongly recommended it to Labour Minister Ray Gunter in an attempt – unsuccessful as it happened – to break the strike deadlock. I suggested that a thorough and impartial investigation of the industry was long overdue. Like the Investors' and Shareholders' Association I had looked at the industry, though for many years longer, and had not liked what I saw either. I mention these issues purely to illustrate that my concern for shipping has deep roots.

In fact, it goes back farther still. I am well aware that others, with far greater knowledge than mine, share my concern but, unfortunately, are not in the independent position to express it publicly.

My company is as stated on the List of Participants. Its title is somewhat misleading for its consultancy work is negligible nowadays and will soon be non-existent. Although it has been established for 30 years it remains a very small, very private, very unimportant 'family' firm. It is also very unusual, probably unique, because almost all its assets are invested in the equities of many quoted shipping companies or industrial companies with shipping subsidiaries. Shipping is the only business we know something about, and the only one that interests us.

These remarks were distributed at the meeting and not included in the original programme.

We usually avoid shipping conferences, seminars and so on like the plague. Why then are we here? Simply because a conference with the main ingredients and potential of this one appealed to us enormously. First, it was to be *the* first of its kind, impartial and quite uncommercial. Second, it had the active support of the Royal Navy with its unparalleled organizational ability, resources and facilities. Third, it had at its disposal the trained, disciplined and incisive minds of Forum academics *from outside the industry* – independent thinkers who, with no axe to grind and able to take an objective posture, would, we understood, combine with industry experts over three days to 'examine the various problems which will confront our shipping concerns in ten years' time'.

We had our misgivings. We were puzzled by the involvement in a conference, with its main focus on *British* Shipping, of the *International* Chamber of Shipping, the *International* Shipping Federation, the EEC and the *United Nations* agencies, – UNCTAD, IMCO and ILO. Further, we knew the industry's traditional antipathy towards academics and serious researchers. We particularly had in mind Political and Economic Planning in 1959, Professor Sturmey in the early 1960s, and the Rochdale Committee in the late 1960s. We wondered how leaders of what is universally regarded as an ultra-conservative industry would react to a Forum largely manned by academics.

When we read the first document, 'The Present Position', we sensed that the Forum had ventured into far deeper water than it realized. It did not describe a position that *we* recognized. It read almost like a fairy story, in the 'fairies at the bottom of the garden' sense. This reminds us of a news item in the *Daily Express*, 25 October 1979, which explained that the name of the Portsmouth–Gosport ferry *Gay Enterprise* had been changed to *Solent Enterprise* because, when it was launched nine years earlier, a director said, 'the word 'gay' had no obvious connotations'. Surely it cannot be true that 'our traditional ports are almost empty of ships?' Surely, 'the modern shipowner' is not as described? Surely, as a *general* proposition, hazards have *not* been increased because crews have been reduced.

On the subject of reduced crews we drew the Department of Trade's attention to a recent, quite extraordinary case. This concerned the calls made by a small (500-ton deadweight) Panamanian-flag vessel at three British ports. She had a crew of only three, which included the young captain's young wife! The vessel was trading in the Baltic and North Sea at the time, among the oil rigs! Perhaps a DoT representative here will explain how this could be allowed to happen. We asked on 18 February 1980 when we furnished full details of ship, ports visited and cargoes carried, but have yet to receive even an acknowledgment, let alone reply. After all, coming from abroad she had to report to UK Customs and Immigration. Number of crew had to be stated on separate documents. She had to clear outwards with Customs and here again the number of crew had to be stated. If this was an example of Department of Trade alertness and supervision in the UK, as we believe it to be, we had better think of something rather more effective, and quickly.

It would be too easy to dismiss this incident by saying this could only happen under a foreign flag of convenience. Unfortunately, it can also happen under the British flag of convenience, in fact, under UK registry. In December 1979 a UK vessel, only slightly smaller than the Panamanian mentioned, was wrecked on the South Coast soon after leaving Par with a cargo of china clay for Rotterdam. She, too, had a complement of only three, though this had nothing to do with the casualty, as far as we are aware. She, too, had reported the number of crew on Customs documentation.

Claims are often made for British shipping to distinctions it does not possess – world leadership etc. The small ship just mentioned gave British shipping a distinction it did possess but did not even know it had! She was part-owned by a lady who, although she was not on board at the time, was her regular Master. Furthermore, at one stage in 1979 she also had a lady First Mate!

Reverting to the document 'The Present Position', there is nothing whatsoever in it to indicate awareness of the industry's plight, referred to by Professor Watt in his opening remarks. Nor of its absolute decline in the past five years – in round figures by some 500 ships and 7 million gross tons to 1500 of 24.75 million at the present time. No appreciation of the fact that without foreign-owned or controlled tonnage the UK would rank not only after Liberia, Japan and Greece, as at present, but also after Norway, Panama, the USA, and the USSR. Of course, the foreign-owned proportion has been increasing for many years, although it is rarely mentioned publicly here. We wonder why. Are we ashamed? The fact remains that today, around 27% of the fleet in ship terms and 44% in gross tonnage terms are owned or controlled overseas. In addition, many overseas companies have an equal or minority interest in a considerable number of UK-registered ships and volume of tonnage through joint ventures with UK companies. We asked in *Lloyd's List* on 29 February 1980, 'How British is British?' From the heavy volume of correspondence and telephone calls we received from people within the industry few realized the extent of foreign ownership.

As we have said, there is no inkling in 'The Present Position' that its compilers comprehend the seriousness of the present position. Even the Chairman of the Furness Withy group observed a month ago that he was 'disturbed' by the fact that the amount of dry cargo imports carried by UK-registered ships had been declining by between 2½% and 3% per annum over the past ten years. Perhaps he would have been even more 'disturbed' if he had realized the declining proportion of UK-*owned* ships among the UK-*registered* ships he mentioned. Mr Peter Sharpe has gone so far as to suggest that only the appointment of a Shipping Supremo, probably by the government, could save British shipping – and it would take that Maritime Messiah 10-15 years! He spoke of the industry as a possible survivor, not as a world leader. At least he is giving the matter serious thought.

When we read 'The Present Position' our enthusiasm gave way to depression, almost despair. It seemed to us absolutely essential to know where we were before we could set course for where we wanted to go. We sensed that whatever the quality of the papers eventually presented, however distinguished and expert the participants, however lively the question and answer sessions, this Conference, a splendid conception, could not possibly achieve its objectives. It seemed to us then as it does now, that there was not the remotest prospect of 'what needs to be done from now on to ensure the health of the industry in the closing years of the 20th century and beyond' being even touched on, let alone discussed. In our view there was no chance whatsoever of this conference doing what *Lloyd's List* said it would only last Friday, namely 'thrash out British maritime policy'.

We recently provided most of the documentation for a private meeting of businessmen and others to discuss various aspects of British shipping. It included a lengthy, hypercritical look at the industry as we saw it. We readily accept that our vision may have been blurred by bias. Nevertheless, it occurred to us that an updated, modified version might be of limited use to the Forum, if only as a starting point. We deleted sections suitable for a small private meeting but not for a large public gathering and introduced a few iconoclastic cartoons, many carefully selected quotations (some by participants, incidentally), Press headlines, etc. Also, very many critical observations from the Rochdale Report which seemed to escape notice in 1970 and have escaped it ever since. The result is *British Shipping: an Independent Study*. Independent, but decidedly not objective. It attempts to portray the industry as it is and, very briefly, how it got here. It does not suggest where it is going though the front cover may provide a pointer to the future. It depicts a sinking ship, Ensign at half-mast, and across her stern the name *British Shipping*.

The study begins with the following quotation from the Rochdale Report which, we suggest, is apposite and topical today: 'Shipping ranks as one of our major industries. The efficient use of the capital and labour it employs is therefore properly of concern to the whole nation, as well as to those directly-engaged in the industry or relying on its services'. It ends with the statement: 'If this study inspires further thought and discussion about the industry and its future it will have achieved its purpose'.

IV. Chairman's Conclusion

CLOSING ADDRESS

Professor Donald Cameron Watt (Chairman, Greenwich Forum)

When we set up this Conference, we had the idea that in ten to 15 years time the crisis which had already overtaken British shipping would be very much worse. We thought that there was very little lead time; but we thought too that today's middle management in the shipping industry, in politics and elsewhere, might have a chance now, with time to think, of developing some thoughts, if subjected to some intellectual stimulus, as to how to deal with problems that they might well be wringing their hands over in 15 years time. We hoped that as a result of this Conference those concerned with British shipping could subject themselves to what might perhaps be described as pre-match training, and possibly even develop some pre-match discussion on strategy. We saw the challenges being faced by shipping as involving both political and technological aspects: political in the challenges from the Soviet bloc, in the continuing challenge from the USA in its efforts to impose its own way of doing things on everbody else, and from what we still persist in calling the Third World, although I must say that to lump it all together seems now to have reached the stage of being totally misleading.

We thought in terms of the technological challenges which arise partly out of the anticipated energy shortages in the 1990s, and partly from the communications revolution already overtaking us. We hoped – although we would possibly not elicit a whole set of replies to these challenges, and accepted that any idea that out of this Conference would come a blueprint for the 1990s or something like that, was obviously far too ambitious – we hoped, however, that we would elicit something more than a preliminary clearing of throats before the answer itself began to emerge.

Speaking as somebody who has attended one of the groups and listened to the conversations here – both formal and informal – I feel remarkably pleased with the outcome of the Conference. There has been a considerable degree of communication. Some issues have emerged quite clearly, and I hope when the papers are published the participants will agree that they attended something that was worth attending – if they do not hold that conviction already.

We have, of course, regrets. The representation from the shipping industry was not perhaps as full as we should have liked it to have been. It certainly was not as full on the trades union side as we should have liked it to have been, and port management – with the exception of somebody from the Port of London Authority – is almost entirely absent. Another very conspicuous absentee from this discussion, as indeed from all discussions so far, has been anybody from marine insurance, and I do wonder how much longer, in the light of the increased disasters that are overtaking the marine insurers, they can go on taking the attitude they have taken hitherto that their job is simply and purely a commercial operation of calculating and spreading risks. I wonder too how it is that the possible actions they might themselves take to diminish such risks is not something that they are prepared to think about, or if they do think about it, to discuss it with anybody else.

I see signs in the work of the International Maritime Insurance Forum and other bodies that minds are being changed, but if minds need to be changed fast anywhere, it is possibly in that corner. As there are no representatives from marine insurance present I feel I can perhaps be a little more free on this subject than I might be on others.

As to what has emerged from the Conference as it struck me as a Chairman, and observer, a lot of it was very familiar ground. Or possibly I can put it this way; the ground was not familiar, but the formation of the terrain was only too familiar – policy-making problems, problems of communication, and a rather horrible feeling that everyone was sitting around saying that somebody else should do something.

The Forum, or rather the proposals that led to the setting up of the Forum, stemmed from a very similar experience centred more on the offshore business than anything else, but I had an extraordinary feeling of *déjà vu* many times during the Conference, perhaps no more so than when sitting in – not at Mr Heathcote's Paper, which was comparatively calm – but sitting in on Group 5 listening to Mr Heathcote and his colleagues outlining the extraordinary position that relates in the matter of security and safety in ports; the multiplication of authorities, the overlapping, the lack of clear division of responsibility, the extraordinary procedures by which nobody can talk to somebody else unless they go through some intermediary, and so on. This was all very familiar.

If I may sum up the specifics. The first, and most serious, point to emerge – as a result of the discussion on the first paper – was this. If there is a need for British policy, facing the challenge from the Group of 77-plus at UNCTAD and elsewhere, as it were to anticipate the formulation of proposals by the UNCTAD staff by 'educating' them (and I put that rather carefully in quotation marks) in the realities of the shipping world before their proposals come to be too clearly formulated and become too much a part of the political bargaining process to be very easily moderated, then it seems to me there is going to be a need for some kind of enhanced machinery of cooperation between the shipping industry and government, and between those and the other parts of the political party process in the UK, so that a definite strategy may be evolved. So far as I understand it, at this stage there has been a fair amount of consultation, but it is clearly going to have to be deepened and developed. It will have to find much more of a political echo in Parliament and elsewhere than it has done so far, and in the press outside the shipping press than it has so far, because it is, after all, not merely a technical issue. It is an issue on which the wealth, employment and the future security of the country depend to a considerable extent, and it is no longer a matter for a fairly small number of people who have been in the industry all their lives, and a fairly small part of the machinery of government, which from the point of view of their political overlords regards this as a technical matter, as though it was something to do with the rates of postage on international stamps, or something of that sort.

I think this applies equally to the evolution of a British policy in what might be described as the European interface. That message seemed to come very clearly out of Group 1, and I hope it will be noticed. Equally it seemed to me that in the pleas that are being put forward from interested parties – and we are all interested parties in our own sense here – the idea of the academic as in some way a sort of slightly empty-brained unrealistic outside observer with no interests of his own who can therefore decide issues without being complicated by personal feelings (which always was an unrealistic idea) is particularly unrealistic today. Academics, especially engineers and technologists, are as interested as anyone today. There is nevertheless obviously a gap in communication at present between government and industry on the question of the commissioning of research, not perhaps so much on the scientific side, but on the side of the human and social implications and inhibitions on commercial, economic and technological developments.

Some discussions raised in my mind the question of whether industry was perhaps as well staffed at the level of a military General Staff as it might be. The role of a General Staff officer in the Armed Forces is of course not to take decisions. It is to provide alternative decisions, and a reasonable case for them, for the man in command to reach a decision. It does not always work as well as it might in the Armed Forces, but on occasion, given the right personnel and the right staff, it does work and has worked extremely well. It did cross my mind while listening to some of the discussion as to whether some parts of the shipping industry were not confusing the two and overloading their principal decision makers so that they had neither the time nor the inclination to listen to staffs, nor indeed had the staffs of the right quality at their disposal. Whether this is a matter for individual companies, or whether it is a matter for the General Council of British Shipping, or whether individual companies do not use the General Council of British Shipping's facilities as well as they might, or what that is, is a question which I simply pose. I certainly do not know anything like enough about it to answer it, and nor indeed do I think it would be my place to do so unless I was either asked to look at it or could speak with a great deal more authority than I would dream of assuming at present.

The third point which seemed to emerge, is that one very severe aspect of the 1990s, the energy crisis, will not be met by any single new set of developments. It will be met by a mix, the precise nature of which is something that we still have a little time – not very much perhaps – to think about. There is a need now to prepare for the strategy of the mix, or the different kinds of mixes which are likely to be put together at that time. The world of oil propulsion will not end with a bang. It will end with phut-phut-phut like any tank that runs out of petrol, but before that phut-phut period eventuates a lot of serious thinking can be done now to prevent being caught short at the wrong moment.

When it comes to the question of training in preparation for that, we have Captain Holder's reminder that the lead time in education is perhaps longest of all. I was impressed by how short the design time appears to be in shipping. If one thinks of lead time in design in terms of the air industry or other high technological areas, one is talking in terms of ten years' lead time between a design and any new concept actually coming into operation. Two-and-a-half years is remarkable. If it is true, it is a great compliment to the way in which the shipbuilding and the shipping industry work together. But in educational terms ten years is but as yesterday, and fifteen years is not very long, and it is now that the thinking has to be done since the universities and the technical colleges – and where shipping is concerned, far more work is being done in the technical colleges than the universities at the moment – do not have very much time to prepare for this. They are entering a period, not in which there is going to be no growth whatever, but one of very great contraction, and one in which any new developments will require some very special extra efforts and some injection of emergency funds from somewhere to bring them about.

I know this very well because the course that we introduced at the London School of Economics last year for trying to train people to run 200-mile zones on their own could not possibly have taken place on existing university funds. It could only be done on a basis of a grant from a foundation to prime the pump, and it must be self-financing when the grant runs out. There was no way I could have got the proposals accepted without their being put on that basis. It also required an enormous amount of goodwill and a great deal of extra energy. That, academics – particularly the best kind who are represented in the Greenwich Forum – can produce, but they need to know that the rest of the support will be forthcoming, and they need to know, if anything is to be done in time, in a very, very short period of time from now.

The last point that occurred to me – and again it is a question mark which I put here rather than anything else – is that it is easier to see the problem than to see how genuine proposals for initiatives can be put forward in such a way that they will be acted upon. The Forum has been criticized in the past for being a talking shop. Businessmen have said with some force that we have three nice days at Greenwich; we spend three days away from our offices, and then at the end, what have we got out of it? Why do we not do something? Well, we try to do what we can. At least we are now publishing our papers, which we never succeeded in doing before, but we are a very small organization with no money, all of whose members are operating full-time in at least two or three other walks of life apart from their responsibilities in the Forum.

Within this whole world of Britain's shipping and maritime interests, it is not enough, clearly, for this, and other conferences to produce proposals unless, somehow or other, goodwill and machinery can be evolved for taking advantages of them and putting them into action. The proposals put forward in such conferences do not always commend themselves to the people concerned. They are not well enough informed; they come quite possibly from people outside the industry; the inhibitions are not there. Nevertheless, industry and government must take advantage of them and talk to one another so that they can evolve their own own way of taking initiatives and their own way of translating suggested initiatives into action, otherwise the reaction to the challenges that come will be, as everybody has said, piecemeal. It will be too late. It will be as the reaction to the *Amoco Cadiz* crisis. It will come as a result of public outrage. And although perhaps we are not getting the best example at present from across the Atlantic, staggering from one crisis to another or from one disaster to another like an old beat-up drunk is neither a very happy nor a very fitting path for the inhabitants of Britain, with its long and excellent maritime tradition and record (and the pride, I hope, that still goes with it). It is not the example that we want to give to the rest of the world, and I, for one, am not at all happy with being regarded as the sick old man of Europe, admired because we have the *Cutty Sark,* we have the beautiful buildings of Greenwich, we have the wonderful ships of the past. But as to the present, being made to take second place, or third place, or seventh place to Koreans, to Japanese, to our fellows on the European mainland, and so on, I do not think is a good thing. I do not think that anybody in the Greenwich Forum thinks it is a good thing. And I see no reason why it should be if we can only evolve ways of translating the initiatives that are suggested – and there is certainly no lack of intellectual ability and farsightedness here – to take advantage.

That concludes the sermon. There will be no collection. It remains my very pleasant and happy duty to express our thanks to the Admiral President of the Royal Naval College, Greenwich, for the superb hospitality that we have enjoyed, and for the care and efficiency with which his staff have looked after us, and all the other care and attention that has been put into making this Conference a success. We are very grateful to them, and without the support that we have enjoyed from the Royal Naval College, this Conference and its predecessors, and I hope its successors, would not be possible.

I have also to express our thanks to the speakers, to the chairmen of the Groups, to the rapporteurs, who have worked under such pressure to produce their reports. I have also to express personal thanks to Mr Farthing and to the General Council of British Shipping for the aid and advice that he gave in setting up the Conference, and our thanks to the Ship and Maritime Transport Requirements Board for the support they gave in staging this Conference.

This has been a very enjoyable Conference; one of the best we have had in terms of warmth of personal relations and liveliness of discussions. It has been a remarkable personal educational experience for me, and speaking for myself – not for the Forum or for anybody else – I am very grateful.

Dr Clive Archer	Lecturer in International Relations University of Aberdeen
Mr Albert J. Almond	Engineer The Marconi International Marine Co Ltd
Dr S.H. Amin	Economics Department Dundee College of Technology
Mr Michael Baily	Shipping Correspondent *"The Times"*
Mr D.J. Ball	Senior Project Developer Ocean Marine Division Ocean Transport
Professor J.H. Bird	Professor of Geography University of Southampton
Mrs P. Birnie (Greenwich Forum)	Lecturer in Public International Law University of Edinburgh
Professor R.E.D. Bishop CBE FRS (Greenwich Forum)	Kennedy Research Professor of Mechanical Engineering University College London
Mr Charles Blyth OBE	Chairman National Dock Labour Board
Sir Frederick Bolton MC	President, International Shipping Federation Chairman, Ship and Marine Technology Requirements Board
Mr George J. Bonwick	Director Mercantile Consultants and Investments
Mr A.P.F. Brown	Senior Lecturer Department of History and International Affairs Royal Naval College
Mr Maxwell Bruce QC	Member of Planning Council International Ocean Institute
Mr P.J.A. Burnyeat	Secretary General International Ship Suppliers Association

Mr Michael St E. Burton	Head of Maritime, Aviation and Environment Department Foreign and Commonwealth Office
Mr Alan W. Cafruny	Graduate Student Cornell University, USA
Mr Brian Cain	General Manager (Sales) Offshore Supply Association Ltd
Lieutenant Commander C.R.K. Cameron RN Honorary Secretary Greenwich Forum	Senior Lecturer Department of History and International Affairs Royal Naval College
Mr A.S. Carter	Managing Director F.I. Trewent & Proctor Ltd
Mr Stanley Clinton Davis MP	Member of Parliament (L) for Hackney Central and Opposition Spokesman on Trade
Rear Admiral A.J. Cooke	Admiral President Royal Naval College
Mr T.A. Coombs	Manager, Mechanical and Civil Engineering Group National Research Development Corporation
Professor A.D. Couper (Greenwich Forum)	Professor of Maritime Studies UWIST
Dr C.T. Cragg	Associate Editor *Sea Trade*
Mr Peter R. Crewe	Head of Research British Hovercraft Corporation Ltd
Captain T.K. Cropper RN	Dean of the College Royal Naval College
Dr K.D. Crosbie	Marine Technology Directorate Science Research Council
Miss Aline F.M. De Bievre	London School of Economics and Political Science
Mr Nigel Despicht	Specialist Adviser to House of Lords Select Committee on the European Communities

Mr John Edmondson	Managing Editor *Marine Policy*
Captain R.K.N. Emden DSC RN	Regional Controller HM Coastguard Dover
Mr Roy Farndon	Editor *Lloyd's List*
Mr C.R. Ford	Head of Marine Technology and Naval Architecture Southampton College of Higher Education
Mr Richard J. Gage	Maritime Administration Representative United States Embassy London
Dr T.F. Gaskell	Executive Secretary E & P Forum
Mr D.L. Giles	Giles Thorneycroft Associates Ltd
Mr David Goodrich	Director and General Manager British Ship Research Association
Mr Peter Goodwin	Consultant Economist Intelligence Unit Ltd
Mr Michael Graham	Overseas Containers Ltd
Mr D.P. Green	Sub-Editor *Marine Policy*
Mr Michael Grey	Managing Editor *Fairplay International Shipping Weekly*
Mr Colin Grimsey	Assistant Secretary, Ports Directorate Department of Transport
Rear Admiral E.F. Gueritz CB OBE DSC	Director Royal United Services Institute for Defence Studies
Mr William Hall	Shipping Correspondent *Financial Times*
Mr C.P.B. Hardcastle (Greenwich Forum)	Managing Director Scrimgeour Hardcastle & Co
Mr K.A. Heathcote	Joint Secretary National Ports Council

Captain Leonard Holder (Greenwich Forum)	Head of Maritime Studies Liverpool Polytechnic
Miss Anne Holmes	News Editor *Marine Week*
Mr John Holt	Senior Lecturer in Maritime Economics Liverpool Polytechnic
Mr A.H.E. Hood	Member of Executive Committee United Kingdom Pilots' Association
Mr H.C. Hooper	Member of Executive Committee United Kingdom Pilots' Association
Captain G.L. Hope RN	Assistant Hydrographer Ministry of Defence (Navy)
Mr L.G. Hudson OBE	Past Chairman Indian Conferences
Dr N.M. Hunnings	Editorial Director European Law Centre
Reverend Glyn Jones	Senior Chaplain Port of London (Missions to Seamen)
Mr L.G. Jeffreys	Assistant General Manager The Salvage Association
Mr George Kejoa	London School of Economics and Political Science
Dr J.F. Kemp	Head of School of Navigation City of London Polytechnic
Lord Kennet	Member of House of Lords
Lady Kennet (Elizabeth Young) (Greenwich Forum)	Writer
Mr J. Kinahan	Special Services Officer National Union of Seamen
Professor J.R.A. Lakey	Department of Nuclear Science and Technology Royal Naval College
Mr J.P. Lancaster-Smith	Director of the Passenger Shipping Association

Mr F.G. Larminie (Greenwich Forum)	General Manager Environment Control Centre British Petroleum Company Ltd
Captain P.A. Leighton	Director of Marine Operations Port of London Authority
Mr D.E. Lennard Honorary Treasurer Greenwich Forum	Director D.E. Lennard and Associates Ltd
Mr Eric Loewy	Partner – Sir William Halcrow and Partners
Captain B.R. Longworth RN	Director The University of Manchester
Captain B.R. Longworth RN	Director Royal Naval Staff College
Dr A.V. Lowe	Faculty of Law The University of Manchester
Mr P.R. Lyon	Principal Marine Officer National Ports Council
Dr I.R. McCallum	Department of Maritime Studies UWIST
Mr T. Macduff	Chief Representative for the United Kingdom Bureau Veritas
Vice Admiral Sir Ian McGeoch KCB DSO DSC (Greenwich Forum)	Editor: *The Naval Review* Editorial Director: *Naval Forces*
Mr G.L. Marchand	Maritime Counsellor French Embassy London
Dr C.M. Mason (Greenwich Forum)	Lecturer in Politics Glasgow University
Mr Marshall Meek	Technical Director British Shipbuilders
Mr T. John Metcalf R.D.	Personal Assistant to the Chairman Gulf Shipping Lines Ltd
Mr Iain Millar	Head of Ship Support Unit National Maritime Institute

Mr A.F. Molland	Lecturer in Ship Science University of Southampton
Mr K.A. Moore	Assistant Manager General Council of British Shipping
Professor Peter Nailor (Greenwich Forum)	Professor of History and International Affairs Royal Naval College
Mr Christopher Nevill	Assistant to the Manager – Commercial Division Marine Navigation Co Ltd
Mr G.B.M. Oliver	Assistant Director, Technical Services National Ports Council
Mr J.A.H. Paffett (Greenwich Forum)	General Manager National Martime Institute
Mr C.J. Parker	Secretary The Nautical Institute
Dr Roy Pearson	Marine Transport Centre University of Liverpool
Mr Robin Pender	Managing Director Stag Line Limited
Mr Francis E. Phillips	Associate Editor *Containerisation International*
Mr R.Y. Pritchard	Chairman and Managing Director Canadian Pacific Steamships Limited
Mr Peter C. Quine	Assistant Manager International and Government Affairs British Petroleum Co Ltd
Professor Bryan Ranft (Greenwich Forum)	Senior Research Fellow in War Studies King's College London
Commander M.B.F. Ranken (Greenwich Forum)	Chairman and Managing Director Aquamarine International
Mr A.J. Renouf	Contributing Editor *Sea Trade*
Mr Colin Rhodes	Technical Committee International Maritime Pilots Association
Miss Jacqueline A. Richardson	Planning and Development Manager Panocean-Anco Limited

Lt Cdr R.B. Richardson

Dr Viktor Sebek

Mrs B.G. Segal

Mr Peter Sharpe

Superintendent
   M. Sherriff WRNS

Mr J. McN Sidey DSO
   (Greenwich Forum)

Mr R.W. Simpson

Dr L.M. Skinner

Mr C.T.B. Smith

Sir Philip Southwell

Mr G.J. Stafford

Professor Susan Strange

Commander Karl F. Strom-Pedersen

Lt Cdr J.S. Thomson RN

Mr Neville Trotter MP

Marine Consultant

Secretary
Advisory Committee on Oil Pollution of
the sea

Assistant to the Secretary General
International Ship Suppliers Association

Freelance Organisation Consultant

Assistant Director of Manpower Planning
Ministry of Defence (Navy)

Director
P & O Energy

Assistant Secretary
Department of Trade
Shipping Policy Division

Director
Research Vessel Services
Natural Environment Research Council

Senior Economic Adviser for Aviation
Shipping and Competition Policy
Department of Trade

President
Brown & Root (UK) Limited

Managing Director
Stephenson Clarke Shipping Limited

Montague Buton Professor of International
Relations
London School of Economics and Political
Science

Managing Director
Jebsens (UK) Limited

Senior Lecturer
Department of History and International
Affairs Royal Naval College

Member of Parliament (C)
for Tynemouth

Mr Jeff G. Usher

Senior Lecturer
Faculty of Maritime Studies
Plymouth Polytechnic

Mr Henk Van Hoorn

North Sea Working Group

Captain G.R. Villar DSC RN

Naval Advisor to
British Aerospace Dynamics Group

Mr H. Watson

Henry Watson Consultants

Professor D.C. Watt
   Chairman
   Greenwich Forum

Professor of International History
London School of Economics and Political
Science

Mr M. Willingale

Department of Geography
Southampton University